Dear Reader,

Congratulations! Your college career is here, and now it's time to bury your nose in piles of textbooks, tailgates, and takeout. Your food choices may seem like a giant playground filled with fast food and unhealthy meals: pizza in the dining hall, late-night burgers, a quick snack of processed popcorn loaded with salt and butter.

It doesn't have to be. College is a time when you can decide how you want to live the rest of your life. You're learning new skills in the classroom, and gaining knowledge that will help you thrive out in the real world. Cooking healthy meals is also **a learning experience**. Instead of loading up on trans fats and high sodium, you can learn to make **easy, delicious, and healthy recipes** in no time at all, recipes that you'll be making long after you graduate. Now is the perfect time to learn to cook, and it will serve you well throughout your life.

In this book, you'll find **all the tips and tools** you need to succeed to create cheap, nutritious meals while in school. It's filled with hundreds of recipes that are a breeze for any beginner to make, ranging from "good for the soul" foods like hamburgers and chocolate brownies to gluten-free, dairy-free, keto, vegan, Paleo, and vegetarian recipes. Thank you for picking up this book on your way to college health and happiness! Enjoy every bite.

Best,
Emma Lunsford

Welcome to the Everything® Series!

These handy, accessible books give you all you need to tackle a difficult project, gain a new hobby, comprehend a fascinating topic, prepare for an exam, or even brush up on something you learned back in school but have since forgotten.

You can choose to read an Everything® book from cover to cover or just pick out the information you want from our four useful boxes: Questions, Facts, Alerts, and Essentials. We give you everything you need to know on the subject, but throw in a lot of fun stuff along the way too.

question	fact
Answers to common questions.	Important snippets of information.

alert	essential
Urgent warnings.	Quick handy tips.

We now have more than 600 Everything® books in print, spanning such wide-ranging categories as cooking, health, parenting, personal finance, wedding planning, word puzzles, and so much more. When you're done reading them all, you can finally say you know Everything®!

PUBLISHER Karen Cooper

MANAGING EDITOR Lisa Laing

COPY CHIEF Casey Ebert

PRODUCTION EDITOR Jo-Anne Duhamel

ACQUISITIONS EDITOR Zander Hatch

DEVELOPMENT EDITOR Lisa Laing

EVERYTHING® SERIES COVER DESIGNER Erin Alexander

THE
EVERYTHING®
COLLEGE
COOKBOOK

2ND EDITION

EMMA LUNSFORD

300 EASY AND BUDGET-FRIENDLY RECIPES FOR BEGINNER COOKS

ADAMS MEDIA

NEW YORK   LONDON   TORONTO   SYDNEY   NEW DELHI

Dedication

To Mom and Dad,

Thank you for your support, generosity, and wisdom throughout the toughest of times and beyond.
Your unconditional love brings me more peace than you will ever know. I love you so much.

Acknowledgments

I would like to thank my parents for letting me take over their kitchen, and my editor,
Zander Hatch, for helping me bring this book to life.

Adams Media
An Imprint of Simon & Schuster, Inc.
57 Littlefield Street
Avon, Massachusetts 02322

An Everything® Series Book.
Everything® and everything.com® are registered trademarks of
Simon & Schuster, Inc.

This Adams Media trade paperback edition April 2020

ADAMS MEDIA and colophon are trademarks of
Simon & Schuster.

For information about special discounts for bulk purchases,
please contact Simon & Schuster Special Sales at 1-866-506-
1949 or business@simonandschuster.com.

The Simon & Schuster Speakers Bureau can bring
authors to your live event. For more information or to
book an event contact the Simon & Schuster Speakers
Bureau at 1-866-248-3049 or visit our website at www
.simonspeakers.com.

Interior design by Colleen Cunningham
Photographs by James Stefiuk

Manufactured in the United States of America

10 9 8 7 6 5 4 3 2 1

Library of Congress Cataloging-in-Publication Data
Names: Lunsford, Emma, author.
Title: The everything® college cookbook, 2nd edition / Emma
Lunsford.
Description: 2nd edition. | Avon, Massachusetts: Adams
Media.
Series: Everything® | Revised edition of: The everything®
college cookbook: 300 hassle-free recipes for students on the go
/ Rhonda Lauret Parkinson. c2005.
Includes index.
Identifiers: LCCN 2019046170 | ISBN 9781507212769 (pb) |
ISBN 9781507212776 (ebook)
Subjects: LCSH: Quick and easy cooking. | LCGFT:
Cookbooks.
Classification: LCC TX833.5 .L87 2020 | DDC
641.5/12--dc23
LC record available at https://lccn.loc.gov/2019046170

ISBN 978-1-5072-1276-9
ISBN 978-1-5072-1277-6 (ebook)

Contains material adapted from the following title published
by Adams Media, an Imprint of Simon & Schuster, Inc.: *The
Everything® College Cookbook* by Rhonda Lauret Parkinson,
copyright © 2005, ISBN 978-1-59337-303-0.

Contents

Introduction

Living on your own at college can make it tough to eat healthy. You're trying to manage your busy schedule, and fast-food chains are scattered across campus. It's almost too easy to grab a giant pizza and bucket of French fries from the dining hall and call it a day. The best way to avoid those unhealthy meals is to learn how to cook easy, healthy food you can whip up in a flash.

Fortunately, with *The Everything® College Cookbook, 2nd Edition*, cooking doesn't have to be difficult, and it shouldn't be a chore. You don't have to create extravagant or difficult meals to eat healthy and smart. With a few simple tools like a mixing bowl, a wooden spoon, a good knife set, and some decent-quality pots and pans, you can learn to cook hundreds of wonderful meals.

With a few common and extremely useful appliances, you can make even more. The Instant Pot® can make a juicy pork tenderloin that will melt in your mouth in just 20 minutes or perfectly cooked rice to serve as a quick side dish for dinner. And an air fryer can take some of your favorite unhealthy foods, like fried chicken or French fries, and make them healthy! By frying with spinning hot air instead of fattening oil, the air fryer gives you all of the flavor and crunch without the grease.

You don't need hard-to-find or expensive ingredients to make a good meal either. Simple staples like flour, salt, and olive oil are going to be much more useful and helpful for you on a day-to-day basis. Having these ingredients in your cupboard means you don't have to run to the grocery store in the middle of cooking. Chapter 1: Getting Started will lead you through everything you need to stock for success in the kitchen.

After that, you'll find three hundred easy, healthy recipes you can put together in your dorm room or apartment kitchen. Start with a few simple recipes, like Teriyaki Chicken in Chapter 3 or Honey Mustard Chicken in Chapter 10, and go from there. If you're vegan, vegetarian, gluten-free, or following another diet, you can find great recipes to fit your lifestyle, like Gluten-Free Blueberry Poppy Seed Muffins in Chapter 2 or Vegan Lasagna in Chapter 9. To make them easy to find, keep an eye out for these icons:

- **VE** **VEGETARIAN**
- **VG** **VEGAN**
- **K** **KETOGENIC DIET**
- **GF** **GLUTEN-FREE**
- **DF** **DAIRY-FREE**
- **P** **PALEO DIET**

Whatever diet you prefer, focus on using fresh ingredients and the right portion size. The more you cook, the easier it will be and the better you'll feel.

So let's get cooking!

CHAPTER 1

Getting Started

College isn't just about learning things in the classroom. It's also about learning life skills out of the classroom—how to be a good roommate, how to manage your own schedule, and, yes, how to cook. For students who don't have any experience in the kitchen, learning basic cooking skills along with everything you need to learn in your classes can seem overwhelming. It's all too easy to give in to the lure of the dining hall or food court. However, these basic tips will help turn cooking from a chore into a creative, stress-free break from studying.

The ABCs of Stocking the Kitchen

There are a few basic pieces of equipment that every well-equipped kitchen should have. Of course, whether or not you bring all of them to college will depend on your specific circumstances. For example, residences with communal kitchens often provide pots, pans, and other cooking essentials. And there is no point in bringing a heavy-duty frying pan if you're going to be relying on a microwave as your only heat source. But, for the most part, you should expect to use everything on this list, and then adjust based on what you need.

Useful Utensils

When stocking your kitchen, start with the utensils. Fortunately, most are pretty inexpensive and can be found at almost any discount store. Items you absolutely need for cooking include:

- Large plastic mixing bowls for mixing ingredients and serving dishes
- Wooden spoons for stirring and mixing
- A heatproof rubber spatula for mixing, flipping, and turning ingredients
- A colander for draining washed, blanched, and boiled food
- A good knife set, particularly a good French knife for cutting meat
- A plastic or wooden cutting board for cutting, chopping, and mincing ingredients
- Measuring spoons and measuring cups

- A vegetable peeler and a can opener
- A grater for grating, shredding, and slicing cheese and other foods
- A wire whisk for whisking sauces and eggs
- Oven mitts or pot holders for grabbing hot pots and pans

Mix It Up!

While those utensils are absolute staples that you'll use almost every time you cook, there are a few other non-staples that will make your cooking experience much easier. Many recipes call for food to be beaten, blended, whipped, processed, or crushed. You can get devices that are perfectly designed for doing just that, like an eggbeater, also called a hand mixer. It's fine for beating eggs, whipping cream, and mixing salad dressing.

A blender can also make your life in the kitchen much easier. It's perfect for health-conscious students, as it's compact, inexpensive, and easy to clean. It can do everything from mixing smoothies and puréeing vegetables to grinding up oats into flour. Even if your only cooking will be throwing together smoothies for breakfast on busy weekdays, a blender will help you put together a tasty and nutritious meal in mere minutes. You can even drink it on the way to class!

Blender or Food Processor?

Besides the basic blender, another option for mixing food is a food processor. A food processor performs all of the functions of a blender and more. However, for most students, these extra options don't justify the food processor's higher price tag. Also, the blender's tall shape means it can hold more liquid, which makes it a better choice for preparing smoothies and other drinks. If you have the space and can afford it, a food processor is a useful addition to your kitchen, but it's not essential. You should prioritize a blender when putting together a list of kitchen items to buy.

Electric Extras

Some college dorms allow students to keep small electrical appliances in their room or residence kitchen. A coffee maker allows you to have a cup of joe ready as soon as you wake up in the morning. Tea drinkers will want a kettle for boiling water, and a toaster or toaster oven will help you make a quick breakfast in the morning.

When it comes to larger appliances, definitely consider a microwave if possible. They make reheating leftovers a breeze, and you can even make full meals using just a microwave (see Chapter 5). Today, you can find compact microwave and refrigerator combinations, designed specifically for dormitories. Some even come with a small freezer attached.

If you have some extra space, an Instant Pot® can save you an enormous amount of time in the kitchen, often cooking your meal in 10 minutes or less. The Instant Pot® has a number of different functions, including acting as a pressure cooker, slow cooker, steamer, or rice cooker. It's perfect for busy nights when you need a quick, healthy meal.

Air fryers are another great appliance to own, if you have the space. Instead of having to dip your food in fatty oil, the air fryer circulates hot air around your food extremely rapidly, creating the same crispy, fried texture with far fewer calories. It's a wonderfully healthy way to get your favorite fried food, like chicken tenders and French fries, without ruining your diet with excess oil. You can find quite a few Instant Pot® and air fryer recipes in Chapter 5: Special Devices to get started on these amazing and convenient appliances.

Equipment for the Stovetop

A few good pots are essential for stovetop cooking. Ideally, you should have three different sizes: a smaller pot for sauces, a medium pot for soups and single-serving meals, and a large pot for boiling noodles and potatoes and for cooking for a group. However, quality is more important than quantity. It's better to purchase one pot made of quality material rather than several inexpensive pots that may not heat properly or may be hard to clean. While getting the cheapest pots you can find might make sense, your food will taste better and cooking will be much easier if you get better-quality pots (without breaking the bank, of course).

Once you have your pots handled, you need to get some pans. Just like your pots, quality matters. Make sure the saucepan is made of a heavy material that conducts heat evenly. Cast-iron and copper pots are probably heavier than you need (and probably beyond your budget), but stainless steel wrapped in aluminum or copper is a good choice. While you should always wear oven mitts, cooking will be easier if the pot handles are made of a material that won't heat up, such as wood, plastic, or rubber. Finally, you want to make sure the lid fits tightly so it doesn't release the heat.

Not surprisingly, quality frying pans are made of the same type of material as saucepans because both are designed for stovetop cooking. A medium, 12" frying pan will meet most of your needs for sautéing, braising meat, and cooking eggs. As with a saucepan, it's important to make sure the frying pan comes with a tight-fitting lid.

Oven Cooking

Oven cooking requires its own special equipment that can take the high heats needed for baking, broiling, and roasting. A large, rectangular-shaped metal baking sheet is used for making cookies, while a square, deep-sided metal baking pan is used for roasting meats and baking desserts. When it comes to muffins and cupcakes, there is no substitute for the standard muffin tin. If you really like muffins, consider getting more than one to prevent having to cook in batches. A glass baking dish is used for main dishes such as fish fillets and marinated chicken breasts

that don't need a rack to let the fat drip off. Finally, a deep-sided casserole dish is used for one-pot meals such as rice and noodle-based casseroles.

Kitchen Staples

Once you've purchased the basic tools needed for cooking, it's tempting to start stocking up your refrigerator. But try to hold off until you've purchased a few staple ingredients. A pantry stocked with basic ingredients that are common to quite a few recipes will keep you from making repeat trips to the grocery store every time you need to cook a meal. Here are the essentials:

> **alert**
>
> Dried herbs are more concentrated than fresh herbs, so you can't simply substitute one for the other in equal proportion. If a recipe calls for fresh herbs, you can use ⅓ the amount of dried herbs instead.

- **Flour:** All-purpose flour is used for almost every type of baking.
- **Sugar:** Regular granulated white sugar is used both as a sweetener at the table and in cooking.
- **Brown sugar:** Molasses-based brown sugar is used in baking, sauces, and wherever a recipe calls for a stronger flavor than granulated sugar.

- **Olive oil:** Olive oil is used for sautéing and frying, as well as for salad dressings and marinades.
- **Broth:** Chicken, beef, and vegetable broths are used in soups, casseroles, and other dishes.
- **Dried herbs and spices:** Dried herbs and spices lend flavor to soups, stews, and other slow-cooked dishes.
- **Salt and pepper:** Standard table salt and ground black pepper should meet all your cooking needs.
- **Noodles:** Italian pasta noodles like linguine, penne, or spaghetti are cheap, quick, and an easy source of healthy complex carbs.
- **Rice:** White long-grain is the standard, but you can experiment with different types such as brown and scented rice.
- **Miscellaneous flavoring agents:** Lemon juice, tomato sauce, and soy sauce will allow you to create a number of different dishes.

fact

Not only is olive oil healthier than vegetable oil—its monounsaturated fats can help ward off heart disease—it's also much more versatile. Besides being an excellent cooking oil, olive oil lends a delicate flavor to salad dressings and marinades and can even serve as a substitute for butter on toasted bread.

Time-Saving Ingredients

While nothing beats the flavor of fresh herbs or chicken broth prepared from scratch, packaged and instant ingredients will save you time on busy weeknights. For example, don't let recipes that call for fresh lemon juice put you off—grocery stores carry packaged bottles of lemon juice that work just as well. Canned tomato sauce made with oregano, basil, and other seasonings can also save you from the work of having to boil, crush, and season tomatoes. Usually these cans will keep for several months in a cool, dry place, which means you don't have to worry about them going bad.

essential

You can find dozens of spices in the supermarket, most of which you'll never use. A good tip when trying to decide which ones to get is to think Italian. Spices like dried oregano, dried basil, and dried parsley bring a lot of flavor to simmered and slow-cooked dishes.

Instant broth comes in cubes, packets, cans, and ready-to-use cartons. All are equally convenient. However, the carton types need to be refrigerated and used within two weeks after they are opened. They're usually a little better for you though, as they contain fewer preservatives.

Getting the right kind of noodles can also save you a lot of time. Many types of Asian noodles, such as rice noodles, don't need to be boiled. Just soak them in hot or warm water until they soften. And precooked (also called "oven-ready") lasagna noodles can go straight from the package to the casserole dish.

Shelf Life

Even staples like these go stale eventually and need to be replaced. Expect flour, baking powder, and baking soda to last for up to one year. White granulated sugar has a longer shelf life than other dry ingredients—it will last up to eighteen months. On the other hand, brown sugar lasts for only six months.

Of course, improper storage will cause ingredients to go stale more quickly. Worse, certain types of small bugs—such as the flour beetle—feed on ingredients like these. For best results, store your staples in tightly sealed canisters. Don't worry about blowing your budget on a matching set of fancy chrome or other metal canisters. Plastic is fine, as long as it has a tight seal. Don't have room in your dorm for a full set of canisters? Set one canister aside to serve as a storage space for smaller amounts of various ingredients. Store each ingredient in a plastic bag, seal it, and place the bag in the container.

Meal Planning 101

Preparing a detailed grocery list makes it so much easier to stick to a budget. It can keep you from grabbing whatever catches your eye (or your stomach) on the way through the grocery store. The best way to start is by preparing a meal plan for one or two weeks. Try to pick more than one recipe that uses the same ingredients so you can save money by purchasing in bulk. Let's say, for example, you decide to cook two recipes, both containing ground beef and tomato sauce. Since you're shopping for both recipes in the same trip, you can buy larger portions of the beef and tomatoes.

Of course, you'll want to incorporate leftovers into your meal plan (and we have some great recipes to help with that in Chapter 6). It's easier to make one large dish and reheat the second half the next day than to have to cook a fresh meal from scratch every single night.

You can also change up some recipes to add variety to your meals. For recipes that provide two or more servings, you could cook two half-portions of the recipe, slightly altering the ingredients for each half. This makes it easier to resist the temptation to skip dinner in favor of the dining hall down the street.

When halving or doubling a recipe, it's helpful to know how to convert cups into tablespoons, tablespoons into teaspoons, and vice versa. This table contains several conversions.

Equivalent Measures	
Measurement	**Equivalent**
3 teaspoons	1 tablespoon
4 tablespoons	¼ cup
5 tablespoons + 1 teaspoon	⅓ cup
8 tablespoons	½ cup
10 tablespoons + 2 teaspoons	⅔ cup
12 tablespoons	¾ cup
16 tablespoons	1 cup
1 cup	8 ounces
1 quart	32 ounces

Shopping Tips

When writing up a grocery list, it can be helpful to list your items in the same order they are organized in the grocery store. Group together fresh vegetables, which will be in the produce section, and do the same with canned soups, frozen foods, and meat products. Put items located at either end of the store first or last on the list. Writing the grocery list in this way ensures that you're moving efficiently from one end of the store to the other, instead of having to go back and forth between aisles. Here are tips for cutting costs at the grocery store:

- Avoid shopping when you're tired or hungry, which can lead to expensive "impulse buying."
- Always bring a list and stick to it.

- Check the "sell by" and "use by" dates on perishable items such as milk and meat. Always purchase food with the date that's furthest away so it will last longer.
- Be sure to ask for a rain check if the store is out of an advertised special.
- Always store perishable goods in the refrigerator or freezer as soon as possible so there is no danger of spoilage.
- Many larger grocery stores have frequent-shopper programs that give substantial discounts to regular shoppers.
- If you have a freezer, use it to freeze individual portions of fresh meat and seafood in bulk.

Staying Healthy

Staying healthy is easier said than done, but that doesn't mean it's particularly difficult. It comes down to mindful eating. Be aware of the ingredients you're eating, and how much you eat each day. It's okay to eat a McDonald's hamburger for lunch one day, but not every single day (or even most days).

Here are a few tips for staying healthy: First and foremost, stick to a regular meal schedule. If you are planning a lengthy study session away from your dorm, prepare healthy snacks to take with you. Simple snacks such as Granola Biscotti, Apple Cinnamon Muffins, and Homemade Trail Mix (all found in Chapter 4: Simple Snacks on the Go) can provide energy without the extra empty calories found in potato chips and chocolate.

Plan your meals at least one week in advance. One option is to cook ahead, making all your weekly meals on the weekend. It's much easier to stick to a healthy meal plan on a busy weeknight when all you need to do is heat up dinner instead of cooking it. Finally, take time to exercise. Many colleges and universities have excellent exercise facilities right on campus that are free for students. With a little planning, you can fit an exercise session into your daily schedule, whether it's lifting weights, going for a run, heading to the pool, or taking a class such as boxing or yoga.

Special Diets

There are dozens of different diets out there. Keto, vegetarian, vegan, gluten-free, dairy-free, Paleo…it's hard to know exactly what you should be eating. The first step to figuring that out is learning what each diet is about.

Ketogenic Diet

The ketogenic diet, or keto diet, is a high-fat, low-carb diet that replaces most of your carb intake with fat. This might sound a bit counterintuitive at first. If you want to lose fat, why eat more of it? Carbs are the first source of energy your body burns for fuel. If you don't have any carbs to burn, your body will start burning fat instead in a metabolic state called ketosis. By burning fat instead of carbs, you lose weight quickly. This is different than a standard low-carb diet because keto replaces the lost carbs with fat, whereas low-carb diets have nothing to replace the hole in their diet.

Vegetarian

Vegetarians don't eat meat, poultry, or fish. Instead, they fill their meals with plant-based protein, fiber, whole grains, and plenty of fruits and vegetables. Vegetarians tend to have lower cholesterol and less risk of heart disease because their diet is low in saturated fat and animal protein. This diet can be a good stepping stone for anyone thinking about becoming vegan. To start, try having a meatless Monday, and then slowly work your way up to a whole week of no meat.

Vegan

Vegans don't eat anything that comes from an animal, so in addition to avoiding meat, poultry, and fish, vegans also choose not to eat dairy products, eggs, and honey. Instead, vegans stick mostly to fruits, vegetables, nuts, beans, and plant-based proteins like tofu. Because vegans focus on eating healthier proteins and avoid red meat, they typically have less risk of heart disease and inflammation, not to mention positive environmental impacts. This diet is great for those wanting to be more environmentally conscious or for those looking to incorporate healthier alternatives.

Gluten-Free

A gluten-free diet is exactly what its name says: no gluten. Those who follow this diet don't eat wheat, barley, rye, or oats unless they're specified gluten-free. This diet has grown in popularity over the past few years as awareness of celiac disease, an intense allergy to gluten, and gluten sensitivities are becoming more recognized. Even if you don't have a gluten allergy, cutting down on gluten in your diet can have health benefits, such as reduced inflammation, improved digestion, and increased energy levels.

Dairy-Free

Just like a gluten-free diet removes gluten, a dairy-free diet simply removes dairy such as milk, cream, cheese, butter, and yogurt. Dairy-free diets are essential to those with a lactose allergy or a lactose intolerance. Dairy can contribute to inflammation, acne, eczema, and bloating. If you don't have an allergy, you don't have to eliminate it entirely, but there are benefits to reducing your intake.

Paleo

The Paleo diet is built on the idea of getting back to our dietary roots and eating like our ancestors did. It focuses primarily on meats, fruits, and vegetables, while eliminating grains and refined sugar. Processed foods are kept at a minimum, which can have a positive impact on weight loss, heart health, and inflammation. Because it's high in protein, this diet is great for athletes or those looking to build or maintain muscle, or people looking to add more whole foods into their lifestyle.

Basic Techniques

When you're just getting started in the kitchen, there are so many techniques and terms that you just don't know. Everyone has to start somewhere, and now that you're on your own, it's the perfect time to learn these new cooking skills.

Cutting an Onion

Start by trimming off one end of the onion with a large, sharp knife, making sure to leave the root end intact to keep the onion together while chopping. Slice the onion in half lengthwise (through the rood end) and peel away the skin. Lay the two halves cut-side down. With your knife pointing to the root end, slice it evenly to within ½" of the root. Rotate the onion 90° and slice again, ending about ½" from the root. Discard the root and and repeat with the other half. Voilà! You have beautiful, even pieces.

How to Mince Garlic

Trim off the root of a garlic clove, then put your knife on top of it, flat-side down, and press hard against the knife. Remove the knife and peel off the skin. Place your knife on the side of the garlic, ready to cut. With one hand holding the knife handle and the other firmly holding the knife tip in place, begin to chop the garlic, moving the handle north and south over the garlic. When you get to the top, wipe the blade clean of any garlic that may have gotten stuck there, collect the garlic into a small pile, and repeat until you reach a very fine consistency.

---

question

Chopped, Diced, or Minced?

These cutting methods are similar but are differentiated by how large the pieces end up. Chopped refers to a larger cut, usually about ¾". Diced is a bit smaller, around ¼". Minced should be very finely chopped, around ¹⁄₁₆".

How to Check Baked Goods

It can be difficult to tell when something has finished baking, as the part that cooks last is the middle, which you can't see. The best way to tell if something is done is by inserting a toothpick into the middle. If the toothpick comes out with wet batter or some crumbs, more oven time is needed. If the toothpick is clean, your baked good is ready to be pulled out.

How to Separate an Egg

Some recipes call for the yolk to be separated from the egg white. To do this, set out two small bowls. Crack your egg on a hard, flat surface, then, with your hand over one of the bowls, pour the egg into your hand, letting the white fall between your fingers into the bowl, and then place the yolk into the other bowl. If you don't want to use your hands, you can crack the egg and pour the yolk back and forth between the two shell halves over a bowl, letting the white fall through and then place the yolk in a separate bowl.

How to Handle Raw Meat

If you've never cooked with raw meat, it might seem intimidating. Always remember to wash your hands before and after handling raw meat, so you don't spread diseases like salmonella. Designate a cutting board only for handling meat and make sure to wash it thoroughly after each use. Never cut vegetables on the same cutting board raw meat was on, or else you risk cross-contaminating the vegetables. When you're done cooking, you may want to disinfect the area where the meat was to ensure everything is properly cleaned.

CHAPTER 2

Breakfast

Bagel with Walnut-Raisin Cream Cheese

SERVES 1

Per Serving:

Calories	433
Fat	14g
Protein	11g
Sodium	595mg
Fiber	4g
Carbohydrates	70g
Sugar	18g
Net Carbs	66g

Got a sweet tooth? Feel free to add a teaspoon of honey to the cream cheese mixture. It will add an extra kick of sweetness and pairs perfectly with the cinnamon.

1 plain bagel

2 teaspoons chopped raisins

2 teaspoons chopped walnuts

2 tablespoons cream cheese

½ teaspoon ground cinnamon

1 Cut bagel in half and place in a toaster. In a small bowl, mix together raisins, walnuts, and cream cheese. Stir in cinnamon.

2 Spread cream cheese mixture on toasted bagel. Serve warm.

Hard-Boiled Eggs

SERVES 1

Per Serving:

Calories	144
Fat	10g
Protein	13g
Sodium	140mg
Fiber	0g
Carbohydrates	1g
Sugar	0g
Net Carbs	1g

The trick to perfect hard-boiled eggs is to start with cold water, and then remove the pan from the burner as soon as the water reaches a rolling boil. This prevents rubbery eggs.

2 large eggs

1 Place eggs in a medium saucepan and cover with cold water to at least ½" above eggs. Cover the pan with a lid and bring to a rolling boil over high heat.

2 Remove pan from heat. Let eggs stand in the hot water for 17–20 minutes, then remove from saucepan and place in a small bowl filled with cold water for at least 2 minutes or until cool enough to handle. Peel off shells and serve immediately or refrigerate for up to 1 week.

Soft-Boiled Eggs

Soft-boiled eggs are delicious sprinkled with "everything" bagel seasoning and served on avocado toast with slices of tomato. You can even add some cooked spinach if you're feeling extra healthy.

2 large eggs

1 Fill a medium saucepan with enough cold water so there will be at least ½" of water above eggs. Bring water to a rolling boil over high heat. Place eggs in pan and cook 3–5 minutes, depending on how soft you want the yolks.

2 Remove eggs from saucepan and place in a small bowl filled with cold water for at least 2 minutes or until cool enough to handle. Peel off shells and serve immediately or refrigerate for up to 1 week.

SERVES 1	
Per Serving:	
Calories	144
Fat	10g
Protein	13g
Sodium	140mg
Fiber	0g
Carbohydrates	1g
Sugar	0g
Net Carbs	1g

Poached Egg

For best results, use the freshest egg possible. For an extra pop of flavor, try poaching the egg in milk or broth instead of water.

½ teaspoon salt

1 large egg

1 In a medium saucepan over high heat, bring 3" water to a boil and add salt. Break egg into a small bowl.

2 When the water reaches a boil, reduce heat until it's just simmering. Gently slide egg into the water and cook 3–5 minutes, depending on how firm you want it.

3 Remove egg from water with a slotted spoon, letting any excess water drain into the saucepan. Use the slotted spoon to gently push aside any "threads" from the egg white. Serve immediately.

SERVES 1	
Per Serving:	
Calories	72
Fat	5g
Protein	6g
Sodium	85mg
Fiber	0g
Carbohydrates	1g
Sugar	0g
Net Carbs	1g

Savory Scrambled Eggs

SERVES 1

Per Serving:

Calories	324
Fat	27g
Protein	15g
Sodium	953mg
Fiber	2g
Carbohydrates	8g
Sugar	4g
Net Carbs	6g

You can easily turn these eggs into a breakfast burrito. Try adding some medium-hot salsa and a handful of Cheddar cheese before removing the eggs from the pan. Sprinkle on some fresh cilantro, transfer to a warm tortilla, and voilà! Your Mexican breakfast burrito is served.

2 large eggs
2 tablespoons whole milk
¼ teaspoon salt
¼ teaspoon ground black pepper
10 capers
4 tablespoons unsalted butter, divided
½ medium tomato, chopped
1 medium scallion, chopped

1 In a small bowl, beat eggs, milk, salt, pepper, and capers. Set aside.

2 In a small frying pan, melt 2 tablespoons butter over low heat. Add tomato and scallion. Sauté until tomato is tender but still firm, about 2–4 minutes. Remove from pan and set aside. Clean and dry pan.

3 Melt remaining 2 tablespoons butter in the pan over low heat. Increase heat to medium-low and add egg mixture.

4 Cook eggs, using a spatula to stir egg mixture so the uncooked egg on top flows underneath.

5 When eggs are nearly cooked, after about 5 minutes, return tomato and scallion to the pan. Cook until eggs are firm but still a bit moist, about 1 minute. Serve immediately.

Turkey Avocado Toast

The seasoning mix in this recipe can be made in larger batches and stored in a glass jar. It can flavor lots of dishes, like broiled chicken breasts or steamed vegetables. Add poppy seeds to the mix, and you'll have a homemade version of "everything" bagel seasoning.

½ teaspoon salt

¼ teaspoon ground black pepper

¼ teaspoon garlic powder

¼ teaspoon onion powder

½ teaspoon sesame seeds

1 (1-ounce) slice whole-wheat bread, toasted

½ medium avocado, peeled, pitted, and mashed

3 (2-ounce) slices deli turkey

SERVES 1	
Per Serving:	
Calories	354
Fat	17g
Protein	32g
Sodium	2,850mg
Fiber	7g
Carbohydrates	22g
Sugar	6g
Net Carbs	15g

1   In a small bowl, mix together salt, pepper, garlic powder, onion powder, and sesame seeds.

2   Spread toasted bread with mashed avocado. Sprinkle seasoning mixture over avocado and top with turkey slices. Serve immediately.

Blueberry Smoothie Bowl

You can easily turn this Blueberry Smoothie Bowl into a classic acai bowl. Just add 1 heaping tablespoon of acai powder to the blender and watch it turn into that gorgeous, purple, Instagram-*worthy color.*

½ cup unsweetened almond milk

1 cup ice

¾ cup frozen blueberries

1 tablespoon honey

1 medium banana, peeled

2 tablespoons shredded coconut

¼ cup frozen pineapple chunks

¼ cup frozen strawberry slices

2 tablespoons chia seeds

SERVES 1	
Per Serving:	
Calories	476
Fat	14g
Protein	9g
Sodium	109mg
Fiber	20g
Carbohydrates	87g
Sugar	51g
Net Carbs	67g

1   Add milk, ice, blueberries, honey, and banana to a blender and blend until smooth.

2   Transfer to a serving bowl and top with coconut, pineapple, strawberries, and chia seeds. Serve immediately.

VE

French Toast

SERVES 1

Per Serving:

Calories	627
Fat	34g
Protein	20g
Sodium	679mg
Fiber	2g
Carbohydrates	59g
Sugar	33g
Net Carbs	57g

FEELING FESTIVE?

One of the best things about making pancakes, waffles, and French toast is that you can easily change up the flavors. Top them off with your favorite jam, fresh fruit, peanut butter, chocolate chips, or sprinkles. You can toss these extras right into the batter before cooking to add a burst of color to your plate.

You can use sourdough or French bread for some extra-fancy French Toast, and if you end up with leftover egg mixture, scramble it up at the end for a side of protein. Talk about a gourmet breakfast!

2 large eggs
⅛ teaspoon salt
¼ cup whole milk
2 tablespoons unsalted butter
2 (1-ounce) slices honey-wheat bread
¼ teaspoon ground cinnamon
2 tablespoons maple syrup

1 In a small bowl, beat eggs, salt, and milk. Heat butter in a medium frying pan over medium-low heat.

2 Take a slice of bread and dip one side into beaten egg mixture, letting it sit for a few seconds to soak up the liquid. Turn bread over and repeat with the other side. Lay bread flat in the frying pan. Repeat with remaining slice of bread.

3 Cook until bread is browned on the bottom, about 3–4 minutes. Flip over and cook the other side 1–2 minutes more until browned. Remove from the frying pan and sprinkle with cinnamon. Serve with syrup.

Jazzed-Up Peanut Butter Toast

SERVES 1

Per Serving:

Calories	290
Fat	9g
Protein	7g
Sodium	221mg
Fiber	6g
Carbohydrates	51g
Sugar	32g
Net Carbs	45g

This recipe is perfect for when you're running out the door with only a little time before class. It's a quick, well-balanced breakfast that will keep you full until lunchtime.

1 (1-ounce) slice whole-wheat bread, toasted

1 tablespoon peanut butter

½ medium banana, peeled and sliced

¼ teaspoon ground cinnamon

1 tablespoon honey

Spread toast with peanut butter and top evenly with banana slices. Sprinkle cinnamon over banana slices and drizzle honey over top. Serve immediately.

Paleo Raspberry Oatmeal

SERVES 1

Per Serving:

Calories	317
Fat	4g
Protein	8g
Sodium	91mg
Fiber	8g
Carbohydrates	69g
Sugar	35g
Net Carbs	61g

Gluten-free oats can usually be found in the health food aisle at your local grocery store. If you're not a fan of raspberries, you can replace them with your favorite fruit. This hearty breakfast can easily be dessert because it's so sweet and delicious!

½ cup quick-cooking gluten-free oats

1 cup water

½ cup unsweetened almond milk

½ cup raspberries

2 tablespoons honey

1. Place oats and water in a large microwave-safe bowl and cook on high for 1–2 minutes.

2. Remove from microwave and add almond milk, raspberries, and honey. Stir to combine. Serve warm.

Easy Pancake Roll-Ups

Try adding ¼ cup chocolate chips to the pancake batter before cooking for a peanut butter cup surprise. Serve these Easy Pancake Roll-Ups alone or top them with butter and syrup.

2 teaspoons baking powder

⅛ teaspoon salt

1 cup all-purpose flour

2 tablespoons granulated sugar

1 large egg

1½ tablespoons canola oil

1 cup whole milk

6 tablespoons peanut butter

SERVES 2	
Per Serving:	
Calories	751
Fat	41g
Protein	23g
Sodium	959mg
Fiber	5g
Carbohydrates	76g
Sugar	25g
Net Carbs	71g

1　Heat a griddle or heavy skillet over medium-high heat, making sure it is very hot (water should sizzle when dropped on it).

2　In a medium bowl, stir baking powder and salt into flour, blending thoroughly. Stir in sugar. In a small bowl, add egg, oil, and milk and beat until combined.

3　Add egg mixture to flour mixture. Do not overmix. (Don't worry about lumps.) The batter should be runny.

4　Spray griddle or skillet with nonstick cooking spray. Pour batter into the pan in ¼-cup portions. Cook until pancakes are browned on the bottom and bubbling on top, about 3–4 minutes. Flip over and cook the other side 1–2 minutes more until browned. Remove pancakes from the skillet or griddle and keep warm. Repeat with remaining batter.

5　Spread peanut butter on pancakes and roll up. Serve hot.

VE

Buckwheat Pancakes

These blueberry-filled pancakes are as healthy as it gets. You can easily make them gluten-free by replacing the all-purpose flour with gluten-free flour. The buckwheat is already celiac-friendly.

SERVES 4

Per Serving:

Calories	361
Fat	9g
Protein	7g
Sodium	735mg
Fiber	2g
Carbohydrates	64g
Sugar	39g
Net Carbs	62g

HOW TO FREEZE PANCAKES

Cool the cooked pancakes before freezing. Once cooled, stack them by placing a layer of wax paper between each pancake. Place the stacked pancakes in the freezer. Once frozen, unstack and place them in a resealable plastic bag, and return them to the freezer. Frozen pancakes will keep for 1–2 months.

¾ cup all-purpose flour

¼ cup buckwheat flour

2 teaspoons baking powder

1 teaspoon baking soda

⅛ teaspoon salt

3 tablespoons granulated sugar

1 large egg

1½ tablespoons canola oil

1 cup buttermilk

¾ cup frozen blueberries

½ cup maple syrup

1 Heat a griddle or heavy skillet over medium-high heat, making sure it is very hot (water should sizzle when dropped on it).

2 In a medium bowl, mix together all-purpose flour and buckwheat flour. Stir baking powder, baking soda, salt, and sugar into flour, blending thoroughly. In a small bowl, combine egg, oil, and buttermilk.

3 Add milk mixture to flour mixture and stir to combine. Do not overmix. (Don't worry about lumps.) The batter should be runny. Gently stir in blueberries.

4 Spray the griddle or skillet with nonstick cooking spray. Pour batter into the pan in 2-tablespoon portions. Cook until pancakes are browned on the bottom and bubbling on top, about 3–4 minutes. Flip over and cook the other side 1–2 minutes more until browned. Remove pancakes from the skillet or griddle and keep warm. Repeat with remaining batter. Serve warm with maple syrup.

Waffles

Don't have a waffle iron? Cook these pancake-style in a griddle or heavy skillet at high heat. You can top these with other fruits as well, like strawberries or blueberries. Don't forget the butter and syrup! Maple syrup is the obvious choice, but you can also try honey, molasses, or agave nectar.

1 large egg, separated

¼ cup unsalted butter, melted

¾ cup plus 2 tablespoons whole milk

1½ teaspoons baking powder

⅛ teaspoon salt

2 tablespoons granulated sugar

½ teaspoon ground cinnamon

1 cup all-purpose flour

½ cup fresh raspberries

SERVES 2

Per Serving:

Calories	580
Fat	28g
Protein	13g
Sodium	612mg
Fiber	4g
Carbohydrates	67g
Sugar	21g
Net Carbs	63g

1 Preheat waffle iron. In a small bowl, use a whisk to beat egg white until stiff, about 12–18 minutes. In another small bowl, beat egg yolk well and mix in butter and milk.

2 In a medium bowl, stir baking powder, salt, sugar, and cinnamon into flour, blending thoroughly.

3 Make a well in the middle of flour mixture by pushing the flour to the edges of the bowl and leaving about ½" of space in the middle. Pour egg yolk mixture into the well and stir to combine with flour mixture until it forms a thick batter. Gently fold in egg white.

4 Pour batter into waffle iron and cook according to the manufacturer's instructions. Top with raspberries and serve hot.

Oatmeal with a Twist

SERVES 2

Per Serving:

Calories	307
Fat	15g
Protein	11g
Sodium	369mg
Fiber	5g
Carbohydrates	35g
Sugar	16g
Net Carbs	30g

You can mix and match ingredients with this versatile oatmeal. Instead of raisins, use peaches or apples, or try almond butter instead of peanut butter. When you're shopping for apple juice, choose a brand with the least amount of added sugars.

1 tablespoon apple juice

2 tablespoons raisins

3 tablespoons part-skim ricotta cheese

¼ teaspoon salt

1 cup water

½ cup rolled oats (not the quick-cooking type)

2 tablespoons unsweetened almond milk

1 tablespoon honey

1 tablespoon peanut butter

¼ cup slivered almonds

1 teaspoon ground cinnamon

¼ teaspoon ground nutmeg

⅛ teaspoon ground cloves

1 In a small bowl, stir together apple juice, raisins, and ricotta. Set aside.

2 Add salt and water to a medium saucepan and bring to a boil. Stir in oats. Cover, reduce heat to low, and simmer for 5 minutes or until oats have absorbed most of the water.

3 Stir in almond milk, honey, peanut butter, and ricotta mixture. Transfer to two serving bowls and sprinkle with almonds, cinnamon, nutmeg, and cloves. Serve hot.

Gluten-Free Baked Apple Oatmeal

This Gluten-Free Baked Apple Oatmeal is the epitome of a crisp fall Saturday morning. It tastes like apple pie but is actually a healthy, nutritious breakfast. For a Paleo version, replace the whole milk with ½ cup of sweetened almond milk and use an extra egg instead of butter.

1½ cups gluten-free rolled oats (not the quick-cooking kind)

½ cup light brown sugar

1 teaspoon ground cinnamon

½ teaspoon ground nutmeg

¼ teaspoon ground cloves

1 teaspoon baking powder

½ teaspoon salt

1 cup whole milk, divided

1 large egg

¼ cup melted unsalted butter

1 teaspoon vanilla extract

1 cup chopped green apple

1 Preheat oven to 350°F and grease an 8" × 8" baking dish.

2 In a large mixing bowl, combine oats, sugar, cinnamon, nutmeg, cloves, baking powder, and salt.

3 Add in ½ cup milk, egg, butter, and vanilla, and mix with a large spoon until fully combined.

4 Gently fold apples into oat mixture, then pour into prepared baking dish.

5 Bake 30–35 minutes or until a knife inserted in the center comes out clean. Divide between four serving bowls and top with remaining ½ cup milk. Serve warm.

SERVES 4

Per Serving:

Calories	382
Fat	17g
Protein	7g
Sodium	461mg
Fiber	4g
Carbohydrates	52g
Sugar	31g
Net Carbs	48g

ROLLED OATS FAQ

If you're having trouble finding rolled oats in the grocery store, try looking for "old-fashioned oats" instead. Quick-cooking oats are a type of rolled oat, but they're rolled thinner and cut into smaller pieces than old-fashioned oats, so they cook much faster.

Keto Quiche Muffins

These delicious and convenient egg muffins store well in the freezer for up to 2 months. Make a batch on a Sunday, and you'll have breakfast ready for the entire week ahead.

6 strips bacon

8 large eggs

¼ cup whole milk

¼ cup chopped red onion

¼ cup chopped chives

¼ cup chopped red bell pepper

1 teaspoon salt

1 teaspoon ground black pepper

¾ cup shredded Cheddar cheese

1 Heat oven to 350°F and spray a 12-cup muffin tin with nonstick cooking spray.

2 Heat a large frying pan over medium-high heat. Add bacon and cook 4–5 minutes. Using a fork, flip bacon and cook another 2–3 minutes until crispy. Drain bacon on paper towels until cool, then crumble and set aside.

3 In a large bowl, whisk together eggs, milk, onion, chives, bell pepper, salt, and black pepper. Add bacon and mix well.

4 Pour egg mixture evenly into muffin tin. Bake 15 minutes or until egg mixture is no longer runny in the middle (a knife or toothpick inserted in the center should come out clean). Top each muffin evenly with cheese, then bake another 5 minutes or until cheese is melted. Serve immediately or store in the refrigerator for up to 5 days. Muffins can also be frozen for up to 8 weeks.

MAKES 12 MUFFINS

Per Serving (1 muffin):

Calories	85
Fat	6g
Protein	6g
Sodium	342mg
Fiber	0g
Carbohydrates	1g
Sugar	1g
Net Carbs	1g

QUICHE ORIGINS

Quiche dishes are often considered to be part of French cuisine, but they actually originated in Germany in the Middle Ages. The word *quiche* is from the German word *kuchen*, meaning "cake." A quiche pie is the perfect dish for any time of the day, as they're so easy to personalize.

Cheese Omelet

SERVES 1

Per Serving:

Calories	393
Fat	31g
Protein	22g
Sodium	1,037mg
Fiber	1g
Carbohydrates	8g
Sugar	4g
Net Carbs	7g

The sharpness of the Cheddar cheese pairs nicely with the chili powder and salsa, but a milder cheese like Swiss would also work well.

2 large eggs

2 tablespoons whole milk

⅛ teaspoon salt

⅛ teaspoon ground black pepper

¼ teaspoon chili powder

1 tablespoon unsalted butter

¼ cup shredded Cheddar cheese

¼ cup mild salsa

1 In a small bowl, beat eggs, milk, salt, pepper, and chili powder.

2 Melt butter in a medium frying pan over low heat. Pour egg mixture into the pan and cook, without stirring, for 1–2 minutes. Sprinkle cheese over half of the omelet. Lift the edges of the omelet with a spatula so that the uncooked egg runs underneath.

3 When eggs are cooked evenly throughout, about 1 minute more, carefully slide the spatula underneath the omelet and fold it in half. Slide it onto a plate and top with salsa. Serve immediately.

Sweet Potato Hash

SERVES 1

Per Serving:

Calories	341
Fat	14g
Protein	11g
Sodium	686mg
Fiber	8g
Carbohydrates	46g
Sugar	12g
Net Carbs	38g

With the savory flavors of garlic, onion, and bacon, this sweet potato delight will melt in your mouth.

2 strips bacon

1 teaspoon olive oil

1 large sweet potato, peeled and diced

¼ cup chopped yellow onion

¼ cup chopped green bell pepper

⅛ teaspoon salt

⅛ teaspoon ground black pepper

¼ teaspoon garlic powder

¼ teaspoon paprika

1 Heat a medium frying pan over medium-high heat. Add bacon and cook 4–5 minutes, then flip and cook another 2–3 minutes until crispy. Drain bacon on paper towels, then crumble and set aside.

2 Heat oil in a large frying pan over medium-high heat. Add sweet potatoes and cook 10–15 minutes, stirring occasionally.

3 Add onion, bell pepper, salt, black pepper, garlic powder, and paprika. Reduce heat to medium-low and sauté for 5–7 minutes. Serve warm with crumbled bacon pieces on top.

Eggs Benedict

This classic brunch recipe is so simple and cost-effective that you might want to start brunching from your own kitchen instead of going out. Spice it up with a little salt and cayenne pepper and add a tomato slice for some extra texture.

1 tablespoon unsalted butter

1 English muffin, halved and toasted

2 tablespoons plain full-fat Greek yogurt

1 teaspoon Dijon mustard

1 Poached Egg (see recipe in this chapter)

1 Spread butter evenly on both halves of English muffin.

2 In a small bowl, mix together yogurt and mustard. Spread yogurt mixture on 1 muffin half and top with poached egg. Place remaining muffin half on top and serve immediately.

VE

SERVES 1	
Per Serving:	
Calories	327
Fat	19g
Protein	13g
Sodium	403mg
Fiber	1g
Carbohydrates	26g
Sugar	2g
Net Carbs	25g

Mocha Protein Smoothie

Instead of drinking your morning coffee right away, you can turn it into a nutritious breakfast. Put a few ice cubes in it and store in the freezer for 15 minutes before adding it to your smoothie.

½ cup whole milk

1 cup cold coffee

1 medium banana, peeled

1 teaspoon cocoa powder

1 tablespoon peanut butter

1 cup ice

½ teaspoon vanilla extract

2 tablespoons honey

1 tablespoon chia seeds

Combine milk, coffee, banana, cocoa powder, peanut butter, ice, vanilla, and honey in a blender. Blend until smooth. Transfer to a tall glass and stir in chia seeds. Serve immediately.

SERVES 1	
Per Serving:	
Calories	474
Fat	17g
Protein	14g
Sodium	128mg
Fiber	10g
Carbohydrates	78g
Sugar	55g
Net Carbs	68g

Keto Sausage Breakfast Bowl

SERVES 1

Per Serving:

Calories	632
Fat	51g
Protein	31g
Sodium	1,323mg
Fiber	3g
Carbohydrates	14g
Sugar	5g
Net Carbs	11g

Not sure what kind of sausage to buy? You can buy precooked, frozen sausage that you pop in the microwave, or you can buy fresh sausage and fry it up in a skillet. The type of sausage doesn't make a significant difference in this recipe. Use breakfast sausage or sweet Italian sausage if you like milder flavors or spice it up with some hot sausage!

2 large eggs
2 tablespoons whole milk
½ cup sliced scallions, divided
1 tablespoon unsalted butter
½ cup crumbled cooked breakfast sausage
¼ cup shredded Cheddar cheese
¼ teaspoon salt
¼ teaspoon ground black pepper
¼ teaspoon garlic powder
¼ teaspoon onion powder
¼ cup mild salsa

1 In a large bowl, whisk together eggs, milk, and ¼ cup scallions.

2 Melt butter in a large frying pan over medium-low heat and swirl to coat the entire pan.

3 Pour egg mixture into the pan and cook, stirring, until almost set (about 2 minutes). Stir in sausage, cheese, salt, pepper, garlic powder, and onion powder. Continue to cook and stir until eggs are set and cheese is melted, about 1 minute more.

4 Transfer to a serving bowl and top with salsa and remaining ¼ cup scallions. Serve immediately.

Healthy Green Breakfast Bowl

If you need some more greens in your diet and you're not quite sure how to incorporate them, this Healthy Green Breakfast Bowl is the perfect start. The zucchini, spinach, green peppers, avocado, and cilantro make up a healthy and delicious combo.

1 tablespoon unsalted butter

½ medium zucchini, sliced

2 large eggs, beaten

2 cups baby spinach leaves

¼ cup chopped red onion

¼ cup chopped green bell pepper

½ cup diced cooked ham

⅛ teaspoon salt

¼ teaspoon ground black pepper

¼ teaspoon garlic powder

¼ cup shredded Cheddar cheese

½ medium avocado, peeled, pitted, and sliced

1 tablespoon chopped fresh cilantro

¼ cup mild salsa

1 Melt butter in a large frying pan over medium-low heat and swirl to coat the entire pan. Add zucchini and sauté 6–8 minutes until softened.

2 Add eggs, spinach, onion, bell pepper, ham, salt, black pepper, and garlic powder. Using a spatula, continue to stir until eggs are fully cooked and spinach is wilted, about 2 minutes.

3 Add cheese and cook until just melted. Immediately transfer to serving bowl and top with avocado, cilantro, and salsa. Serve warm.

SERVES 1

Per Serving:	
Calories	687
Fat	48g
Protein	47g
Sodium	2,178mg
Fiber	11g
Carbohydrates	30g
Sugar	8g
Net Carbs	19g

DON'T SKIMP ON THE SPINACH

It's hard to believe that the small pile of cooked spinach on your plate came from several cups of fresh leaves. But it's true. Spinach retains a lot of water, which is released during cooking, reducing its size. When cooking with spinach, count on using at least 1 cup of freshly packed spinach leaves per person.

On-the-Go Green Smoothie

SERVES 1

Per Serving:

Calories	461
Fat	22g
Protein	11g
Sodium	261mg
Fiber	22g
Carbohydrates	60g
Sugar	24g
Net Carbs	38g

MAKE YOUR OWN ALMOND MILK

Although there are a number of almond milks on the market, you can make your own version at home. Combine ½ cup water and 1 cup almonds in a blender and blend thoroughly. Strain before using.

Add 1 cup of vanilla Greek yogurt to this recipe for an extra protein punch. You can make your smoothie the night before and store it in the refrigerator, so you have a few extra minutes to sleep before getting to class in the morning.

1 cup unsweetened almond milk

2 cups baby spinach leaves

½ medium avocado, peeled and pitted

½ cup frozen pineapple chunks

1 medium banana, peeled and chopped

1 cup ice

2 tablespoons chia seeds

In a blender, combine milk, spinach, avocado, pineapple, banana, and ice. Blend until smooth. Pour into a large glass and stir in chia seeds. Serve immediately.

Fresh Fruit Granola

SERVES 1

Per Serving:

Calories	670
Fat	22g
Protein	15g
Sodium	80mg
Fiber	13g
Carbohydrates	104g
Sugar	58g
Net Carbs	91g

This is an easy version of muesli, the popular Swiss oatmeal dish. Feel free to add your own favorite fruits, or mix in yogurt instead of milk. You can eat this for breakfast or skip the milk and take it as a snack for later in the day.

½ medium Gala apple, cored and chopped
¼ cup chopped dried dates
1 cup granola
½ cup whole milk
1 tablespoon honey

Combine apple, dates, and granola in a serving bowl and pour milk over the top. Drizzle honey over granola mixture and serve.

Breakfast Banana Parfait

SERVES 1

Per Serving:

Calories	615
Fat	20g
Protein	28g
Sodium	98mg
Fiber	13g
Carbohydrates	82g
Sugar	38g
Net Carbs	69g

Instead of grabbing a fast-food yogurt parfait, which is usually loaded with added sugars, make your own version! The Greek yogurt in this parfait guarantees less added sugar.

¾ cup granola
¾ cup plain low-fat Greek yogurt
¼ small banana, peeled and sliced
1 tablespoon honey
1 tablespoon chia seeds

Place 2 tablespoons granola in the bottom of a tall glass. Add 2 tablespoons yogurt. Continue layering by alternating even portions of granola and yogurt. Top with banana, honey, and chia seeds. Serve immediately.

Gluten-Free Blueberry Poppy Seed Muffins

Be careful when you're zesting the lemon, as the grater is sharper than it looks! You can use the leftover lemon to squeeze some lemon juice over your muffins for a little extra flavor.

1 cup gluten-free all-purpose flour

⅓ cup granulated sugar

½ teaspoon salt

1 teaspoon baking powder

1 large egg

½ cup whole milk

¼ cup unsalted butter, melted

1 teaspoon vanilla extract

1 cup fresh blueberries

1 teaspoon lemon zest

2 tablespoons poppy seeds

MAKES 6 MUFFINS

Per Serving (1 muffin):	
Calories	238
Fat	11g
Protein	4g
Sodium	306mg
Fiber	1g
Carbohydrates	33g
Sugar	14g
Net Carbs	32g

1 Preheat oven to 375°F and grease a 6-cup muffin tin with non-stick cooking spray.

2 In a medium bowl, combine flour, sugar, salt, and baking powder. Set aside.

3 In a large mixing bowl, whisk together egg, milk, butter, and vanilla.

4 Add flour mixture to egg mixture and mix for 1 minute, making sure to scrape the sides of the bowl. Gently fold in blueberries, lemon zest, and poppy seeds.

5 Pour batter into muffin tin, filling each well about ⅔ full. Bake 20–25 minutes or until a toothpick inserted into the middle of a muffin comes out clean. Cool in pan for 5 minutes, then transfer muffins to a wire rack. Serve warm or at room temperature.

VE

Easy Crepes

Making crepes doesn't have to be a big production. These crepes are a cinch to whip up and are best served with some fresh fruit and syrup right when they come off the pan, but you can have them later for a study-break snack.

SERVES 4

Per Serving:

Calories	223
Fat	8g
Protein	9g
Sodium	214mg
Fiber	1g
Carbohydrates	27g
Sugar	6g
Net Carbs	26g

2 large eggs
¼ teaspoon salt
½ tablespoon granulated sugar
1 cup all-purpose flour
1¼ cups whole milk
1 tablespoon unsalted butter

1 In a small bowl, beat eggs, salt, and sugar.

2 In a large bowl, add flour and make a well by pushing the flour to the edges of the bowl and leaving about ½" of space in the middle. Gradually whisk egg mixture into the middle of the well until eggs and flour are fully combined.

3 Gradually whisk milk into flour mixture. Add more milk if needed to create a thin consistency. Let batter sit at room temperature for at least 30 minutes or until it starts to bubble at the top.

4 Melt butter over medium heat in a small frying pan. Add ¼ cup batter to the pan and swirl so the batter covers it entirely. Cook 2 minutes on one side, flip, then cook 2 minutes on the other side. Repeat with remaining batter. Serve warm or at room temperature.

CHAPTER 3

Lunch

Baked Pita Chips with Yogurt Dressing

SERVES 1

Per Serving:

Calories	395
Fat	18g
Protein	17g
Sodium	1,202mg
Fiber	2g
Carbohydrates	42g
Sugar	5g
Net Carbs	40g

Got a full day of classes ahead with no time for lunch? Just place the yogurt sauce in a to-go container and the chips in a plastic bag to take with you.

1 (8") pita bread
1 tablespoon olive oil
½ cup plain low-fat Greek yogurt
¼ teaspoon garlic salt
1 teaspoon lemon juice

1 tablespoon chopped red onion
2 sprigs fresh parsley, finely chopped
¼ teaspoon salt
¼ teaspoon ground black pepper

1 Preheat oven to 350°F.

2 Cut pita into six wedges. Brush both sides of each wedge with oil, place them on a baking sheet, and bake 8–10 minutes, turning once.

3 Combine yogurt, garlic salt, lemon juice, onion, parsley, salt, and pepper in a small bowl. Mix well. Serve with chips.

Mu Shu Chicken Wraps

SERVES 2

Per Serving:

Calories	189
Fat	7g
Protein	10g
Sodium	471mg
Fiber	1g
Carbohydrates	17g
Sugar	8g
Net Carbs	16g

For extra pops of flavor, replace the napa cabbage with a packaged coleslaw mixture and use a flavored tortilla wrap, such as red pepper.

4 teaspoons hoisin sauce
4 teaspoons low-sodium chicken broth
1 teaspoon honey
2 teaspoons olive oil

3 ounces boneless, skinless chicken breast, thinly sliced
¼ cup shredded napa cabbage
2 (6") flour tortillas

1 In a small bowl, combine hoisin sauce, broth, and honey. Set aside.

2 Heat oil in a medium frying pan over medium heat. Sauté chicken 5 minutes. Add cabbage and sauté 1 minute. Stir in hoisin sauce mixture. Remove pan from heat and cool 2 minutes.

3 Lay tortillas flat on a work surface. Spread ½ cup chicken mixture onto the bottom half of the wrap, spreading toward the edges. Roll each tortilla up tightly, cut wraps in half, and serve.

Asian Chicken Wraps

Make this dish even easier to prepare by using leftover cooked chicken, or buy a rotisserie chicken at the grocery store. Just chop the chicken into bite-sized pieces and add to the frying pan during the final stages of cooking to heat through.

2 teaspoons rice vinegar

2 teaspoons low-sodium soy sauce

2 teaspoons honey

2 tablespoons vegetable oil, divided

1 clove garlic, peeled and minced

1 (4-ounce) boneless, skinless chicken breast, cut into bite-sized pieces

3 tablespoons chopped yellow onion

⅓ cup chopped red bell pepper

¼ cup bean sprouts

⅛ teaspoon sesame oil

2 (8") flour tortillas

½ cup shredded romaine lettuce

DF

SERVES 2	
Per Serving:	
Calories	397
Fat	21g
Protein	17g
Sodium	906mg
Fiber	2g
Carbohydrates	41g
Sugar	9g
Net Carbs	39g

1 In a small bowl, combine rice vinegar, soy sauce, and honey, and set aside.

2 Heat 1 tablespoon vegetable oil in a large frying pan over medium-high heat. Add garlic and sauté 1 minute. Add chicken and sauté until no pink remains, about 5 minutes. Remove garlic and chicken from the pan and set aside.

3 Heat remaining 1 tablespoon vegetable oil in the same pan over medium-high heat. Add onion and sauté for about 1 minute. Add bell pepper and sauté for another minute, then add bean sprouts.

4 Stir in rice vinegar mixture. Cook, stirring constantly, until mixture boils. Add chicken and stir. Sprinkle sesame oil over the top. Remove from heat.

5 Place tortillas on a work surface. Top each with ¼ cup lettuce and half the chicken mixture. Roll each tortilla up tightly, cut wraps in half, and serve.

Dairy-Free Italian Pasta Salad

Before buying the salami, make sure to check the ingredient list. Some salami brands contain lactic acid, which originates from milk.

6 ounces rotini

1 tablespoon olive oil

1 medium zucchini, sliced

½ medium green bell pepper, seeded and chopped

¼ cup chopped red onion

½ cup steamed broccoli

½ cup sliced cherry tomatoes

¼ teaspoon salt

½ teaspoon ground black pepper

½ teaspoon dried oregano

2 ounces Genoa salami, chopped

⅓ cup Italian salad dressing

1 Cook rotini according to package instructions. Drain, then rinse with cold water and drain again. Set aside.

2 Heat oil in a medium frying pan over medium heat. Add zucchini, bell pepper, onion, broccoli, tomatoes, salt, black pepper, and oregano. Cook 10–15 minutes, stirring occasionally, until zucchini and onion are soft.

3 Add cooked rotini and zucchini mixture to a large mixing bowl. Mix well, then add salami and Italian dressing. Stir until fully combined. Refrigerate at least 2 hours before serving.

SERVES 2

Per Serving:

Calories	603
Fat	26g
Protein	19g
Sodium	1,181mg
Fiber	6g
Carbohydrates	76g
Sugar	12g
Net Carbs	70g

GENOA SALAMI

What makes Genoa salami different from hard salami or other cured meats like sop-pressata? Along with the traditional seasonings for salami like garlic and salt, Genoa salami adds some black and white peppercorns and red wine. It also usually has a higher fat content, giving the meat a richer flavor.

Greek Salad Pita Sandwich

Greek salad is super-easy to make and requires very few ingredients. If you're not a fan of feta cheese, try substituting with ricotta cheese instead.

SERVES 1	
Per Serving:	
Calories	408
Fat	32g
Protein	5g
Sodium	1,130mg
Fiber	3g
Carbohydrates	26g
Sugar	3g
Net Carbs	23g

½ medium tomato, sliced into thin wedges

1 cup shredded romaine lettuce

8 medium cucumber slices

¼ cup crumbled feta cheese

6 whole black olives, pitted and chopped

2 tablespoons extra-virgin olive oil

¼ teaspoon salt

¼ teaspoon ground black pepper

1 (4") pita bread, halved

1 In a medium bowl, toss tomato, lettuce, and cucumber together. Add cheese, olives, and oil, and toss again. Sprinkle with salt and pepper.

2 Fill each pita pocket with half of the salad and serve.

Classic BLT

You can replace the mayonnaise with mashed avocado for a healthier but still flavorful alternative.

SERVES 1	
Per Serving:	
Calories	330
Fat	20g
Protein	12g
Sodium	714mg
Fiber	5g
Carbohydrates	30g
Sugar	13g
Net Carbs	25g

2 strips bacon

1 tablespoon mayonnaise

2 (1-ounce) slices whole-wheat bread, toasted

4 slices tomato

2 large romaine lettuce leaves

1 Heat large frying pan over medium-high heat. Add bacon and cook 4–5 minutes. Using a fork, flip bacon and cook another 2–3 minutes until crispy. Drain bacon on paper towels and cut into strips about 3" long.

2 Spread mayonnaise on both slices of bread. Lay bacon on 1 slice of bread on top of the mayonnaise. Lay tomato slices on top of bacon and top with lettuce. Place remaining slice on top to close the sandwich, cut in half, and serve.

Grilled Cheese Sandwich

Ever put ketchup on a grilled cheese? Try it! You'll be surprised at how it transforms this humble sandwich.

2 teaspoons ketchup

2 (1-ounce) slices whole-wheat bread

2 (2-ounce) slices American cheese

1½ tablespoons softened unsalted butter, divided

SERVES 1	
Per Serving:	
Calories	581
Fat	39g
Protein	22g
Sodium	1,402mg
Fiber	4g
Carbohydrates	37g
Sugar	18g
Net Carbs	33g

1 Spread ketchup on 1 slice of bread. Place cheese slices over ketchup and top with remaining slice of bread.

2 Melt 1 tablespoon butter in a large frying pan over medium heat.

3 Add sandwich to the frying pan. Cook until bottom is golden brown, about 3–4 minutes.

4 Push sandwich to the edge of the pan and add remaining ½ tablespoon butter. Turn sandwich over and cook 3–4 minutes until cheese is melted. Remove from pan and cut in half. Serve immediately.

Simple Stuffed Pita Sandwich

This Simple Stuffed Pita Sandwich will be your new go-to lunch. Make the filling the night before to save some time the next day. You can also toss in some leftover chicken if you have it.

½ small Gala apple, cored and finely chopped

½ medium celery stalk, chopped

½ cup shredded romaine lettuce

¼ cup shredded Cheddar cheese

1 tablespoon Thousand Island salad dressing

1 tablespoon chopped walnuts

1 (4") pita bread, halved

SERVES 1	
Per Serving:	
Calories	335
Fat	18g
Protein	11g
Sodium	514mg
Fiber	3g
Carbohydrates	32g
Sugar	11g
Net Carbs	29g

1 Mix apple, celery, lettuce, cheese, dressing, and walnuts in a small bowl. Cover and refrigerate at least 2 hours.

2 Fill each pita pocket with half the salad and serve.

Meatless Mexican Taco Salad

SERVES 1

Per Serving:

Calories	739
Fat	52g
Protein	30g
Sodium	1,092mg
Fiber	11g
Carbohydrates	45g
Sugar	10g
Net Carbs	34g

Don't have time to cook ground beef? No problem! This one-step recipe includes extra cheese instead of meat, so you'll save time and have a tasty alternative to a heavier meat dish. If you like your tacos extra spicy, slice up a jalapeño to toss in or use a medium or hot salsa instead of mild.

1 cup shredded romaine lettuce

½ small red bell pepper, seeded and chopped

½ small green bell pepper, seeded and chopped

1 small tomato, chopped

1 cup shredded Monterey jack cheese

3 tablespoons mild salsa

½ medium avocado, peeled, pitted, and sliced

1 ounce (about 12) tortilla chips

1 Combine lettuce, bell peppers, tomato, and cheese in a small salad bowl. Stir in salsa and top with avocado.

2 Serve salad with tortilla chips.

Deviled Egg Sandwich

SERVES 1

Per Serving:

Calories	394
Fat	22g
Protein	18g
Sodium	1,954mg
Fiber	5g
Carbohydrates	30g
Sugar	12g
Net Carbs	25g

This classic egg sandwich is perfect if you have some leftover hard-boiled eggs in the refrigerator. Add chopped pickles and celery for some extra crunch and a little more paprika for extra spice.

2 Hard-Boiled Eggs (see recipe in Chapter 2), peeled and roughly chopped

1 tablespoon mayonnaise

2 teaspoons Dijon mustard

⅛ teaspoon paprika

½ teaspoon salt

½ teaspoon ground black pepper

½ cup shredded romaine lettuce

¼ small tomato, seeded and finely chopped

2 (1-ounce) slices whole-wheat bread, toasted

1 In a small bowl, add eggs, mayonnaise, and Dijon mustard and mash to combine. Stir in paprika, salt, pepper, lettuce, and tomato. Mix well.

2 Spread half of the mixture on 1 slice of bread. Place remaining slice on top to close the sandwich, cut in half, and serve.

Herbed Tomato Soup

Don't let the lengthy ingredient list throw you! This is a classic one-pot dish that will pair perfectly with a grilled cheese or crackers. For extra creaminess, use an electric blender before serving to give it that characteristic tomato soup texture.

2 tablespoons olive oil

½ medium yellow onion, peeled and chopped

½ small green bell pepper, seeded and chopped

1 cup stewed tomatoes, with juice

1 small celery stalk, thinly sliced

¼ teaspoon celery salt

¼ teaspoon dried thyme

1 bay leaf

2 cups low-sodium chicken broth

1 cup water

¼ teaspoon salt

½ teaspoon ground black pepper

½ teaspoon light brown sugar, divided

1 Heat oil in a large saucepan over medium heat. Add onion and green pepper. Reduce heat to medium-low and sauté about 5 minutes until onion is soft and translucent.

2 Add tomatoes, celery, celery salt, thyme, and bay leaf. Simmer 5 minutes.

3 Add broth, water, salt, and black pepper. Bring to a boil, reduce heat, and simmer for another 10 minutes. Remove bay leaf.

4 Transfer to serving bowls and stir in brown sugar. Serve immediately.

SERVES 2

Per Serving:

Calories	219
Fat	14g
Protein	3g
Sodium	735mg
Fiber	5g
Carbohydrates	21g
Sugar	15g
Net Carbs	16g

BELL PEPPER TYPES

Ever wonder what the difference is between green, orange, yellow, and red bell peppers? Actually, each type comes from the same plant. Red peppers are left to ripen longer on the vine than green, so they are sweeter. The orange and yellow peppers are not as bitter as green peppers but are not as sweet as red.

Corn Tortilla Chicken Quesadilla

SERVES 1

Per Serving:

Calories	406
Fat	28g
Protein	16g
Sodium	512mg
Fiber	2g
Carbohydrates	20g
Sugar	4g
Net Carbs	18g

You can use rotisserie chicken from the grocery store, bake some chicken breasts, or sauté some chicken tenders for this delicious quesadilla. For extra flavor, toss the chicken with salsa before placing it on top of the tortilla and use guacamole as a dipping sauce.

¼ cup shredded cooked chicken breast

⅛ teaspoon chili powder

1 tablespoon unsalted butter

1 (8") corn tortilla

4 tablespoons shredded Cheddar cheese, divided

1 large fresh button mushroom, sliced

½ medium scallion, diced

2 tablespoons sour cream

¼ cup mild salsa

1　In a small bowl, toss chicken with chili powder. Set aside.

2　Melt butter in a medium frying pan over low heat and swirl to coat the entire pan, then add tortilla. Cook 1 minute, then sprinkle 2 tablespoons cheese on half of the tortilla. Heat until cheese melts, about 2 minutes, then add chicken on top. Lay mushroom slices on top of chicken and add scallions. Fold tortilla in half.

3　Cook tortilla until browned on the bottom, about 3 minutes, then flip and cook another 5 minutes. Sprinkle remaining 2 tablespoons cheese over tortilla and cook 1 minute, then remove from pan. Serve hot with sour cream and salsa on the side for dipping.

The Ultimate Sub Sandwich

This hearty sub sandwich is perfect for tucking into your backpack and eating on your lunch break or between classes.

1 (8") whole-wheat sub roll

1 tablespoon mustard

1 tablespoon mayonnaise

1½ tablespoons peeled and finely chopped red onion

1 large romaine lettuce leaf

2 (2-ounce) slices deli ham

1 (2-ounce) slice Cheddar cheese

2 (2-ounce) slices deli turkey

1 (2-ounce) slice mozzarella cheese

½ medium tomato, seeded and sliced

4 dill pickle slices

SERVES 1	
Per Serving:	
Calories	1,112
Fat	52g
Protein	76g
Sodium	5,177mg
Fiber	7g
Carbohydrates	72g
Sugar	15g
Net Carbs	65g

1 Slice roll in half lengthwise, making sure to not cut all the way through. Spread mustard on one half and mayonnaise on the other.

2 Fill roll with onion, lettuce, ham, Cheddar cheese, turkey, mozzarella cheese, tomato, and pickles. Cut in half and serve.

Middle Eastern Hummus

Hummus makes for the perfect addition to your lunch, as it's high in protein and fiber. It's also tasty, versatile, and easy to transport.

1 (19-ounce) can chickpeas, with liquid

2 large cloves garlic, peeled and finely chopped

2 tablespoons plus 1 teaspoon lemon juice

2 tablespoons tahini

¼ teaspoon ground cumin

2 (8") pita breads

SERVES 2	
Per Serving:	
Calories	491
Fat	13g
Protein	24g
Sodium	529mg
Fiber	21g
Carbohydrates	68g
Sugar	10g
Net Carbs	47g

1 Drain chickpeas, reserving 4 tablespoons liquid. Rinse chickpeas and drain again. Transfer chickpeas to a blender. Pulse two or three times until smooth.

2 Add reserved chickpea liquid, garlic, lemon juice, tahini, and cumin to blender and blend until smooth.

3 Cut pitas into six wedges each. Spread hummus evenly on each wedge and serve.

(GF) Loaded Sweet Potatoes

This is the ultimate healthy comfort food recipe. Top it off with some Greek yogurt for a healthier sour cream alternative and add some shredded chicken for extra protein.

Per Serving:

Calories	224
Fat	10g
Protein	11g
Sodium	370mg
Fiber	5g
Carbohydrates	26g
Sugar	7g
Net Carbs	21g

HOW TO STEAM SWEET POTATOES

Steaming sweet potatoes is easy! All you need to do is prick each potato several times with a fork, put them on a microwave-safe plate, and pop them in the microwave for 7–9 minutes or until cooked through. Use tongs to pick them up. They'll be hot!

2 large sweet potatoes, steamed (see sidebar on this page)
4 strips bacon
½ cup canned black beans, drained and rinsed
½ cup shredded Cheddar cheese
¼ cup chopped scallions
½ teaspoon paprika
½ teaspoon garlic powder
¼ teaspoon salt
½ teaspoon ground black pepper
2 tablespoons sour cream

1 Preheat oven to 375°F.

2 Cut sweet potatoes in half and scoop out the flesh, leaving only a thin layer of potato and skin. Put flesh in a medium mixing bowl. Place skins on an ungreased baking sheet and set aside.

3 Heat a large frying pan over medium-high heat. Add bacon and cook 4–5 minutes. Using a fork, flip bacon and cook another 2–3 minutes until crispy. Drain bacon on paper towels until cool, then crumble and add to mixing bowl with potatoes.

4 Add beans, cheese, scallions, paprika, garlic powder, salt, and pepper to sweet potato mixture and mix well.

5 Transfer sweet potato mixture back into potato skins and bake 5 minutes or until cheese is melted. Top with sour cream and serve.

Whole-Wheat Pasta with Basil and Tomato Pesto

SERVES 4

Per Serving:

Calories	580
Fat	40g
Protein	14g
Sodium	195mg
Fiber	4g
Carbohydrates	47g
Sugar	3g
Net Carbs	43g

This simple pasta dish is a breeze to make and is filled with delicious earthy flavors.

8 ounces whole-wheat rigatoni

3 cloves garlic, peeled and chopped

⅓ cup pine nuts

1 cup chopped tomato

¼ cup chopped fresh basil

½ cup olive oil

½ cup grated Parmesan cheese

1 Cook rigatoni according to package instructions. Drain.

2 Process garlic and pine nuts in a food processor until pine nuts are finely chopped. Add tomato and basil and process again. Slowly add oil and continue processing until thick and creamy. Add cheese and pulse until combined.

3 Pour pesto sauce over rigatoni and stir to combine. Serve immediately.

Roasted Pepper and Chickpea Soup

SERVES 2

Per Serving:

Calories	257
Fat	13g
Protein	10g
Sodium	1,064mg
Fiber	7g
Carbohydrates	26g
Sugar	6g
Net Carbs	19g

This healthy soup makes a high-protein lunch, thanks to the chickpeas.

1 tablespoon olive oil

1 clove garlic, peeled and chopped

¼ cup chopped yellow onion

1 cup sliced fresh button mushrooms

2½ cups low-sodium chicken broth

1½ cups chopped roasted red bell peppers

¾ cup canned chickpeas, drained and rinsed

¼ teaspoon salt

¼ teaspoon ground black pepper

1 Heat oil in a medium saucepan over medium heat. Add garlic and onion and sauté about 5 minutes until onion is soft and translucent. Add mushrooms and cook 1–2 minutes, stirring occasionally.

2 Add broth and increase heat to medium-high. Bring to a boil, then add roasted peppers and chickpeas. Reduce heat to medium-low and simmer 5 minutes. Stir in salt and pepper and serve immediately.

Keto Taco Salad

This taco salad is great for a quick, delicious, and healthy lunch.

½ pound 85% lean ground beef

1 (1-ounce) packet taco seasoning mix

4 cups chopped romaine lettuce

½ cup mild salsa

¼ cup chopped fresh cilantro

1 cup shredded Cheddar cheese

½ cup sour cream

1 medium avocado, peeled, pitted, and sliced

SERVES 4	
Per Serving:	
Calories	369
Fat	29g
Protein	20g
Sodium	475mg
Fiber	4g
Carbohydrates	10g
Sugar	4g
Net Carbs	6g

1 Heat a medium frying pan over medium heat and add ground beef. Sauté, using a large spoon to break up beef. Cook until no longer pink, about 5 minutes. Add taco seasoning and cook 5–7 minutes, stirring occasionally.

2 Add lettuce to a large serving bowl, then add beef, salsa, cilantro, cheese, and sour cream. Mix well. Top with avocado and serve.

Greek Yogurt Chicken Salad

You can eat this chicken salad on a sandwich, in a pita pocket, in a wrap, with crackers, or just on its own. The best part? It's so full of protein, you won't be hungry until dinner.

1 (6-ounce) boneless, skinless chicken breast

1 cup plain low-fat Greek yogurt

1 medium celery stalk, chopped

¼ cup chopped red onion

1 cup chopped green grapes

½ teaspoon garlic salt

1 teaspoon ground black pepper

SERVES 2	
Per Serving:	
Calories	230
Fat	5g
Protein	31g
Sodium	363mg
Fiber	1g
Carbohydrates	15g
Sugar	10g
Net Carbs	14g

1 Fill a medium saucepan with water and bring to a boil over medium-high heat. Add chicken, reduce heat to medium-low, and simmer 20–25 minutes until cooked through. Remove chicken from pan.

2 Cut chicken into 1" cubes and transfer to a small mixing bowl. Add yogurt, celery, onion, grapes, garlic salt, and pepper. Mix well. Refrigerate at least 1 hour before serving.

Hummus and Vegetable Wraps

SERVES 2

Per Serving:

Calories	304
Fat	13g
Protein	9g
Sodium	825mg
Fiber	8g
Carbohydrates	40g
Sugar	5g
Net Carbs	32g

This hummus wrap lets you load up on your vegetables in one delicious sandwich! Not only is this wrap portable and easy to eat on the go; it's the perfect way to sneak some nutritious greens into your diet. Try a flavored hummus like garlic or spicy red pepper.

2 (10") flour tortillas

4 tablespoons hummus

2 teaspoons lemon juice

¼ teaspoon salt

¼ teaspoon ground black pepper

½ teaspoon garlic powder

2 teaspoons sesame seeds

1 cup baby spinach leaves

½ small green bell pepper, seeded and thinly sliced

½ small cucumber, thinly sliced

½ small carrot, peeled and grated

¼ cup shredded cabbage

½ small tomato, thinly sliced

½ medium avocado, peeled, pitted, and sliced

1   Place tortillas on a work surface. In a small bowl, combine hummus and lemon juice. Spoon hummus mixture onto tortillas, spreading outward, making sure to leave 1" of room around the edges. Sprinkle salt, black pepper, garlic powder, and sesame seeds over hummus.

2   Divide spinach, bell pepper, cucumber, carrot, cabbage, tomato, and avocado between the 2 tortillas. Roll tortillas up tightly, cut in half, and serve.

Paleo Avocado and Shrimp Wraps

You can find precooked shrimp in the freezer section of the grocery store. Just thaw as much as you'll need at a time. If the lettuce doesn't cooperate with you as a wrap, you can always turn this recipe into a healthy shrimp salad.

20 small cooked shrimp, peeled and deveined

¼ cup chopped red onion

⅛ cup chopped fresh cilantro

1 tablespoon lime juice

1 tablespoon grated lime zest

½ cup chopped cherry tomatoes

1 medium avocado, peeled, pitted, and cubed

½ teaspoon garlic power

¼ teaspoon cayenne pepper

½ teaspoon paprika

¼ teaspoon salt

½ teaspoon ground black pepper

6 large iceberg lettuce leaves

¼ cup sliced scallions

1 In a large bowl, combine shrimp, onion, cilantro, lime juice, lime zest, tomatoes, avocado, garlic powder, cayenne pepper, paprika, salt, and black pepper. Mix well and refrigerate at least 20 minutes.

2 Put lettuce on a large plate and carefully spoon in an even amount of shrimp mixture onto each leaf. Garnish with scallions and serve immediately.

SERVES 2

Per Serving:

Calories	238
Fat	14g
Protein	20g
Sodium	303mg
Fiber	7g
Carbohydrates	12g
Sugar	2g
Net Carbs	5g

Hot Turkey, Apple, and Cheddar Sandwich

You can heat this up in a panini press if you have one. The cheese will melt in your mouth, and the apples will soften and be easier to bite into. If you want some extra sweetness, drizzle more honey over the cheese before serving.

1 tablespoon mayonnaise

¼ teaspoon garlic powder

¼ teaspoon celery salt

1 teaspoon honey

½ teaspoon lemon juice

2 (1-ounce) slices whole-wheat bread, toasted

1 tablespoon mustard

1 tablespoon unsalted butter

3 (2-ounce) slices deli turkey

4 thin slices medium Gala apple

2 (1-ounce) slices Cheddar cheese

2 slices tomato

2 thin slices peeled red onion

3 large romaine lettuce leaves

1 In a small bowl, combine mayonnaise, garlic powder, celery salt, honey, and lemon juice. Mix well, then spread onto 1 slice of bread. Spread mustard on the other slice.

2 Heat a small frying pan over medium-low heat and add butter, swirling to coat the entire pan.

3 Add turkey slices, one on top of the other, to the pan. Layer apples and cheese on top of turkey. Cook 5 minutes until cheese begins to melt. Transfer turkey, apple, and cheese stack to the slice of bread spread with mayonnaise mixture. Top with tomato, onion, and lettuce. Place slice of bread with mustard on top to close the sandwich, cut in half, and serve.

SERVES 1	
Per Serving:	
Calories	600
Fat	32g
Protein	33g
Sodium	2,608mg
Fiber	4g
Carbohydrates	37g
Sugar	19g
Net Carbs	33g

SANDWICH DEFINED

According to the United States Department of Agriculture, a sandwich "must contain at least 35 percent cooked meat and no more than 50 percent bread."

Tuna Salad Sandwich

DF

Add a slice of cheese on top, then pop the sandwich in the toaster oven for 2 minutes to create a delicious tuna melt version.

SERVES 1	
Per Serving:	
Calories	418
Fat	24g
Protein	23g
Sodium	1,286mg
Fiber	5g
Carbohydrates	28g
Sugar	12g
Net Carbs	23g

1 (3-ounce) can solid white tuna, drained

2 tablespoons mayonnaise

¼ cup chopped gherkin pickles

2 teaspoons pickle brine

2 tablespoons chopped scallions

¼ teaspoon salt

¼ teaspoon ground black pepper

¼ teaspoon garlic powder

½ teaspoon sesame seeds

2 (1-ounce) slices whole-wheat bread, toasted

2 large romaine lettuce leaves

1 Combine tuna, mayonnaise, pickles, pickle brine, scallions, salt, pepper, garlic powder, and sesame seeds in a small bowl.

2 Spread tuna mixture onto 1 bread slice and top with lettuce. Place remaining bread slice on top, cut in half, and serve.

Keto Egg Salad

Egg salad is already keto-friendly, but the avocado adds even more healthy fats. You can add a ¼ teaspoon of lemon juice to prevent the avocado from browning.

SERVES 1	
Per Serving:	
Calories	313
Fat	26g
Protein	14g
Sodium	245mg
Fiber	3g
Carbohydrates	5g
Sugar	1g
Net Carbs	2g

2 Hard-Boiled Eggs (see recipe in Chapter 2), peeled and roughly chopped

¼ medium avocado, peeled, pitted, and roughly chopped

1 tablespoon mayonnaise

¼ cup chopped gherkin pickles

2 teaspoons pickle brine

1 tablespoon chopped parsley

1 tablespoon chopped dill

1 tablespoon chopped scallions

¼ teaspoon paprika

Combine eggs, avocado, mayonnaise, pickles, pickle brine, parsley, dill, and scallions in a medium mixing bowl. Mash together with a fork until there are no large egg or avocado pieces. Sprinkle paprika on top and serve.

Rainbow Beet and Goat Cheese Salad

This salad is a treat for your eyes and your taste buds! The fruits and vegetables are bursting with healthy colors, and the sweet maple syrup complements the goat cheese perfectly.

2 large sweet potatoes, peeled and cubed

4 tablespoons olive oil, divided

½ teaspoon salt

½ teaspoon ground black pepper

1 teaspoon garlic powder

¼ teaspoon cayenne pepper

1 (15-ounce) can sliced beets, drained and chopped

10 ounces baby arugula

½ cup crumbled goat cheese

½ cup fresh raspberries

1 medium Granny Smith apple, cored and chopped

1 medium avocado, peeled, pitted, and diced

¼ cup finely chopped pecans

2 tablespoons balsamic vinegar

2 teaspoons maple syrup

SERVES 4	
Per Serving:	
Calories	427
Fat	26g
Protein	8g
Sodium	393mg
Fiber	9g
Carbohydrates	39g
Sugar	19g
Net Carbs	30g

1 Preheat oven to 375°F and line a large baking sheet with parchment paper.

2 Place sweet potatoes on prepared baking sheet and toss with 1 tablespoon oil. Bake 25–30 minutes until crispy. Transfer to a large bowl and sprinkle with salt, black pepper, garlic powder, and cayenne pepper. Mix well.

3 Carefully stir in beets, arugula, cheese, raspberries, apple, avocado, and pecans.

4 In a small bowl, mix together vinegar, maple syrup, and remaining 3 tablespoons oil. Drizzle over salad and toss. Serve immediately.

DF

Teriyaki Chicken

HOT AND STEAMY VEGETABLES

To get the most nutritional benefit out of your vegetables, it's best to steam them. This is easier than ever these days! You can buy frozen, steamable bags of vegetables that you can pop in the microwave for 5 minutes or less. Top with a little salt and pepper and voilà! You have hot and steamy vegetables.

This classic Asian recipe works for either lunch or dinner. While the chicken is cooking, make a side of rice and broccoli for a full meal. This is an easy recipe to double so you can save the leftovers for the next day!

3 tablespoons low-sodium soy sauce

1 tablespoon honey

1 tablespoon light brown sugar

½ teaspoon ground ginger

1 teaspoon garlic powder

1 tablespoon rice wine vinegar

2 teaspoons sesame oil

1 teaspoon salt

1 teaspoon ground black pepper

1 tablespoon canola oil

2 (6-ounce) boneless, skinless chicken breasts, cut into 1" cubes

1 tablespoon sesame seeds

1 medium scallion, sliced

1 In a small mixing bowl, combine soy sauce, honey, brown sugar, ginger, garlic powder, rice wine vinegar, sesame oil, salt, and pepper. Mix well until brown sugar is dissolved. Set aside.

2 Heat oil in a medium frying pan over medium heat, then add chicken. Sauté 10 minutes or until no longer pink.

3 Add soy sauce mixture to the pan, increase heat to medium high, and bring to a boil. Reduce heat to medium-low and simmer 10 minutes.

4 Remove from heat, top with sesame seeds and scallions, and serve immediately.

Gluten-Free Quinoa Salad

This salad is packed with powerful proteins to keep you feeling full throughout the entire day. The chickpeas, feta, and quinoa will give you the energy you need to power through those late afternoon lectures without falling asleep.

¼ cup uncooked rinsed quinoa

½ cup water

1 tablespoon unsalted butter

2 cups baby spinach leaves

½ cup canned chickpeas, drained and rinsed

1 small cucumber, peeled and sliced into half moons

¼ cup sliced cherry tomatoes

¼ cup diced red onion

¼ cup crumbled feta cheese

½ teaspoon garlic powder

1 teaspoon dried parsley

¼ teaspoon salt

½ teaspoon ground black pepper

SERVES 2

Per Serving:

Calories	294
Fat	12g
Protein	14g
Sodium	830mg
Fiber	7g
Carbohydrates	32g
Sugar	4g
Net Carbs	25g

1 Combine quinoa and water in a small saucepan. Bring to a boil over medium-high heat, then reduce heat to low and simmer 10–15 minutes or until quinoa has absorbed most of the water. Remove from heat, put a lid on the saucepan, and let rest for 5–10 minutes until quinoa has fluffed up. Set aside.

2 Heat a medium frying pan over medium heat and add butter, swirling to coat the entire pan. Add spinach and cook 5 minutes or until wilted. Remove from heat and set aside.

3 In a large serving bowl, add chickpeas, cucumber, tomatoes, onion, cheese, garlic powder, parsley, salt, and pepper. Mix well. Add quinoa and spinach, stirring to combine. Serve warm or cold.

Gluten-Free Hummus Roll-Ups

SERVES 2

Per Serving:

Calories	236
Fat	12g
Protein	10g
Sodium	688mg
Fiber	4g
Carbohydrates	29g
Sugar	6g
Net Carbs	25g

You can find gluten-free tortillas next to the regular tortillas or in the health food aisle of your grocery store. You can also use coconut wraps or almond flour wraps. For a spicier roll-up, use a flavored hummus.

¼ cup hummus

1 tablespoon lime juice

1 tablespoon grated lime zest

2 tablespoons chopped fresh cilantro

¼ teaspoon salt

¼ teaspoon ground black pepper

¼ cup shredded Swiss cheese

2 (8") gluten-free tortillas

½ medium cucumber, peeled and sliced

¾ cup baby spinach leaves

½ medium green bell pepper, seeded and sliced

1. In a small mixing bowl, combine hummus, lime juice, lime zest, cilantro, salt, black pepper, and cheese. Mix well.

2. Lay tortillas flat on a large serving plate. Spoon half the hummus mixture onto each wrap, spreading outward, making sure to leave 1" of room around the edges.

3. Layer cucumber, spinach, and bell pepper on top of hummus. Roll each tortilla up tightly, then slice into pinwheels, putting a toothpick in each one to hold in place. Serve immediately or refrigerate up to 8 hours.

CHAPTER 4

Simple Snacks on the Go

Supreme Pizza Crackers

SERVES 1

Per Serving:

Calories	389
Fat	18g
Protein	35g
Sodium	2,175mg
Fiber	3g
Carbohydrates	25g
Sugar	3g
Net Carbs	22g

Like to load up on extra pizza toppings? Choose whichever ingredients you like best on a pizza and throw them on. The classic cheese and tomato sauce combo works just as well, if you prefer.

3 tablespoons tomato sauce

1 (6") pita bread

2 (2-ounce) slices deli ham

2 large fresh button mushrooms, sliced

2 tablespoons sliced black olives

⅓ cup shredded Cheddar cheese

1 Preheat oven broiler.

2 Spread tomato sauce on pita bread. Lay ham on top, then add mushrooms and olives. Sprinkle cheese over top. Broil for about 2–3 minutes, until cheese melts. Cut into wedges and serve.

Healthy Popcorn with Yogurt

SERVES 1

Per Serving:

Calories	145
Fat	2g
Protein	6g
Sodium	21mg
Fiber	2g
Carbohydrates	29g
Sugar	18g
Net Carbs	27g

Use unbuttered popcorn and your favorite flavor of Greek yogurt for this healthy alternative to movie popcorn saturated in fake butter. Feel free to add nuts or dried fruit to the mix for some extra flavor.

1½ cups popped popcorn

3 tablespoons plain low-fat Greek yogurt

1 tablespoon honey

¼ teaspoon ground nutmeg

Place popcorn in a large bowl. In a small bowl, combine yogurt and honey. Add to the popcorn, tossing to mix. Sprinkle with nutmeg and serve.

Banana Muffins

If you like banana bread, you'll love these easy muffins. You can make them ahead of time, store them in the freezer, and pop them in the microwave whenever you want a sweet snack. Spread some cream cheese, butter, or apple butter over the top for some extra sweetness.

1 large egg

1 cup whole milk

¼ cup canola oil

¾ teaspoon baking soda

¾ teaspoon baking powder

⅛ teaspoon salt

1½ cups all-purpose flour

3 tablespoons honey

1 cup mashed banana (about 2 medium peeled bananas)

¼ teaspoon ground cinnamon

1 Preheat oven to 375°F and spray a 12-cup muffin tin with non-stick cooking spray.

2 In a small bowl, beat together egg, milk, and oil. Set aside.

3 In a large bowl, stir baking soda, baking powder, and salt into flour until well-blended.

4 Add egg mixture to flour mixture and stir to form batter. Be careful not to overmix batter; don't worry if there are lumps. Stir in honey, banana, and cinnamon until combined but do not beat.

5 Spoon batter into muffin tin wells until about ⅔ full. Bake 20–25 minutes or until a toothpick inserted into the middle of a muffin comes out clean. Cool in pan for 5 minutes, then transfer muffins to a wire rack. Serve warm or at room temperature.

MAKES 12 MUFFINS

Per Serving (1 muffin):

Calories	147
Fat	6g
Protein	3g
Sodium	150mg
Fiber	1g
Carbohydrates	21g
Sugar	8g
Net Carbs	20g

Blueberry Muffins

MAKES 12 MUFFINS

Per Serving (1 muffin):

Calories	139
Fat	5g
Protein	3g
Sodium	152mg
Fiber	2g
Carbohydrates	21g
Sugar	8g
Net Carbs	19g

LET'S GET BAKED!

Muffins get their distinctive domed shape from the addition of baking powder. When baking powder comes into contact with wet ingredients, carbon dioxide gas is released. This causes the batter to expand. The reaction is quick, so it's important to get muffins in the oven as quickly as possible after making the batter. Otherwise, too much gas escapes before they're heated, leading to flat-topped muffins.

If you don't have buttermilk, just add 1 tablespoon lemon juice to 1 cup whole milk and let it sit for a minute.

1 large egg

1 cup buttermilk

3 tablespoons canola oil

¾ cup all-purpose flour

¾ cup whole-wheat flour

¼ cup rolled oats

¾ teaspoon baking powder

½ teaspoon baking soda

⅛ teaspoon salt

⅓ cup light brown sugar

1 cup blueberries

1 Preheat oven to 375°F and spray a 12-cup muffin tin with non-stick cooking spray.

2 In a small bowl, beat together egg, buttermilk, and oil. Set aside.

3 In a large bowl, combine all-purpose flour, whole-wheat flour, and oats. Stir in baking powder, baking soda, salt, and brown sugar until well blended.

4 Add egg mixture to flour mixture and stir to form a batter. Be careful not to overmix batter; don't worry if there are lumps. Gently stir in blueberries.

5 Spoon batter into muffin tin wells until about ⅔ full. Bake 20–25 minutes or until a toothpick inserted into the middle of a muffin comes out clean. Cool in pan for 5 minutes, then transfer muffins to a wire rack. Serve warm or at room temperature.

Apple Cinnamon Muffins

MAKES 12 MUFFINS

Per Serving (1 muffin):

Calories	166
Fat	6g
Protein	3g
Sodium	183mg
Fiber	1g
Carbohydrates	24g
Sugar	11g
Net Carbs	23g

HEALTHIER OILS

It's often essential to include some sort of oil while baking or cooking. However, a lot of oils, like vegetable oil, contain high amounts of trans and saturated fats. Opt instead for olive, canola, flaxseed, grapeseed, avocado, or coconut oil. They're healthier alternatives that won't totally tank your nutrition.

There's nothing better than sweet apple and cinnamon combined in a soft, delicious muffin to warm you up on a cold day. For extra flavor, add some cranberries or walnuts and drizzle honey over the top before serving.

1 large egg
1 teaspoon vanilla extract
1 cup buttermilk
¼ cup canola oil
1½ teaspoons baking powder
½ teaspoon baking soda
⅛ teaspoon salt
½ cup granulated sugar
1¾ cups all-purpose flour
¾ teaspoon ground cinnamon
½ teaspoon ground nutmeg
1½ cups diced apple

1 Preheat oven to 375°F and spray a 12-cup muffin tin with non-stick cooking spray.

2 In a small bowl, beat together egg, vanilla, buttermilk, and oil. Set aside.

3 In a large bowl, combine baking powder, baking soda, salt, sugar, flour, cinnamon, and nutmeg and mix well.

4 Add egg mixture to flour mixture and stir to form a batter. Be careful not to overmix batter; don't worry if there are lumps. Stir in apple.

5 Spoon batter into muffin tin wells until about ⅔ full. Bake 20–25 minutes or until a toothpick inserted into the middle of a muffin comes out clean. Cool in pan for 5 minutes, then transfer muffins to a wire rack. Serve warm or at room temperature.

Cinnamon Raisin Granola

Try adding 3 tablespoons shredded coconut halfway through cooking and 3 tablespoons chocolate chips once cooled.

2 cups rolled oats

¼ cup slivered almonds

1 teaspoon ground cinnamon

6 tablespoons apple juice

2 tablespoons canola oil

1 tablespoon unsalted butter

1 teaspoon salt

2 tablespoons light brown sugar

1 cup raisins

SERVES 4	
Per Serving:	
Calories	426
Fat	17g
Protein	8g
Sodium	601mg
Fiber	6g
Carbohydrates	66g
Sugar	32g
Net Carbs	60g

1 Preheat oven to 250°F. Line a baking sheet with parchment paper.

2 In a large bowl, combine oats, almonds, and cinnamon. Stir in juice, oil, butter, and salt. Spread mixture on baking sheet. Bake 15 minutes, stirring regularly. Pour granola back into bowl. Stir in brown sugar and raisins. Spread mixture on baking sheet and cook, stirring occasionally, 15–20 minutes until granola is golden brown. Cool before serving.

Dairy-Free No-Bake Energy Bites

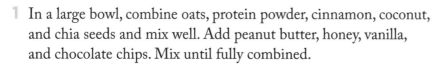

Need something quick, filling, and delicious to hold you over through a long study session? Here's your solution.

¾ cup rolled oats

2 tablespoons vanilla protein powder

¼ teaspoon ground cinnamon

2 tablespoons sweetened shredded coconut

2 teaspoons chia seeds

¼ cup peanut butter

2 tablespoons honey

½ teaspoon vanilla extract

¼ cup dairy-free mini semisweet chocolate chips

2 tablespoons unsweetened almond milk

SERVES 12	
Per Serving:	
Calories	113
Fat	5g
Protein	3g
Sodium	34mg
Fiber	2g
Carbohydrates	15g
Sugar	10g
Net Carbs	13g

1 In a large bowl, combine oats, protein powder, cinnamon, coconut, and chia seeds and mix well. Add peanut butter, honey, vanilla, and chocolate chips. Mix until fully combined.

2 Stir in almond milk. Form dough into twelve balls. Refrigerate at least 2 hours before serving.

Chewy Granola Bars

SERVES 16

Per Serving:

Calories	183
Fat	10g
Protein	4g
Sodium	25mg
Fiber	2g
Carbohydrates	21g
Sugar	13g
Net Carbs	19g

Having trouble getting the granola bars to hold their shape after baking? Let the bars cool, cut lightly with a knife while still in the pan, and freeze for about 30 minutes until they are firm but not frozen. You can store these in a sealed container or plastic bag.

2 cups rolled oats

2 tablespoons flaxseeds

¾ teaspoon ground cinnamon

1 tablespoon sesame seeds

½ cup unsalted butter

¼ cup plus 2 tablespoons honey

¼ cup light brown sugar

2 large eggs

½ cup raisins

½ cup chopped peanuts

1 Preheat oven to 300°F. Line a 9" × 9" baking pan with parchment paper.

2 In a large bowl, combine oats, flaxseeds, cinnamon, and sesame seeds.

3 Melt butter with honey and sugar in a small saucepan over low heat, stirring continuously.

4 Add butter mixture to oat mixture and stir to mix. Add eggs, mix well, then stir in raisins and peanuts.

5 Spread mixture in prepared baking pan, pressing down with a spatula to spread evenly. Bake 15 minutes or until golden brown. Cool in pan completely and cut into sixteen bars. Serve immediately or store in a sealed container for up to 1 week.

Granola Biscotti

If there's such a thing as healthy cookies, these Granola Biscotti fit the bill. They are perfect for when you're craving something sweet in the middle of the day but want to avoid the vending machine candy bars.

4 large eggs

1 teaspoon vanilla extract

½ teaspoon almond extract

1½ cups all-purpose flour

1 cup rolled oats

½ teaspoon baking powder

⅛ teaspoon salt

½ cup light brown sugar

¼ cup granulated sugar

½ cup toasted almonds

½ cup chopped dates

⅓ cup honey

MAKES 30 COOKIES	
Per Serving (2 cookies):	
Calories	172
Fat	4g
Protein	4g
Sodium	42mg
Fiber	2g
Carbohydrates	30g
Sugar	18g
Net Carbs	28g

1 Preheat oven to 325°F. Spray a large baking sheet with nonstick cooking spray.

2 In a small bowl, beat together eggs, vanilla, and almond extract. In a large bowl, combine flour, oats, baking powder, salt, brown sugar, and granulated sugar. Blend thoroughly. Add egg mixture and stir to form a sticky dough. Stir in almonds and dates.

3 Cut dough in half. Flour your hands and shape each half into a 14" log. Place logs on prepared baking sheet, flatten slightly, and bake 30 minutes or until a toothpick inserted into the center comes out clean. Let cool on baking sheet for 10 minutes.

4 Cut dough diagonally into slices about ½" thick. Place slices cut-side down on two ungreased baking sheets. Bake 15 minutes, removing baking sheets from oven at the halfway point and flipping the biscotti.

5 Cool biscotti on baking sheets for 5 minutes, then transfer to a wire rack. Drizzle honey over the tops. Serve immediately or store in a sealed container for up to 1 week.

BISCOTTI

An Italian creation, biscotti are crunchy, oblong-shaped biscuits that are perfect for dunking in tea or coffee. The secret to biscotti lies in baking the dough twice: first to cook it through, and then a second time to add extra crispness. (The word *biscotti* means "twice-baked" in Italian.)

Tropical Pineapple Smoothie

SERVES 2

Per Serving:

Calories	228
Fat	6g
Protein	5g
Sodium	69mg
Fiber	4g
Carbohydrates	39g
Sugar	27g
Net Carbs	35g

Garnish this sweet smoothie with a lime wedge and banana slices to feel like you're at some spring break tropical paradise. You can also add a scoop of your favorite vanilla protein powder for an extra protein punch.

1 cup frozen strawberries

1 cup whole milk

1 cup frozen pineapple chunks

1 medium banana, peeled, sliced, and frozen

2 tablespoons sweetened shredded coconut

1 teaspoon lime juice

½ teaspoon ground cinnamon

½ cup crushed ice

Process strawberries in a blender or food processor until finely chopped. Add milk and pineapple and process again for about 20 seconds. Add banana, coconut, lime juice, cinnamon, and ice, and process again until smooth. Serve in two chilled glasses.

Homemade Trail Mix

MAKES 1¾ CUPS

Per Serving (¼ cup):

Calories	163
Fat	11g
Protein	3g
Sodium	60mg
Fiber	2g
Carbohydrates	16g
Sugar	7g
Net Carbs	14g

Sweet chocolate and salty peanuts combine with healthy granola to make a nutritious and tasty backpack snack. You can substitute coconut flakes or sunflower seeds for the banana chips and add almonds or walnuts instead of hazelnuts. Make it your own!

1 cup granola

½ cup salted peanuts

¼ cup semisweet chocolate chips

¼ cup dehydrated banana chips

2 tablespoons hazelnuts

Combine all ingredients in a medium bowl. Pack in a resealable plastic bag or container for easy carrying and storing.

Supersized Oatmeal Cookies

When you're hangry, it's hard to resist those yummy-looking cookies all around campus. But why not bring your own instead? Pack one (or two) to take with you while you're out and about, so when snack time comes around, you don't have to buy a treat. You've already got one!

¾ cup unsalted butter

1 cup light brown sugar

1 large egg

1 teaspoon vanilla extract

½ teaspoon baking soda

½ teaspoon salt

1 cup all-purpose flour

1 teaspoon ground cinnamon

1 cup quick-cooking oats

¾ cup semisweet chocolate chips

¾ cup chopped walnuts

MAKES 12 COOKIES

Per Serving (1 cookie):

Calories	336
Fat	21g
Protein	3g
Sodium	161mg
Fiber	3g
Carbohydrates	36g
Sugar	21g
Net Carbs	33g

1 Preheat oven to 350°F. Line two large baking sheets with parchment paper.

2 Cream together butter and brown sugar in a large bowl, then beat in egg and vanilla.

3 In a small bowl, combine baking soda, salt, flour, and cinnamon. Add flour mixture to egg mixture and mix well. Stir in oats and chocolate chips.

4 Shape dough into balls about 2" in diameter. Place on prepared baking sheets, set well apart, about six balls per tray. Press down gently on each ball with your finger. Press a few walnut pieces in the middle of each cookie.

5 Bake 13–15 minutes. Cool 1 minute on baking sheets, then transfer to a wire rack to cool completely. Serve immediately or store in an airtight container.

Blueberry Smoothie

This delightful purple drink is an antioxidant booster due to the blueberry and honey combination. The milk gives it a creamy texture, while the yogurt provides an amazing protein content. Add ½ cup crushed ice at the end if you're in the mood for a real chiller.

²⁄₃ cup frozen unsweetened blueberries

½ cup plain low-fat Greek yogurt

½ cup unsweetened almond milk

1 medium banana, peeled, sliced, and frozen

1 teaspoon honey

Process blueberries in a blender or food processor until finely chopped. Add yogurt and almond milk and process again for about 20 seconds. Add banana and honey and process until smooth. Serve in a chilled glass.

SERVES 1

Per Serving:

Calories	284
Fat	4g
Protein	13g
Sodium	141mg
Fiber	6g
Carbohydrates	53g
Sugar	32g
Net Carbs	47g

HEALTHY BLUEBERRIES

Blueberries have a wide variety of health benefits, including healthier bones, better skin, lower blood pressure, and even cancer prevention. They're high in vitamin C, antioxidants, fiber, iron, potassium, and a wealth of other vitamins and minerals.

Stuffed Celery Sticks

SERVES 1

Per Serving:

Calories	430
Fat	31g
Protein	12g
Sodium	603mg
Fiber	6g
Carbohydrates	33g
Sugar	15g
Net Carbs	27g

This recipe is a spin-off of the classic "ants on a log" snack. Try mixing and matching with different ingredients, like almond butter or cream cheese instead of peanut butter and coconut or dried fruit instead of chocolate.

2 medium celery stalks

3 tablespoons peanut butter

3 tablespoons granola

1 tablespoon semisweet mini chocolate chips

⅛ teaspoon salt

Cut each celery stalk into three equal pieces. In a small bowl, mash together peanut butter and granola. Spread granola mixture on each celery piece and top with chocolate chips and salt. Serve immediately.

Picante Sauce

MAKES 3 CUPS

Per Serving (¼ cup):

Calories	71
Fat	7g
Protein	1g
Sodium	197mg
Fiber	1g
Carbohydrates	4g
Sugar	1g
Net Carbs	3g

This salsa is amazing paired with some tortilla chips or as a topping for your favorite Mexican dish. For a less spicy sauce, keep the jalapeño whole and remove it after simmering the mixture.

6 tablespoons olive oil

1 large white onion, peeled and chopped into ¼" pieces

1 small jalapeño pepper, seeded and chopped

6 medium tomatoes, chopped

1 teaspoon salt

1 tablespoon honey

1 tablespoon minced fresh cilantro or 1 teaspoon dried cilantro

1 Heat oil in a large frying pan over medium-high heat. Add onions and sauté for about 5 minutes until soft and translucent.

2 Add remaining ingredients. Reduce heat to medium-low and simmer for about 10 minutes. Remove from heat and cool completely before serving.

Turkey Roll-Ups

This recipe is perfect for those days when you can't get around to lunch. The tortilla, avocado, and turkey combine to make a well-rounded, balanced meal between the carbs, healthy fats, and protein. Plus, it's easy to carry with you and eat between classes!

1 (8") flour tortilla

½ medium avocado, peeled, pitted, and mashed

¼ teaspoon salt

½ teaspoon ground black pepper

½ teaspoon sesame seeds

3 (2-ounce) slices deli turkey

2 (2-ounce) slices Swiss cheese

½ cup baby spinach leaves

¼ medium green bell pepper, seeded and sliced

½ medium cucumber, peeled and sliced

SERVES 1	
Per Serving:	
Calories	901
Fat	54g
Protein	65g
Sodium	2,752mg
Fiber	8g
Carbohydrates	46g
Sugar	5g
Net Carbs	38g

1   Place tortilla on a work surface. Spread avocado evenly around tortilla, leaving about 1" of space from the edges. Sprinkle salt, black pepper, and sesame seeds over avocado.

2   Layer on turkey, cheese, spinach, bell pepper, and cucumber. Roll up tightly, cut wrap in half, and serve.

Baked Banana Chips

SERVES 2

Per Serving:

Calories	116
Fat	0g
Protein	1g
Sodium	0mg
Fiber	4g
Carbohydrates	31g
Sugar	15g
Net Carbs	27g

Banana slices are the perfect alternative to potato chips—they're crispy and crunchy but don't have unnecessary fats and salt. Bake a bunch up in a day and store them for snacking throughout your week.

2 medium ripe bananas, peeled and thinly sliced
1 teaspoon lemon juice
2 teaspoons ground cinnamon

1 Preheat oven to 225°F. Line a baking sheet with parchment paper.

2 Brush both sides of banana slices with lemon juice. Lay slices evenly on prepared pan, making sure they do not touch. Bake 90 minutes or until slices have completely dried out. Sprinkle with cinnamon and cool completely before serving.

Sweet Potato Fries

SERVES 4

Per Serving:

Calories	144
Fat	7g
Protein	3g
Sodium	623mg
Fiber	3g
Carbohydrates	19g
Sugar	6g
Net Carbs	16g

You can dip these fries in ketchup, guacamole, or even ranch dressing as a snack or use them as a side for your lunch.

2 large sweet potatoes, peeled and cut into ¼" wedges
2 tablespoons olive oil
1 teaspoon sea salt
1 teaspoon ground black pepper
½ teaspoon garlic powder
½ teaspoon cayenne pepper

1 Preheat oven to 450°F. Line a baking sheet with parchment paper.

2 In a large bowl, toss sweet potatoes with olive oil and salt. Transfer to prepared baking sheet and spread out in a single layer. Bake 25 minutes or until crispy.

3 As fries cool, sprinkle with black pepper, garlic powder, and cayenne pepper. Serve immediately.

Bruschetta with Tomatoes and Herbs

This classic recipe is perfect for when you just need something light to hold you over. The fresh summer flavors are sure to bring some sunshine to your meal, no matter the season!

1 clove garlic, peeled

4 tablespoons olive oil, divided

2 large tomatoes, diced

2 tablespoons minced fresh basil leaves

1 tablespoon chopped fresh cilantro

1 tablespoon balsamic vinegar

1 teaspoon salt

⅛ teaspoon crushed red pepper flakes

½ cup shredded mozzarella cheese

½ (26") baguette loaf, cut into 6 slices

SERVES 6	
Per Serving:	
Calories	167
Fat	12g
Protein	5g
Sodium	550mg
Fiber	1g
Carbohydrates	13g
Sugar	2g
Net Carbs	12g

1 Cut garlic clove in half and mince 1 half. Set remaining half aside.

2 Heat 1 tablespoon oil in a medium frying pan over medium-low heat. Add minced garlic and sauté 4 minutes, stirring frequently, then remove from heat. Let cool 5 minutes.

3 In a medium mixing bowl, combine cooked garlic, tomatoes, basil, cilantro, balsamic vinegar, salt, red pepper flakes, and cheese. Mix well, cover, and refrigerate at least 30 minutes.

4 Preheat oven to 400°F.

5 Brush baguette slices with remaining 3 tablespoons olive oil and rub with the cut side of remaining half clove garlic. Place bread slices on an ungreased baking sheet and bake for 10 minutes or until golden.

6 Spoon tomato mixture onto baguette slices and serve immediately.

Quesadilla Triangles

AVOCADO LIME DIP

For a healthier alternative to sour cream for dipping, blend together ½ cup plain low-fat Greek yogurt, 1 medium avocado, 1 tablespoon lime juice, ¼ cup chopped fresh cilantro, ¼ cup chopped red onion, and 2 teaspoons garlic powder. This version will give you more valuable protein and less unhealthy fats.

Dip these Quesadilla Triangles in sour cream or guacamole for a delicious snack. You can let the salsa mixture sit in the refrigerator for 30 minutes before you add it to the quesadilla to let the flavors marinate.

¼ cup mild salsa

¼ cup diced red onion

¼ cup diced green bell pepper

¼ cup chopped cooked ham

¼ cup black beans, drained and rinsed

¼ cup chopped fresh cilantro

1 tablespoon lime juice

1 teaspoon garlic powder

¼ teaspoon paprika

¼ teaspoon chili powder

¼ teaspoon ground cumin

1 tablespoon unsalted butter

2 (10") flour tortillas

¾ cup shredded Cheddar cheese

1 In a large bowl, combine salsa, onion, bell pepper, ham, beans, cilantro, lime juice, garlic powder, paprika, chili powder, and cumin. Mix well and set aside.

2 Melt butter in a large frying pan over medium heat and swirl to coat the entire pan. Add 1 tortilla to the pan and top with half the cheese. When cheese begins to melt, spread salsa mixture evenly on top. Add remaining cheese on top, then place remaining tortilla on top to close the quesadilla.

3 Cook 5 minutes, then flip and cook another 5 minutes. Remove from heat.

4 Slice into six triangles and serve.

Egg Salad–Stuffed Mini Peppers

The sweet peppers and spicy paprika create an addictive flavor for this simple snack combo. Keep these in the refrigerator for 4 days.

2 Hard-Boiled Eggs (see recipe in Chapter 2), peeled and chopped

1 tablespoon mayonnaise

1 tablespoon plain low-fat Greek yogurt

1 tablespoon chopped chives

2 tablespoons chopped celery

1 tablespoon chopped gherkin pickles

1 tablespoon chopped fresh cilantro

½ teaspoon garlic powder

¼ teaspoon onion powder

¼ teaspoon paprika

4 mini sweet peppers, seeded and halved

SERVES 1	
Per Serving:	
Calories	305
Fat	20g
Protein	16g
Sodium	381mg
Fiber	4g
Carbohydrates	13g
Sugar	6g
Net Carbs	9g

In a small bowl, combine eggs, mayonnaise, yogurt, chives, celery, pickles, cilantro, garlic powder, onion powder, and paprika. Spoon mixture into peppers. Refrigerate at least 1 hour before serving.

Roasted Chickpeas

Chickpeas are loaded with protein, which makes them an exceptional snack.

1 (15-ounce) can chickpeas, drained and rinsed

1 tablespoon olive oil

1 teaspoon paprika

1 teaspoon garlic powder

¼ teaspoon chili powder

½ teaspoon salt

1 teaspoon ground black pepper

SERVES 2	
Per Serving:	
Calories	246
Fat	11g
Protein	11g
Sodium	973mg
Fiber	13g
Carbohydrates	38g
Sugar	2g
Net Carbs	25g

1 Preheat oven to 400°F. Line a baking sheet with parchment paper.

2 Spread chickpeas on a clean kitchen towel and pat dry.

3 Transfer chickpeas to baking sheet and add oil, paprika, garlic powder, chili powder, salt, and pepper. Toss to combine.

4 Bake, stirring occasionally, for 20–25 minutes until crispy. Serve warm or store in a sealed container for up to 1 week.

Loaded Keto Nachos

Per Serving:

Calories	187
Fat	13g
Protein	10g
Sodium	439mg
Fiber	2g
Carbohydrates	8g
Sugar	4g
Net Carbs	6g

HOW SWEET IT IS

Mini bell peppers are grown specifically for their size and flavor. They have thinner skins than mature peppers and a sweeter flavor. Each whole mini pepper contains only 1.7 grams of carbohydrates, so they're an excellent way to get in the micronutrients you need without affecting ketosis.

If you like nachos, you'll love this savory keto spin. Instead of carb-loaded chips, this recipe uses crunchy mini bell peppers. Add salsa or avocado slices on top before serving for extra bursts of flavor.

¼ **pound lean ground turkey**
¼ **cup chopped yellow onion**
½ **cup chopped fresh cilantro, divided**
¼ **teaspoon ground cumin**
¼ **teaspoon garlic powder**
½ **teaspoon salt**
½ **teaspoon ground black pepper**
8 mini sweet peppers, seeded and halved
½ **medium jalapeño, seeded and sliced**
½ **cup shredded Cheddar cheese**
½ **cup sour cream**

1 Preheat oven to 400°F. Line a large baking sheet with parchment paper.

2 Heat a large frying pan over medium-high heat and add ground turkey and onion. Cook 8–10 minutes or until meat is fully cooked through, stirring frequently.

3 Add ¼ cup cilantro, cumin, garlic powder, salt, and black pepper. Mix until fully combined and cook another 5 minutes.

4 Place bell pepper halves on prepared baking sheet and evenly fill each half with ground turkey mixture. Top with jalapeño slices and cheese. Bake 8–10 minutes until cheese is melted.

5 Top with sour cream and remaining ¼ cup cilantro and serve immediately.

Paleo Pumpkin Pecan Muffins

MAKES 6 MUFFINS

Per Serving (1 muffin):

Calories	188
Fat	13g
Protein	6g
Sodium	231mg
Fiber	2g
Carbohydrates	12g
Sugar	8g
Net Carbs	10g

MAPLE MADNESS

Instead of traditional sugars like granulated or brown sugar, pure maple syrup can be used as a natural substitute in many recipes. It actually has antioxidant properties and some nutritional content. However, as with any sweetener, you should use maple syrup in moderation. You can also use agave syrup, rice malt syrup, or coconut sugar.

Make sure to purchase almond flour instead of almond meal, as flour has a much better taste when it comes to baking. If you need more sweetness, drizzle honey over the top before eating or add some dairy-free chocolate chips into the batter before baking.

⅓ cup pumpkin purée

2 large eggs

3 tablespoons 100% pure maple syrup

½ teaspoon vanilla extract

¾ cup almond flour

½ teaspoon baking soda

2 teaspoons ground cinnamon

⅛ teaspoon ground nutmeg

⅛ teaspoon ground cloves

¼ teaspoon salt

3 tablespoons unsweetened almond milk

½ cup chopped pecans

1 Preheat oven to 350°F. Spray 6 cups of a muffin tin with nonstick cooking spray.

2 In a small bowl, combine pumpkin, eggs, maple syrup, and vanilla. Mix well and set aside.

3 In a large bowl, combine almond flour, baking soda, cinnamon, nutmeg, cloves, and salt. Make a well by pushing flour mixture to the edges of the bowl and leaving about ½" of space in the middle. Pour pumpkin mixture into the well and stir thoroughly to incorporate into the flour mixture.

4 Slowly mix in almond milk 1 tablespoon at a time, mixing well after each addition. Gently stir in pecans.

5 Spoon batter into muffin wells until about ⅔ full. Bake 25–35 minutes or until a toothpick inserted in the center of a muffin comes out clean. Cool in pan for 5 minutes, then transfer muffins to a wire rack. Serve warm or at room temperature.

Peanut Butter Chocolate Chip Energy Bars

Quinoa, oats, and peanut butter make these energy bars not only a healthy and delicious snack but also a filling breakfast. You can replace the peanut butter with almond butter and add in ⅓ cup sweetened shredded coconut with the oats and quinoa for an Almond Joy twist.

1 cup rolled oats

½ cup cooked quinoa

½ teaspoon ground cinnamon

¼ teaspoon baking powder

¼ teaspoon baking soda

¼ teaspoon salt

2 large eggs

2 tablespoons melted coconut oil

¼ cup plus 2 tablespoons peanut butter

2 medium bananas, peeled and mashed

¼ cup maple syrup

½ teaspoon vanilla extract

⅓ cup semisweet chocolate chips

SERVES 16

Per Serving:

Calories	136
Fat	7g
Protein	3g
Sodium	101mg
Fiber	2g
Carbohydrates	16g
Sugar	8g
Net Carbs	14g

1. Preheat oven to 375°F. Spray an 8" × 8" baking pan with nonstick cooking spray.

2. In a large bowl, combine oats, quinoa, cinnamon, baking powder, baking soda, and salt. Mix well.

3. In a medium bowl, combine eggs, oil, peanut butter, bananas, maple syrup, and vanilla. Mix well.

4. Pour egg mixture into oat mixture and add chocolate chips. Stir to combine. Transfer dough to prepared baking pan and spread evenly. Bake 25–30 minutes or until edges are golden brown.

5. Cool 30 minutes on a wire rack and then refrigerate another 30 minutes before cutting into sixteen equal bars. Serve immediately or store in an airtight container for up to 5 days.

PEANUT BUTTER NEWS FLASH

Peanut butter is packed with protein and fiber, so it should be good for you. However, a lot of peanut butter brands contain added sugars and artificial preservatives. When you're shopping, look for natural brands and check the nutrition label for high sugar content, extra oils, and chemicals. The ingredient list should be short and sweet.

Healthy Brownie Bites

Got an afternoon sweet tooth craving? Here's the cure. These Healthy Brownie Bites are the perfect alternative to the sugar-loaded brownies found on campus. Add a scoop of your favorite chocolate protein powder for an extra protein boost.

MAKES 12 BROWNIES

Per Serving (1 brownie):

Calories	208
Fat	8g
Protein	4g
Sodium	46mg
Fiber	4g
Carbohydrates	32g
Sugar	17g
Net Carbs	28g

1¾ cup whole-wheat flour

¾ teaspoon baking powder

⅓ cup cocoa powder

¼ cup unsalted butter, melted

2 large eggs

½ cup honey

½ medium banana, peeled and mashed

2 teaspoons vanilla extract

¾ cup shredded zucchini

½ cup semisweet chocolate chips

1 Preheat oven to 350°F and line a 12-cup mini muffin tin with mini muffin liners.

2 In a large bowl, combine flour, baking powder, and cocoa powder. Mix well.

3 In a small bowl, mix together butter, eggs, honey, banana, vanilla, and zucchini. Add butter mixture to flour mixture and stir to combine. Fold in chocolate chips.

4 Spoon batter into muffin wells and bake 15–20 minutes or until a toothpick inserted in the middle of a brownie comes out clean. Cool in pan for 5 minutes, then transfer to a wire rack. Serve warm or at room temperature.

BAKING WITH WHAT NOW?

Did you know you can add zucchini to pretty much any baked good? This vegetable has unique baking properties, like adding moisture and texture to baked goods without any unnecessary fats. It has a mild enough taste to not change the flavor of the recipe so you can sneak some healthy nutrition into your not-so-healthy baking sprees.

CHAPTER 5

Special Devices

Instant Pot® Steamed Jasmine Rice

SERVES 6

Per Serving:

Calories	137
Fat	2g
Protein	2g
Sodium	99mg
Fiber	0g
Carbohydrates	27g
Sugar	0g
Net Carbs	27g

Rice is an easy staple that can be used for almost every meal. It's inexpensive and versatile—have it as a side dish, stirred into a vegetable soup, or as the base of a burrito bowl. Using an Instant Pot® means you can have hot cooked rice in minutes.

1 cup jasmine rice, rinsed

1 cup water

¼ teaspoon salt

1 tablespoon unsalted butter

1 Place rice, water, and salt in the Instant Pot®, making sure rice is submerged in water.

2 Close lid, set steam release to Sealing, and press the Rice button. When the timer beeps, let the pressure release naturally for 10 minutes.

3 Open lid and transfer rice to a serving bowl. Stir in butter and serve warm.

Instant Pot® Steamed Broccoli

SERVES 2

Per Serving:

Calories	28
Fat	0g
Protein	2g
Sodium	327mg
Fiber	3g
Carbohydrates	6g
Sugar	1g
Net Carbs	3g

If you like your broccoli a little crunchier, set the timer for 0 minutes. Add 1 tablespoon butter and ¼ cup shredded Parmesan cheese before serving for some extra flavor.

1 cup chopped broccoli

¼ teaspoon salt

½ teaspoon ground black pepper

Fill Instant Pot® with water to the max fill line and place broccoli in the steamer basket, then place the basket in the Instant Pot®. Close lid, set steam release to Sealing, press the Manual button, and set timer to 1 minute. When the timer beeps, quick-release the pressure. Season with salt and pepper. Serve immediately.

Instant Pot® Turkey Breast

Only have 15 minutes to make dinner? This easy steamed turkey breast is for you. Just steam some vegetables for a side dish, and dinner is served.

1 cup low-sodium chicken broth

1 medium yellow onion, peeled and cut into wedges

1 tablespoon garlic powder

1 tablespoon paprika

½ teaspoon dried thyme

½ teaspoon salt

1 teaspoon ground black pepper

1 tablespoon olive oil

1 (16-ounce) boneless turkey breast tenderloin

SERVES 4	
Per Serving:	
Calories	183
Fat	9g
Protein	29g
Sodium	497mg
Fiber	2g
Carbohydrates	6g
Sugar	2g
Net Carbs	4g

1 Place broth and onion in the Instant Pot®.

2 In a small bowl, combine garlic powder, paprika, thyme, salt, and pepper. Rub oil over turkey, then rub with seasoning mixture.

3 Transfer turkey to the Instant Pot®. Close lid, set steam release to Sealing, press the Manual button, and set timer to 7 minutes. When the timer beeps, let pressure release naturally for 10 minutes.

4 Using a meat thermometer, check turkey at its thickest portion to make sure the internal temperature is at least 165°F. Transfer to a large plate and let rest 10 minutes before serving.

Microwave Black Bean Quesadilla

This hearty quesadilla gives you all the gooey goodness in a fraction of the time it would take to cook on the stove. Add some guacamole on the side for some extra flavor and spice!

½ cup canned black beans, drained and rinsed

¼ cup corn kernels

3 tablespoons chopped red onion

3 tablespoons mild salsa

1 tablespoon chopped fresh cilantro

2 tablespoons taco seasoning mix

1 tablespoon lime juice

2 (8") flour tortillas

½ cup shredded Cheddar cheese

1. In a small mixing bowl, combine black beans, corn, onion, salsa, cilantro, taco seasoning, and lime juice.

2. Place 1 tortilla on a microwave-safe plate. Spread black bean mixture on tortilla, then sprinkle cheese over top. Place remaining tortilla on top to close quesadilla, then microwave for 1–2 minutes or until cheese is melted.

3. Cut into quarters and serve immediately.

SERVES 1

Per Serving:

Calories	750
Fat	26g
Protein	31g
Sodium	1,804mg
Fiber	10g
Carbohydrates	96g
Sugar	7g
Net Carbs	86g

HOMEMADE SALSA

Making your own salsa at home is a breeze if you have the time. Add some diced tomatoes, diced onion, diced bell peppers, cilantro, and corn to a large bowl and stir to combine. Chill for 4 hours and serve.

Instant Pot® Chicken Breasts

THE PERFECT TEMPERATURE

Cooked poultry should reach a temperature of at least 165°F. If your meat is hovering around 160°F after you finish cooking, just put the lid back on and let it sit for 5 minutes. If it's lower than that, close the lid, set the steam release to Sealing, press the Manual button, and set the timer for another 1–2 minutes.

Don't worry if you forgot to defrost your chicken. Frozen chicken works just as well in the Instant Pot®! Just add an extra 3–4 minutes to the cook time. If you have leftovers, you can easily dice them up for a chicken salad for lunch the next day.

½ cup low-sodium chicken broth

1 small yellow onion, peeled and cut into wedges

1 tablespoon garlic powder

2 teaspoons cayenne pepper

½ teaspoon Italian seasoning

¼ teaspoon salt

½ teaspoon ground black pepper

1 tablespoon olive oil

2 (6-ounce) boneless, skinless chicken breasts

1 Place broth and onion in the Instant Pot®.

2 In a small bowl, combine garlic powder, cayenne pepper, Italian seasoning, salt, and pepper. Rub olive oil evenly over chicken breasts, then rub with seasoning mixture.

3 Transfer chicken to Instant Pot®. Close lid, set steam release to Sealing, press the Manual button, and set timer to 6 minutes. When the timer beeps, let pressure release naturally for 10 minutes.

4 Using a meat thermometer, check chicken at its thickest portion to make sure the internal temperature is at least 165°F. Transfer to large plate and let rest for 5 minutes before serving.

Microwave Corn on the Cob

The microwave gives a quick and easy alternative to boiling corn in a large pot of water. If you're cooking 2 ears of corn at once, increase the cooking time to 4–5 minutes.

1 ear corn, husk removed

2 teaspoons unsalted butter, melted

¼ teaspoon salt

¼ teaspoon ground black pepper

SERVES 1	
Per Serving:	
Calories	149
Fat	9g
Protein	3g
Sodium	591mg
Fiber	3g
Carbohydrates	18g
Sugar	5g
Net Carbs	15g

1 Wrap corn in a paper towel and place on a microwave-safe plate. Microwave on high heat 2–3 minutes. Let cool in microwave 5 minutes.

2 In a small bowl, combine butter, salt, and pepper. Mix well, then brush on corn. Serve hot.

Microwave Green Beans

The trick to this recipe is making sure the green beans are fully submerged under the chicken broth. Eat them as a side or pop them in a salad.

3½ ounces fresh green beans

⅓ cup low-sodium chicken broth

¼ teaspoon salt

¼ teaspoon ground black pepper

SERVES 1	
Per Serving:	
Calories	36
Fat	0g
Protein	2g
Sodium	787mg
Fiber	2g
Carbohydrates	7g
Sugar	1g
Net Carbs	5g

Place green beans in a microwave-safe bowl and cover with broth. Cook on high heat 1½–2 minutes until crisp and bright green. Season with salt and pepper. Serve immediately.

Microwave Baked Potato

SERVES 1	
Per Serving:	
Calories	162
Fat	0g
Protein	4g
Sodium	607mg
Fiber	4g
Carbohydrates	37g
Sugar	2g
Net Carbs	33g

Want a bit of melted butter with your baked potato? When it's done cooking, slice it open, add 1 tablespoon butter, and place the potato back in the microwave for about 30 seconds.

1 medium baking potato
¼ teaspoon salt
¼ teaspoon ground black pepper

Pierce potato four times with a fork. Place potato on a microwave-safe plate and cook on high heat 4–6 minutes. Slice potato open and season with salt and pepper. Serve hot.

Lazy Slow-Cooked Chili

SERVES 8	
Per Serving:	
Calories	510
Fat	19g
Protein	33g
Sodium	913mg
Fiber	4g
Carbohydrates	52g
Sugar	7g
Net Carbs	48g

Before you head out the door for your first class, brown the ground beef and toss all the ingredients in a slow cooker.

2 pounds 85% lean ground beef
1 large yellow onion, peeled and chopped
2 (28-ounce) cans crushed tomatoes, with liquid
3 (15-ounce) cans chickpeas, with liquid

2 tablespoons chili powder
1 teaspoon ground cumin
1 teaspoon garlic powder
1 teaspoon salt
1 teaspoon ground black pepper

1 Heat a large frying pan over medium heat and add beef. Sauté, using a large spoon to break up the beef into small chunks. Cook until no longer pink, about 5 minutes. Drain, then transfer beef to slow cooker.

2 Stir in remaining ingredients. Cook on low for 4 hours. Serve hot.

Microwave Garlic Chicken

This healthy dish is perfect for when you only have a few minutes between classes and don't have time to run to the dining hall. If your microwave is large enough, you can microwave the garlic butter with the chicken during the last 30 seconds of cooking.

1½ teaspoons olive oil

1 (6-ounce) boneless, skinless chicken breast

1 teaspoon dried oregano

¼ cup chopped yellow onion

3 tablespoons butter, divided

2 cloves garlic, peeled and chopped

1 Rub olive oil over chicken, then rub dried oregano on both sides of the breast.

2 Place chicken breast in a microwave-safe bowl and loosely cover the bowl with plastic wrap. Microwave on high heat 3 minutes. Turn chicken over and microwave on high heat another 3 minutes. Using a meat thermometer, check chicken at its thickest portion to make sure the internal temperature is at least 165°F.

3 Place onion and 2 tablespoons butter in a microwave-safe bowl. Microwave on high heat 1 minute. Stir and microwave 30 seconds. Stir in garlic and remaining 1 tablespoon butter. Microwave 1–1½ minutes, until onion is tender and garlic is aromatic. Pour garlic butter over chicken and serve.

SERVES 1

Per Serving:

Calories	565
Fat	47g
Protein	34g
Sodium	349mg
Fiber	1g
Carbohydrates	6g
Sugar	0g
Net Carbs	5g

DEFROSTED MEAT WARNING

Most meat packages have instructions for how to defrost frozen meat. The meat should always be cooked immediately after thawing to avoid the risk of bacteria developing on the meat. Many microwaves are set to cook everything at high power, so check the instruction manual to find out how to cook food at lower temperatures.

Microwave Tandoori Chicken

SERVES 2

Per Serving:

Calories	358
Fat	22g
Protein	36g
Sodium	366mg
Fiber	1g
Carbohydrates	10g
Sugar	3g
Net Carbs	9g

This recipe takes some planning ahead, since the chicken must marinate overnight. Curry powder takes the place of a garam masala spice mixture in this quick and easy microwave dish. Canned or fresh pineapple juice can be substituted for the coconut milk.

2 (6-ounce) boneless, skinless chicken breasts
1 teaspoon curry powder
2 teaspoons lemon juice
¼ cup plain full-fat Greek yogurt
½ cup full-fat coconut milk

1 Cut four diagonal slits on the top of each chicken breast, being careful not to cut completely through the meat. Turn breasts over and make two to three more diagonal cuts, again being careful not to cut completely through.

2 In a small bowl, combine curry powder, lemon juice, and yogurt. Mix well, then rub yogurt mixture onto chicken so yogurt fills the cuts. Place breasts in another small bowl, cover with plastic wrap, and refrigerate overnight.

3 Remove chicken from refrigerator and cut into 1" cubes. Place chicken in a large microwave-safe bowl. Add milk, then cover the dish with plastic wrap. Microwave on high heat 5 minutes.

4 Uncover chicken, stir, and microwave another 1–3 minutes, until chicken is cooked but still tender. Serve warm.

Air Fryer French Fries

  VE VG GF DF

These French fries are just as tasty as McDonald's, but they're a lot healthier...and you don't have to leave your apartment! If you somehow have leftovers, you can reheat them by placing them back in the air fryer at 390°F for 5 minutes.

1 medium russet potato, peeled and cut into ¼" slices

1 tablespoon olive oil

½ teaspoon salt

¼ teaspoon ground black pepper

¼ teaspoon paprika

¼ teaspoon garlic powder

SERVES 2

Per Serving:

Calories	146
Fat	7g
Protein	2g
Sodium	596mg
Fiber	2g
Carbohydrates	20g
Sugar	1g
Net Carbs	18g

1 Preheat air fryer to 380°F.

2 In a small mixing bowl, toss potatoes with remaining ingredients until coated. Place slices in air fryer basket and fry for 10 minutes, turning halfway through. Serve immediately.

Microwave Keto Quiche in a Mug

VE GF K

This Keto Quiche is loaded with healthy protein and fats like eggs and Cheddar cheese. This makes for a great breakfast, lunch, or dinner, so make it whenever you need a quick bite.

½ cup baby spinach leaves

2 tablespoons water

1 large egg

¼ cup whole milk

2 tablespoons chopped red onion

⅓ cup shredded Cheddar cheese

¼ teaspoon salt

¼ teaspoon ground black pepper

¼ teaspoon garlic powder

SERVES 1

Per Serving:

Calories	278
Fat	20g
Protein	18g
Sodium	943mg
Fiber	1g
Carbohydrates	7g
Sugar	3g
Net Carbs	6g

1 Add spinach and water to a large, 16-ounce microwave-safe mug. Microwave for 1 minute, then drain excess water.

2 Add egg, milk, onion, cheese, salt, pepper, and garlic powder to the mug. Stir well with a fork, cover with a paper towel, and microwave for 2 minutes. Serve immediately.

Air Fryer Quinoa Burgers

This quinoa burger is easier on the digestive system than its red meat cousin and is loaded with protein and fiber. And since it's cooked in an air fryer instead of on a grill, it's much healthier too! To make it a complete meal, add a side of Air Fryer French Fries (see recipe in this chapter).

QUINOA CONUNDRUM

Quinoa is a healthy gluten-free grain loaded with protein and fiber. You should, however, be aware of cross-contamination when you're shopping for quinoa. Some brands may come in contact with gluten through processing and packaging, so if you have an allergy, do your research and only buy from brands you trust.

½ cup cooked quinoa, cooled

¾ cup dried bread crumbs

2 large eggs

¼ small yellow onion, peeled and minced

2 tablespoons chopped scallions

¼ cup part-skim ricotta cheese

1 teaspoon salt

¼ teaspoon ground black pepper

½ teaspoon garlic powder

1 tablespoon chopped parsley

2 sesame seeded hamburger buns

½ avocado, peeled, pitted, and mashed

4 lettuce leaves

2 slices medium tomato

4 slices red onion, peeled

1 Preheat air fryer to 400°F. Spray the basket with nonstick cooking spray.

2 In a large mixing bowl, combine quinoa, bread crumbs, eggs, yellow onion, scallions, cheese, salt, pepper, garlic powder, and parsley. Shape quinoa mixture into two large patties.

3 Place quinoa patties in the basket. Fry 10 minutes, flipping halfway through.

4 Transfer patties to buns and add avocado, lettuce, tomato, and red onion. Serve immediately.

Air Fryer Chicken Tenders

These Air Fryer Chicken Tenders are the perfect alternative to deep-fried chicken nuggets. You get the same crispy crunch but with way less oil! Serve with your favorite dipping sauce.

4 (2-ounce) skinless chicken tenderloin pieces
2 tablespoons olive oil
⅓ cup dried bread crumbs
½ teaspoon salt
¼ teaspoon ground black pepper
¼ teaspoon garlic powder
¼ teaspoon onion powder
¼ teaspoon Italian seasoning
¼ teaspoon paprika

1 Preheat air fryer to 400°F. Spray the basket with nonstick cooking spray.

2 Coat chicken with olive oil. In a shallow bowl, combine bread crumbs, salt, pepper, garlic powder, onion powder, Italian seasoning, and paprika.

3 Gently press tenders into seasoning, turn, and press again until chicken is fully coated, then shake off excess seasoning. Place chicken in the basket.

4 Fry 10 minutes, flipping halfway through. Serve immediately.

Air Fryer Keto Turkey Meatballs

The air fryer makes these delicious Italian meatballs tender on the inside and slightly crisp on the outside. Serve with a side of cauliflower rice and vegetables or add them to your favorite marinara sauce to serve on top of spaghetti. Freeze any leftovers for up to 1 month.

1 pound ground turkey

1 pound ground pork

¼ cup diced yellow onion

2 tablespoons chopped parsley

2 large eggs

1¼ cups grated Parmesan cheese

1 teaspoon salt

1 teaspoon ground black pepper

2 teaspoons garlic powder

½ teaspoon Italian seasoning

1 tablespoon Worcestershire sauce

SERVES 8	
Per Serving:	
Calories	345
Fat	22g
Protein	34g
Sodium	648mg
Fiber	0g
Carbohydrates	2g
Sugar	1g
Net Carbs	2g

1 Preheat air fryer to 400°F. Spray the basket with nonstick cooking spray.

2 Combine all ingredients in a large mixing bowl.

3 Using your hands, take 2 tablespoons meat mixture, roll into a 1"–2" ball and place in the basket. Repeat with remaining mixture.

4 Cook 10 minutes, rotating halfway through. Using a meat thermometer, check a meatball to make sure the internal temperature is at least 165°F. Serve immediately.

Air Fryer Gluten-Free Fried Chicken

This gluten-free and keto-friendly fried chicken recipe will satisfy any craving, without excess oil and calories! You can make this even healthier by going dairy-free. Just replace the Parmesan cheese with a grated dairy-free cheese.

SERVES 4

Per Serving:

Calories	349
Fat	21g
Protein	37g
Sodium	848mg
Fiber	2g
Carbohydrates	7g
Sugar	1g
Net Carbs	5g

HOW DOES AN AIR FRYER WORK?

An air fryer is basically a miniature convection oven. It heats the air inside and then uses a fan to blow the hot air around the food extremely quickly in a circular motion so it reaches every single crevice of your food. This is what creates that crispy, fried crust you want without all of the extra oil.

4 (4-ounce) boneless, skinless chicken breasts
¾ cup almond flour
¾ cup Parmesan cheese
½ teaspoon salt
½ teaspoon ground black pepper
¼ teaspoon paprika
¼ teaspoon garlic powder
¼ teaspoon onion powder
2 large eggs, beaten

1 Preheat air fryer to 390°F. Spray the basket with nonstick cooking spray.

2 Place chicken breasts in a large plastic bag and pound to ½" thickness.

3 In a shallow bowl, combine flour, cheese, salt, pepper, paprika, garlic powder, and onion powder. Place eggs in a separate shallow bowl.

4 Coat chicken in eggs, then gently press chicken into flour mixture, turn, then press again until chicken is fully coated. Shake off any excess flour. Repeat with remaining chicken pieces.

5 Place chicken in the air fryer basket. Fry 12–14 minutes, flipping halfway through. Using a meat thermometer, check chicken at its thickest portion to make sure the internal temperature is at least 165°F. Serve immediately.

Air Fryer Coconut Shrimp

This shrimp recipe is an easy and delicious way to get some healthy fresh seafood into your diet. The coconut goes really well with a sweet chili sauce, so feel free to add some at the end for dipping.

¼ cup unsweetened shredded coconut

2 tablespoons panko bread crumbs

¼ teaspoon salt

¼ teaspoon ground black pepper

¼ teaspoon red pepper flakes

1 large egg, beaten

¼ cup all-purpose flour

½ pound large shrimp, peeled and deveined with tail on

2 tablespoons fresh lime juice

1 Preheat air fryer to 390°F. Spray the basket with nonstick cooking spray.

2 In a shallow bowl, combine coconut, bread crumbs, salt, pepper, and red pepper flakes. Place egg in a separate shallow bowl. In a third shallow bowl, add flour.

3 Coat shrimp in flour, then egg. Gently press into coconut mixture, turn, then press again until shrimp is fully coated. Shake off any excess coconut mixture. Repeat with the rest of the shrimp.

4 Lay shrimp evenly in the basket. Fry 9 minutes, flipping halfway through. Remove from basket and transfer to serving plate. Sprinkle lime juice over shrimp and serve.

SERVES 2

Per Serving:

Calories	254
Fat	11g
Protein	22g
Sodium	830mg
Fiber	3g
Carbohydrates	19g
Sugar	1g
Net Carbs	16g

RINSING FRESH SHRIMP

Rinsing shrimp in warm salt water brings out their flavor. The idea is to reproduce the salty flavor of the ocean. For every cup of warm water, add at least ½ teaspoon of salt. Let the shrimp stand in the water for 5–15 minutes, then pat dry with paper towels.

Instant Pot® Pork Tenderloin

SERVES 4

Per Serving:

Calories	173
Fat	9g
Protein	22g
Sodium	1,089mg
Fiber	0g
Carbohydrates	4g
Sugar	1g
Net Carbs	4g

This juicy and flavorful pork tenderloin tastes like it took hours to make, but in reality, it takes less than 20 minutes. You don't have to roast pork for hours to get a nice, delicious meal. Serve it up with a side of steamed rice and vegetables for a perfect dinner to end the day.

1 teaspoon salt

1 teaspoon ground black pepper

½ teaspoon garlic powder

½ teaspoon ground cumin

½ teaspoon cayenne pepper

1 tablespoon light brown sugar

2 tablespoons olive oil, divided

1 (1-pound) pork tenderloin

½ cup low-sodium chicken broth

1 In a small bowl, combine salt, black pepper, garlic powder, cumin, cayenne pepper, and brown sugar. Mix well. Rub 1 tablespoon oil over pork, then coat it in seasoning mixture.

2 Press the Sauté button on the Instant Pot® and heat remaining 1 tablespoon oil. Add pork and sear 3 minutes on each side.

3 Press the Cancel button and place the trivet in the Instant Pot®. Add broth to the pot and place pork on the trivet. Close lid, set steam release to Sealing, press the Manual button, and set timer to 5 minutes.

4 When the timer beeps, let pressure release naturally 5 minutes and then slowly start to manually release the pressure. Transfer to a plate and serve hot.

Instant Pot® Spaghetti

Who wants to wash dishes after a long day of classes? When you're done with this hearty spaghetti recipe, you'll only have one pot to clean!

1 pound 85% lean ground beef

2 cups water, divided

1 (24-ounce) jar marinara sauce

8 ounces spaghetti

2 tablespoons grated Parmesan cheese

SERVES 4	
Per Serving:	
Calories	506
Fat	21g
Protein	31g
Sodium	698mg
Fiber	5g
Carbohydrates	50g
Sugar	6g
Net Carbs	45g

1 Press the Sauté button on the Instant Pot® and add ground beef. Sauté, using a large spoon to break up beef into small chunks. Cook until no longer pink, about 5 minutes.

2 Press the Cancel button and add ½ cup water. Scrape the bottom of the pot to remove any pieces that are stuck, then add marinara sauce.

3 Break spaghetti in half and add to pot. Do not stir, or else noodles will stick together. Add remaining 1½ cups water.

4 Close lid, set steam release to Sealing, press the Manual button, and set timer to 8 minutes.

5 When the timer beeps, quick-release the pressure. Stir well and top with Parmesan cheese before serving.

Instant Pot® Chicken Noodle Soup

Feeling a little under the weather? This Instant Pot® Chicken Noodle Soup will help to warm you up and make you feel cozy. Between the chicken broth and vegetables, you'll be on your way to better health in no time.

1 tablespoon olive oil

½ cup chopped yellow onion

½ cup chopped celery

½ cup chopped carrots

1 teaspoon garlic powder

1 teaspoon Italian seasoning

½ teaspoon salt

½ teaspoon ground black pepper

2 (8-ounce) boneless, skinless chicken breasts

2 cups low-sodium chicken broth

2 cups cold water

4 ounces egg noodles

1 Press the Sauté button on the Instant Pot® and heat oil. Add onion, celery, and carrots. Sauté about 5 minutes until onion is soft and translucent.

2 Add garlic powder, Italian seasoning, salt, pepper, chicken, broth, and water. Close lid, set steam release to Sealing, press the Soup button, and set timer to 7 minutes.

3 When the timer beeps, let pressure release naturally for 10 minutes. Transfer chicken to a cutting board, cool slightly, then shred chicken with two forks. Return chicken to the Instant Pot® and add egg noodles.

4 Press the Sauté button and cook 5 minutes (uncovered) or until noodles are fully cooked. Serve warm.

SERVES 4

Per Serving:

Calories	282
Fat	9g
Protein	27g
Sodium	621mg
Fiber	2g
Carbohydrates	24g
Sugar	2g
Net Carbs	22g

THE AMAZING INSTANT POT®

The Instant Pot® is an electric pressure cooker. It works by trapping the steam released by food and building an intense amount of pressure. The pressure causes water to boil at a hotter-than-normal temperature, up to 240°F. This allows food to cook much faster without losing flavor.

Slow Cooker Honey Garlic Chicken

SERVES 4

Per Serving:

Calories	503
Fat	6g
Protein	41g
Sodium	1,832mg
Fiber	4g
Carbohydrates	80g
Sugar	41g
Net Carbs	76g

You have an entire meal right in one pot with this recipe. By throwing everything in at the same time, you get a great harmony of flavors that blend together while cooking.

4 (6-ounce) boneless, skinless chicken breasts

2 large russet potatoes, peeled and cubed

2 cups chopped asparagus

½ cup honey

½ cup low-sodium soy sauce

¼ cup ketchup

2 cloves garlic, peeled and minced

½ teaspoon ground black pepper

1 teaspoon grated ginger

1 teaspoon sesame oil

Add chicken, potatoes, and asparagus to a slow cooker. In a small bowl, combine honey, soy sauce, ketchup, garlic, pepper, ginger, and oil and pour over chicken. Cook on high for 3–4 hours or on low for 7–8 hours until chicken is cooked through. Serve hot.

Slow Cooker Shredded Pork

SERVES 6

Per Serving:

Calories	543
Fat	28g
Protein	41g
Sodium	1,991mg
Fiber	1g
Carbohydrates	10g
Sugar	2g
Net Carbs	9g

Serve this shredded pork with a side of rice for dinner, add some to a salad for lunch, or use it for a flavorful taco filling.

1 tablespoon ground cumin

1 teaspoon garlic powder

1 teaspoon chili powder

1 teaspoon paprika

1 teaspoon dried oregano

1 teaspoon salt

1 (1½-pound) pork shoulder

½ small yellow onion, peeled and chopped

½ cup mild salsa

⅓ cup fresh orange juice

1 In a small bowl, combine cumin, garlic powder, chili powder, paprika, oregano, and salt.

2 Rub spice mixture evenly over pork, then place in a slow cooker. Add onion, salsa, and orange juice.

3 Cook on low for 8 hours or on high for 4 hours. Transfer pork to a cutting board. Cool slightly. Using two forks, shred pork. Serve warm.

Slow Cooker Barbecue Meatballs and Noodles

This dish is perfect for when you're craving some comfort food. And if you need lunch for tomorrow, you can use the leftover meatballs to create a fantastic sub.

1 pound frozen beef meatballs
½ (18-ounce) bottle barbecue sauce
1¼ cups grape jelly
1 pound egg noodles
¼ cup chopped scallions

1 Add meatballs, barbecue sauce, and grape jelly to a slow cooker and stir. Cook on high for 3½ hours, stirring halfway through.

2 Cook egg noodles according to package instructions. Transfer noodles to a serving bowl and top with meatballs and sauce. Top with scallions before serving.

SERVES 4	
Per Serving:	
Calories	1,031
Fat	19g
Protein	42g
Sodium	597mg
Fiber	5g
Carbohydrates	174g
Sugar	83g
Net Carbs	169g

Slow Cooker Sweet Potatoes

Sweet potatoes make a delicious side dish, especially when they're topped with butter, cinnamon, and brown sugar. Or you can scrape out the insides to make mashed sweet potatoes.

4 large sweet potatoes

Using a fork, prick holes all around the sweet potatoes. Add sweet potatoes to a slow cooker and cook 3–4 hours on high or 6–8 hours on low. Serve warm.

SERVES 6	
Per Serving:	
Calories	109
Fat	0g
Protein	3g
Sodium	43mg
Fiber	4g
Carbohydrates	25g
Sugar	7g
Net Carbs	21g

Slow Cooker Asian Lettuce Wraps

SERVES 4

Per Serving:

Calories	340
Fat	16g
Protein	23g
Sodium	1,099mg
Fiber	3g
Carbohydrates	27g
Sugar	19g
Net Carbs	24g

SOY SAUCE AND SODIUM

Too much sodium can be bad for your health, as it causes your body to retain fluid. Unfortunately, soy sauce is loaded with sodium, so when you can, buy the low-sodium version. You can also substitute coconut aminos for a lower-sodium, gluten-free, and soy-free version.

These wraps provide lots of protein and not too many carbs, so they'll fill you up without making you feel stuffed. You can substitute romaine lettuce for the iceberg, but it's important to use a sturdy enough lettuce so the leaves will stand up to the filling.

½ **cup hoisin sauce**

3 **tablespoons low-sodium soy sauce**

2 **teaspoons sesame oil**

½ **teaspoon ground ginger**

1 **teaspoon garlic powder**

¼ **teaspoon ground black pepper**

2 **teaspoons olive oil**

1 **pound ground chicken**

½ **cup chopped yellow onion**

½ **cup chopped red bell pepper**

8 **large iceberg lettuce leaves**

½ **cup sliced scallions**

1 In a small bowl, combine hoisin sauce, soy sauce, sesame oil, ginger, garlic powder, and black pepper. Mix well and set aside.

2 Heat olive oil in a large frying pan over medium heat, then add chicken. Sauté, using a large spoon to break up chicken into small chunks. Cook until no longer pink, about 5 minutes. Add onion and bell pepper and cook 1 minute. Remove from heat and transfer to a slow cooker.

3 Add soy sauce mixture to the slow cooker and mix well. Cook on low 2–3 hours until sauce is thick.

4 Spoon chicken mixture onto lettuce leaves and top with scallions. Serve immediately.

CHAPTER 6

Leftovers

French Toast Sandwich

SERVES 1	
Per Serving:	
Calories	926
Fat	50g
Protein	28g
Sodium	820mg
Fiber	6g
Carbohydrates	96g
Sugar	59g
Net Carbs	90g

Slices of French Toast add a kick of sweetness to an everyday sandwich. For a less breakfasty meal, you can substitute the peanut butter with your favorite sandwich fillings, like ham and Swiss, turkey and Cheddar, roast beef, or chicken salad.

2 tablespoons peanut butter
2 slices French Toast (see recipe in Chapter 2)
½ small banana, peeled and sliced
1 tablespoon honey

Spread 1 tablespoon peanut butter on each slice of French Toast. Lay banana slices on top of peanut butter and drizzle with honey. Close sandwich. If desired, microwave for 30–45 seconds before eating.

Potato Skins with Cheese and Bacon

SERVES 2	
Per Serving:	
Calories	182
Fat	10g
Protein	5g
Sodium	131mg
Fiber	2g
Carbohydrates	19g
Sugar	1g
Net Carbs	17g

Got a leftover baked potato? This recipe transforms your potato into a cheesy, bacon-filled delight. Add a dollop of sour cream for some extra creaminess.

1 medium baked potato
1 tablespoon unsalted butter

2 tablespoons shredded Cheddar cheese
1 slice cooked bacon, chopped

1 Preheat oven broiler and position oven rack about 4"–5" from the heat source.

2 Cut potato in half lengthwise. Scoop out the insides, leaving ¼"–½" of potato filling around the skin. Cut the skin in half, from top to bottom to yield four potato segments.

3 Spread butter on the inside of the potato skins, then place on an ungreased baking sheet, skin-side down. Sprinkle cheese and bacon on top. Broil until cheese melts, about 2 minutes. Serve hot.

Mashed Potatoes

Potatoes are cheap and easy to buy in bulk, which means you'll likely always have one or two in your pantry. Spice these Mashed Potatoes up with garlic powder, paprika, or ground nutmeg.

1 large russet potato, peeled and cut into quarters

1 tablespoon unsalted butter

1½ teaspoons whole milk

½ teaspoon salt

½ teaspoon ground black pepper

1 Fill a medium saucepan with enough water to cover potato and bring to a boil.

2 Add potato and boil until tender, about 5 minutes. Drain and transfer potato to a medium bowl.

3 Add butter. Mash potato and butter using a fork. Add milk a bit at a time as you are mashing until potato is fluffy. Stir in salt and pepper and serve.

SERVES 1

Per Serving:

Calories	275
Fat	11g
Protein	5g
Sodium	1,194mg
Fiber	4g
Carbohydrates	40g
Sugar	2g
Net Carbs	36g

Super-Easy Ham and Bean Soup

Refried beans and cooked ham provide the flavor in this easy-to-make dish. If you want the soup to be thicker or thinner, add more or less ham and refried beans than the recipe calls for.

¾ cup chopped cooked ham

¾ cup refried beans

2 cups low-sodium chicken broth

1 cup water

2 tablespoons sour cream

1 Combine ham, beans, broth, and water in a medium saucepan. Bring to a boil over medium-high heat.

2 Reduce heat to medium-low and simmer 5 minutes. Remove from heat and stir in sour cream. Serve hot.

SERVES 2

Per Serving:

Calories	186
Fat	6g
Protein	17g
Sodium	1,169mg
Fiber	4g
Carbohydrates	15g
Sugar	2g
Net Carbs	11g

Shrimp with Simple Cocktail Sauce

SERVES 2	
Per Serving:	
Calories	184
Fat	1g
Protein	24g
Sodium	893mg
Fiber	0g
Carbohydrates	19g
Sugar	15g
Net Carbs	19g

Ketchup and a dollop of horseradish are all you need to spice up leftover shrimp. Serve this with rice, a salad, or steamed vegetables for a nutritious meal. You can store leftover sauce in a sealed container in the refrigerator for up to 7 days.

½ cup ketchup
1½ teaspoons horseradish
1½ teaspoons lemon juice

¼ teaspoon Worcestershire sauce
8 ounces cooked shrimp, peeled and deveined

Combine ketchup, horseradish, lemon juice, and Worcestershire sauce in a small bowl. Chill. Toss cooked shrimp in cocktail sauce. Serve immediately or refrigerate at least 1 hour.

Teriyaki Shrimp with Vermicelli

SERVES 1	
Per Serving:	
Calories	402
Fat	11g
Protein	36g
Sodium	847mg
Fiber	0g
Carbohydrates	37g
Sugar	18g
Net Carbs	37g

Adding pasta to a dish is an easy way to stretch your leftovers. If you have any leftover Air Fryer Coconut Shrimp (see recipe in Chapter 5), you can use it in this recipe.

2 tablespoons pineapple juice
2 tablespoons teriyaki sauce
1 teaspoon light brown sugar
2 teaspoons vegetable oil

2 ounces cooked vermicelli
½ cup baby carrots, cut in half
6 ounces cooked shrimp, peeled and deveined

1 In a small bowl, mix together pineapple juice, teriyaki sauce, and brown sugar. Set aside.

2 Heat oil in a medium frying pan over medium heat, then add vermicelli and cook about 1 minute. Push vermicelli to the sides of the pan and add carrots. Cook 1–2 minutes, then add shrimp and sauce. Cook another 1–2 minutes until warmed through. Serve immediately.

Sesame Chicken Lettuce Wraps

Dinner for four in 10 minutes? Done. Add half a mashed avocado to the yogurt mixture for some extra creaminess.

1/3 cup sesame seeds

1/4 cup plain low-fat Greek yogurt

2 teaspoons honey

1 tablespoon dried dill

1 (5-ounce) cooked boneless, skinless chicken breast, thinly sliced

4 large iceberg lettuce leaves

1 medium cucumber, peeled and thinly sliced

SERVES 2	
Per Serving:	
Calories	308
Fat	13g
Protein	30g
Sodium	86mg
Fiber	4g
Carbohydrates	19g
Sugar	9g
Net Carbs	15g

1 Heat a medium frying pan over medium heat. Toast sesame seeds, shaking continuously, about 1 minute until golden brown. Remove from heat and set aside.

2 In a small bowl, combine yogurt, honey, and dill. Add chicken and toss to coat.

3 Place lettuce leaves on a platter. Divide chicken mixture and cucumber among leaves. Sprinkle with sesame seeds before serving.

Dairy-Free Zucchini Fritters

Whether you're looking for a quick snack, a healthy lunch, or a great appetizer for the tailgate on Saturday, these Dairy-Free Zucchini Fritters won't disappoint.

1 large zucchini, shredded

1 large egg

1/4 cup whole-wheat flour

1/2 teaspoon salt

1/8 teaspoon ground black pepper

1/4 teaspoon garlic powder

2 tablespoons olive oil

SERVES 2	
Per Serving:	
Calories	131
Fat	4g
Protein	7g
Sodium	639mg
Fiber	4g
Carbohydrates	16g
Sugar	5g
Net Carbs	12g

1 Press shredded zucchini between sheets of paper towels to absorb excess moisture. In a large bowl, combine zucchini, egg, flour, salt, pepper, and garlic powder. Mix well.

2 Heat oil in a large frying pan over medium heat. Scoop 2 tablespoons of zucchini mixture and add to the pan. Gently push down with a spatula to form a patty. Cook until golden brown, about 2 minutes, then flip and cook another 2 minutes. Repeat with remaining mixture. Serve warm.

Easy Fried Rice

SERVES 2

Per Serving:

Calories	305
Fat	14g
Protein	9g
Sodium	702mg
Fiber	3g
Carbohydrates	35g
Sugar	2g
Net Carbs	32g

RICE TYPES

Ever wonder what the difference is between long-grain, medium-grain, and short-grain rice? It all comes down to starch. Long-grain rice has more of a type of starch called amylase, which makes it fluff up nicely. At the other end, short-grain rice has a starch called amylopectin, which makes it sticky. Medium-grain rice is a combination of short and long grain.

Fried rice is always best when made with cold, cooked rice. Refrigerating the rice for at least a day helps dry it out, giving you that crunchy texture you want. Add in some leftover shrimp, chicken, or pork for extra protein.

1 large egg
¼ teaspoon salt
½ teaspoon ground black pepper
1 tablespoon canola oil
1 cup cooked white rice
½ cup frozen peas
2 tablespoons diced scallion, divided
1 tablespoon low-sodium soy sauce
1 teaspoon sesame oil
½ teaspoon garlic powder
½ teaspoon ground ginger
1 tablespoon sesame seeds

1. In a small bowl, beat egg, salt, and pepper together. Set aside.

2. Heat oil in a medium frying pan over medium-high heat. Add rice and cook 5 minutes, stirring frequently.

3. Push rice to the edges of the frying pan and add egg mixture to the middle of the pan. Cook 1–2 minutes, stirring with a spatula until set. Mix with rice.

4. Stir in peas, 1 tablespoon scallions, soy sauce, sesame oil, garlic powder, and ginger and cook another 2–3 minutes until heated through.

5. Top with sesame seeds and remaining 1 tablespoon scallions. Serve immediately.

Roasted Chicken Soup

Leftover vegetables make great additions to any soup you're whipping up. They thicken the soup and add a lot of good vitamins and minerals to the meal—and it saves them from sitting in the back of your refrigerator for weeks and weeks. You can substitute 1 teaspoon chili powder if you don't have any Tabasco sauce.

SERVES 2

Per Serving:

Calories	237
Fat	7g
Protein	28g
Sodium	630mg
Fiber	4g
Carbohydrates	11g
Sugar	5g
Net Carbs	7g

2 teaspoons olive oil

1 clove garlic, peeled and chopped

¼ cup chopped yellow onion

½ medium zucchini, thinly sliced

1 medium carrot, peeled and thinly sliced

6 medium fresh button mushrooms, sliced

4 cups low-sodium chicken broth

1 cup chopped roasted chicken breast

1 teaspoon dried oregano

½ teaspoon dried basil

¼ teaspoon Tabasco sauce

¼ teaspoon salt

½ teaspoon ground black pepper

2 scallions, thinly sliced

1 Heat oil in a medium saucepan over medium-low heat. Add garlic and onion and cook until onion is soft and translucent, about 5 minutes. Add zucchini and carrot and cook 1–2 minutes, stirring continuously. Add mushrooms and cook for 1 minute.

2 Add broth and bring to a boil, then add chicken, oregano, basil, Tabasco sauce, salt, pepper, and scallions. Reduce heat and simmer for 15 minutes or until carrots are tender. Serve warm.

Thanksgiving Sandwich

Many people enjoy Thanksgiving leftovers more than the holiday turkey dinner itself! If you'd prefer a cold sandwich, skip the butter and the frying pan.

4 teaspoons mayonnaise

2 (1-ounce) slices whole-wheat bread

2 (6-ounce) slices cooked turkey

1 tablespoon cranberry sauce

2 tablespoons leftover stuffing

2 teaspoons butter

SERVES 1	
Per Serving:	
Calories	878
Fat	39g
Protein	90g
Sodium	1,487mg
Fiber	4g
Carbohydrates	38g
Sugar	17g
Net Carbs	34g

1 Spread 2 teaspoons mayonnaise on each slice of bread. Place turkey on one slice and spread cranberry sauce on top. Spread stuffing on other slice of bread. Close up sandwich.

2 Spread 1 teaspoon of butter on each slice of bread. Heat a small frying pan over medium heat and fry sandwich 3 minutes on each side. Serve immediately.

Noodles with Spinach and Tomato

Add some leftover chicken for a protein-packed pasta meal. Use leftover noodles for an even quicker meal and thawed frozen spinach if you don't have fresh.

1 tablespoon olive oil

2 cloves garlic, peeled and chopped

1 medium tomato, sliced

1½ cups cooked egg noodles

2 cups baby spinach leaves

2 tablespoons grated Parmesan cheese

¼ teaspoon salt

¼ teaspoon ground black pepper

SERVES 2	
Per Serving:	
Calories	253
Fat	11g
Protein	9g
Sodium	432mg
Fiber	3g
Carbohydrates	31g
Sugar	2g
Net Carbs	28g

1 Heat oil in a medium frying pan over medium heat, then add garlic and tomato. Cook 2 minutes, turn heat up to high, and add noodles.

2 Stir in spinach and cook until spinach wilts, about 1 minute. Sprinkle with cheese, salt, and pepper and serve.

Meatball and Cheese Sub

SERVES 1	
Per Serving:	
Calories	794
Fat	21g
Protein	41g
Sodium	1,386mg
Fiber	11g
Carbohydrates	112g
Sugar	5g
Net Carbs	101g

For a heartier sandwich, add 2 or 3 slices of provolone or cooked ham. If you don't have marinara sauce, plain tomato sauce works just as well.

3 tablespoons marinara sauce
1 (12") whole-wheat sub roll
2 tablespoons shredded mozzarella cheese
4 (1-ounce) meatballs

1 Spread sauce on the inside of sub roll, then add cheese. Place meatballs inside the roll.

2 Place sandwich on a paper towel or microwave-safe plate and microwave 1½–2½ minutes on high, until meatballs and sauce are heated through and cheese is melted. Serve immediately.

Apple and Walnut Salad

SERVES 2	
Per Serving:	
Calories	166
Fat	12g
Protein	4g
Sodium	22mg
Fiber	3g
Carbohydrates	13g
Sugar	9g
Net Carbs	10g

This is one of those salads that looks like a bunch of random ingredients were tossed together, but it tastes amazing. Experiment with the recipe by using your favorite flavored Greek yogurt and some Cheddar cheese cubes. If you like red onion, toss that in as well.

1 medium stalk celery, chopped
1 cup chopped apple
⅓ cup roughly chopped walnuts
2 tablespoons vanilla low-fat Greek yogurt

In a small bowl, combine celery, apple, and walnuts, then toss with yogurt. Serve immediately or cover and refrigerate at least 1 hour.

Easy Egg Drop Soup

This Easy Egg Drop Soup is the perfect dish for all that spinach hiding in your refrigerator! It only has five ingredients, and all of them are kitchen staples.

2 cups low-sodium chicken broth

⅛ teaspoon salt

¼ teaspoon ground black pepper

1 large egg, beaten

1 scallion, diagonally sliced

1   Bring broth to a boil in a small saucepan over medium-high heat, then stir in salt and pepper.

2   Remove saucepan from heat and slowly add in beaten egg, stirring rapidly clockwise to form long, thin ribbons. Stir in scallion and serve immediately.

SERVES 1	
Per Serving:	
Calories	97
Fat	5g
Protein	9g
Sodium	1,058mg
Fiber	1g
Carbohydrates	4g
Sugar	1g
Net Carbs	3g

Low-Carb Chicken Pinwheels

These healthy pinwheels are a play on sushi rolls, but instead of fish and rice, they are filled with chicken and avocado. You can even use hummus if you're not feeling the avocado.

2 (8" × 7") nori sheet

1 small avocado, peeled, pitted, and thinly sliced

1 tablespoon sesame seeds

1 cup thinly sliced cooked chicken

¼ cup diced red onion

1   Place nori sheet onto a flat surface. Place avocado evenly on top, making sure to leave 1" of room around the edges.

2   Sprinkle sesame seeds over avocado, then layer on chicken and onion. Roll wrap, then slice into rolls. Serve at room temperature or refrigerate at least 2 hours.

SERVES 2	
Per Serving:	
Calories	276
Fat	16g
Protein	25g
Sodium	73mg
Fiber	7g
Carbohydrates	11g
Sugar	1g
Net Carbs	4g

GF

Herb Risotto

SERVES 2

Per Serving:

Calories	345
Fat	5g
Protein	9g
Sodium	518mg
Fiber	3g
Carbohydrates	65g
Sugar	6g
Net Carbs	62g

This recipe can easily be doubled or halved to serve as many people as needed, and it pairs perfectly with a baked chicken or pork recipe. For a creamier risotto, replace 1 cup of the chicken broth with 1 cup whole milk.

2 teaspoons olive oil

½ cup diced yellow onion

1 cup arborio rice

½ cup water

¼ teaspoon salt

⅛ teaspoon ground black pepper

¼ teaspoon garlic powder

½ teaspoon dried parsley

½ teaspoon dried basil

1 tablespoon chopped chives

2 medium carrots, chopped

2 cups low-sodium chicken broth, divided

1 tablespoon grated Parmesan cheese

1 teaspoon lemon juice

1 Heat oil in a medium saucepan over medium heat. Add onion and cook about 5 minutes until soft and translucent. Stir in rice. Cook 3–4 minutes until rice looks shiny. Reduce heat to medium.

2 Add water and cook 2–3 minutes, until rice has absorbed nearly all of the water. Stir in salt, pepper, garlic powder, parsley, basil, chives, carrots, and ½ cup broth. Cook, stirring constantly, until broth is absorbed.

3 Continue adding broth, ½ cup at a time, stirring constantly until absorbed. This will take about 25 minutes. Stir in cheese and lemon juice and serve immediately.

Shepherd's Pie

Shepherd's Pie is a super-easy casserole dish for those crazy, no-time-to-cook weeknights. You can use leftover ground beef if you have it. For a little bit of extra flavor, add ½ cup shredded Cheddar cheese to the mashed potatoes.

2 teaspoons olive oil

½ pound 85% lean ground beef

¼ cup chopped yellow onion

¼ cup chopped carrots

¼ cup chopped celery

½ cup frozen corn kernels

½ cup frozen peas

3 tablespoons ketchup

2 teaspoons Worcestershire sauce

¼ teaspoon garlic powder

¼ teaspoon salt

¼ teaspoon ground black pepper

1½ cups mashed potatoes

1 Preheat oven to 350°F.

2 Heat oil in a large frying pan over medium heat and add beef. Sauté, using a large spoon to break up beef into small chunks. Add onion, carrots, celery, corn, and peas. Cook 7–9 minutes or until beef is no longer pink and onion is soft and translucent. Drain excess liquid.

3 Transfer ground beef mixture to a small (about 1-quart) casserole dish. Stir in ketchup, Worcestershire sauce, garlic powder, salt, and pepper. Mix well, then spread mashed potatoes on top, completely covering beef mixture. Bake 15 minutes or until heated through. Serve warm.

SERVES 2

Per Serving:

Calories	554
Fat	29g
Protein	27g
Sodium	969mg
Fiber	6g
Carbohydrates	48g
Sugar	13g
Net Carbs	42g

THE LEFTOVER RULE OF THUMB

So you have more food than you need for one meal? Great! Just store it in a tightly sealed container and pop it in the refrigerator. The general rule of thumb for leftovers with meat is that they can last for up to 3 days unless the packaging says otherwise.

Gluten-Free Stuffed Peppers

Stuffed peppers are the perfect dish for using up leftovers. You can add the leftover ground beef from last night's hamburgers or throw in some spaghetti sauce from last week's pasta dish.

4 large green bell peppers

2 tablespoons olive oil, divided

½ cup chopped yellow onion

½ pound 90% lean ground beef

1 tablespoon garlic powder

½ teaspoon dried oregano

¼ teaspoon dried basil

½ teaspoon salt

¼ teaspoon ground black pepper

1 (14.5-ounce) can diced tomatoes, with liquid

3 tablespoons tomato paste

1 cup cooked white rice

¾ cup shredded Cheddar cheese

1 Preheat oven to 350°F.

2 Remove ½" from the top of each bell pepper. Use a metal spoon to carefully remove ribs and seeds from inside the peppers. Lightly brush the outside of peppers with 1 tablespoon olive oil and set aside.

3 Heat remaining 1 tablespoon oil in a large frying pan over medium heat. Add onion and cook about 5 minutes until soft and translucent. Add beef, garlic powder, oregano, basil, salt, black pepper, tomatoes, and tomato paste. Mix well and cook 10 minutes. Stir in rice and cook another 5 minutes or until rice is heated through.

4 Scoop even portions of beef mixture into each bell pepper. Top each pepper with equal amounts Cheddar cheese and transfer to a 3-quart casserole dish. Bake 30 minutes or until cheese starts to brown. Serve hot.

SERVES 4

Per Serving:

Calories	384
Fat	20g
Protein	20g
Sodium	675mg
Fiber	5g
Carbohydrates	33g
Sugar	9g
Net Carbs	28g

GARLIC CLOVES VS. GARLIC POWDER

When a recipe calls for garlic cloves, you can usually use the powder in place of it, and vice versa. Cloves will give you a fresher taste, but the powder has a longer shelf-life. One fresh clove is equal to about ½ teaspoon garlic powder.

Creamy Chicken and Rice Soup

SERVES 4

Per Serving:

Calories	190
Fat	6g
Protein	15g
Sodium	464mg
Fiber	2g
Carbohydrates	17g
Sugar	5g
Net Carbs	15g

MILK ALTERNATIVES

If you prefer a dairy-free soup, you can replace the milk with almond, cashew, coconut, oat, soy, or rice milk. Yes, there are a lot of options. If you're new to the nondairy game, start with soy milk or rice milk. These two tend to taste the most like the dairy milk you're used to.

Don't have leftover chicken? After Step 1, add two large skinless, boneless chicken breasts to the pan with the thyme, basil, parsley, salt, pepper, and chicken broth. Bring to a boil, then simmer for about 30 minutes, until chicken is fully cooked. Remove the chicken, cube it, then return it to the pan with the rice. Continue with Step 3.

2 teaspoons olive oil

½ cup chopped yellow onion

½ cup chopped celery

½ cup chopped carrots

2 cloves garlic, peeled and minced

8 ounces cubed cooked chicken breast

¾ cup cooked white rice

1 teaspoon dried thyme

1 teaspoon dried basil

1 teaspoon dried parsley

½ teaspoon salt

1 teaspoon ground black pepper

3 cups low-sodium chicken broth

1 cup whole milk

¼ cup chopped chives

1 Heat oil in a large saucepan over medium heat. Add onion, celery, and carrots and cook 5–7 minutes until onion is soft and translucent. Add garlic and cook another 30 seconds, continuously stirring.

2 Add chicken, rice, thyme, basil, parsley, salt, and pepper. Mix well and cook 2 minutes. Stir in broth. Reduce heat to medium-low and simmer about 15 minutes.

3 Remove from heat and add milk. Set aside for 5 minutes. Garnish with chives before serving.

Chicken Pot Pie

You can usually find frozen mixed vegetable bags that include peas, carrots, and corn. You can use 3 cups of that instead of buying individual bags.

1 tablespoon olive oil

1 medium yellow onion, peeled and chopped

1 cup frozen peas, thawed

1 cup frozen carrots, thawed and chopped

1 cup frozen corn kernels, thawed

2 cups shredded cooked chicken breast

2 cups low-sodium chicken broth

1 cup whole milk

½ cup plus 6 tablespoons all-purpose flour, divided

¾ teaspoon salt, divided

½ teaspoon ground black pepper

½ cup cold unsalted butter, cubed

1⅓ tablespoons cold water

1 Preheat oven to 375°F and grease an 8" × 8" baking dish.

2 Heat oil in a small frying pan over medium heat. Add onion, peas, carrots, and corn and cook about 5 minutes, until onion is soft and translucent. Add chicken, broth, milk, 6 tablespoons flour, ¼ teaspoon salt, and pepper. Reduce heat to low and simmer 10 minutes, until mixture thickens.

3 In a small bowl, combine remaining ½ cup flour and remaining ½ teaspoon salt. Add butter and, using two knives or your fingers, work butter into flour until mixture has a sand-like texture. Add water and mix just until dough comes together.

4 Roll out dough on a floured surface until it is the size of the baking dish. Spoon chicken mixture into baking dish, then top with dough. Bake 25 minutes or until crust is golden brown. Serve warm.

SERVES 4

Per Serving:

Calories	582
Fat	31g
Protein	31g
Sodium	652mg
Fiber	5g
Carbohydrates	41g
Sugar	10g
Net Carbs	36g

PERFECT DOUGH TIPS

Making pie dough may seem intimidating, but don't worry—it's easier than it looks. Just make sure you use very cold butter and add only the minimum amount of water. Less is more! Use a floured surface and a floured rolling pin when rolling out your dough. It'll help keep the dough from sticking.

Paleo Chicken and Apple Sausage

SERVES 4

Per Serving:

Calories	339
Fat	19g
Protein	22g
Sodium	393mg
Fiber	4g
Carbohydrates	24g
Sugar	16g
Net Carbs	20g

You can make this recipe in large batches, as these patties are super-easy to freeze and reheat as needed.

2 tablespoons olive oil, divided

1 large green apple, peeled, cored, and diced

2 teaspoons ground cinnamon

1 teaspoon ground nutmeg

¼ teaspoon ground allspice

2 tablespoons dried oregano

1 tablespoon dried thyme

3 tablespoons 100% pure maple syrup

1 pound ground chicken

1 tablespoon garlic powder

1 tablespoon onion powder

1 teaspoon ground cumin

½ teaspoon salt

¼ teaspoon ground black pepper

1 Preheat oven to 425°F. Line a baking sheet with foil.

2 Heat 1 tablespoon oil in a small frying pan over medium heat. Add apple, cinnamon, nutmeg, allspice, oregano, thyme, and maple syrup. Cook 5–7 minutes, stirring continuously, until apples are soft. Remove from heat and set aside.

3 In a large mixing bowl, combine chicken, garlic powder, onion powder, cumin, salt, and pepper. Add apple mixture and mix well.

4 Using your hands, form mixture into ½"-thick patties and place them on prepared baking sheet. Bake 20 minutes or until fully cooked through.

5 Heat remaining 1 tablespoon oil in the frying pan over medium heat. Add 1–2 patties and cook 30 seconds on each side, just long enough for patties to brown. Serve warm.

Keto Chicken and Broccoli Casserole

There's something incredibly comforting about a warm, cheesy casserole. Use mozzarella or Parmesan cheese instead of Cheddar if you prefer, and spice it up with a sprinkle of red pepper flakes.

1 tablespoon unsalted butter

2 cups chopped fresh broccoli

12 ounces shredded cooked chicken breast

1 tablespoon garlic powder

2 teaspoons paprika

1 teaspoon salt

1 teaspoon ground black pepper

½ teaspoon dried basil

½ teaspoon dried oregano

4 ounces cream cheese

½ cup low-sodium chicken broth

1 tablespoon dried parsley

¾ cup shredded Cheddar cheese

SERVES 4

Per Serving:	
Calories	360
Fat	21g
Protein	35g
Sodium	925mg
Fiber	2g
Carbohydrates	8g
Sugar	2g
Net Carbs	6g

1 Preheat oven to 400°F. Spray an 8" × 8" baking pan with nonstick cooking spray.

2 Heat butter in a medium frying pan over medium heat. Add broccoli and cook 5 minutes, then set aside.

3 In a large bowl, combine chicken, garlic powder, paprika, salt, pepper, basil, and oregano. Mix well and set aside. In a small bowl, mix together cream cheese, broth, and parsley until creamy.

4 Place chicken mixture in prepared baking pan. Pour cream cheese mixture over chicken, then top with broccoli and Cheddar cheese. Bake 20–25 minutes or until cheese is melted. Serve warm.

Chicken Enchiladas

This Tex-Mex staple is filled with wonderful seasonings and a delicious enchilada sauce to give your leftover chicken a nice kick of flavor. You can usually find the enchilada sauce in the international aisle of your grocery store. Feel free to top with pico de gallo for some fresh flavor.

SERVES 4

Per Serving:

Calories	902
Fat	47g
Protein	59g
Sodium	2,168mg
Fiber	8g
Carbohydrates	65g
Sugar	8g
Net Carbs	57g

ENCHILADA SAUCES

Enchiladas can be made with a wide variety of different sauces, such as salsa roja, mole, or chili con queso. Different sauces work with different fillings, so try a few combinations until you find one you love.

1 tablespoon olive oil

1 cup chopped yellow onion

2 teaspoons garlic powder

½ teaspoon salt

1 teaspoon ground black pepper

½ teaspoon chili powder

½ teaspoon ground cumin

1 (10-ounce) can red enchilada sauce

1 (15-ounce) can crushed tomatoes, with liquid

2 cups shredded cooked chicken

1 (14-ounce) can black beans, drained and rinsed

¼ cup chopped fresh cilantro

2 tablespoons lime juice

2 cups shredded Cheddar cheese, divided

1 cup shredded Monterey jack cheese, divided

4 (8") flour tortillas

1 Preheat oven to 350°F and spray an 8" × 8" baking pan with nonstick cooking spray.

2 Heat oil in a large frying pan over medium heat. Add onion and cook about 5 minutes until soft and translucent. Add garlic powder, salt, pepper, chili powder, cumin, enchilada sauce, and tomatoes. Cook another 5 minutes or until sauce is heated through.

3 In a large bowl, combine chicken, beans, cilantro, lime juice, 1 cup Cheddar cheese, ½ cup Monterey jack cheese, and 1 cup enchilada sauce mixture. Mix well.

4 Place 1 tortilla on a work surface. Add a scoop of chicken mixture to the center of the tortilla, roll tightly, and place seam-side down in prepared baking pan. Repeat with remaining tortillas. Pour remaining enchilada sauce mixture over tortillas and top with remaining 1 cup Cheddar and ½ cup Monterey jack cheese. Bake 10 minutes or until cheese is melted and bubbly. Serve hot.

Leftover Pasta Bake

The two types of cheese in this dish create a flavorful and creamy combo that is used all the time in Italian cooking.

SERVES 2	
Per Serving:	
Calories	432
Fat	18g
Protein	26g
Sodium	598mg
Fiber	4g
Carbohydrates	38g
Sugar	2g
Net Carbs	34g

2 cups cooked ziti

2 large eggs, beaten

½ cup grated Parmesan cheese

1 teaspoon garlic powder

1½ cups marinara sauce

1 cup shredded mozzarella cheese

½ cup sliced scallions

1. Preheat oven to 350°F and grease an 8" × 8" baking dish with nonstick cooking spray.

2. In a large bowl, combine ziti, eggs, Parmesan cheese, garlic powder, and marinara sauce, then transfer to prepared baking dish.

3. Bake 30 minutes, top with mozzarella cheese and bake another 10 minutes. Garnish with scallions. Serve hot.

Ham, Potato, and Vegetable Medley

To make this dish a little creamier, add ½ cup milk and ½ cup shredded Cheddar cheese.

SERVES 4	
Per Serving:	
Calories	226
Fat	13g
Protein	16g
Sodium	592mg
Fiber	2g
Carbohydrates	12g
Sugar	2g
Net Carbs	10g

1 tablespoon olive oil

½ cup chopped yellow onion

¼ cup chopped green bell pepper

1 clove garlic, peeled and minced

½ cup steamed broccoli

1 cup cubed cooked ham

1 cup cubed cooked russet potatoes

¾ cup low-sodium chicken broth

½ cup grated Parmesan cheese

¼ teaspoon paprika

¼ teaspoon cayenne pepper

¼ teaspoon dried oregano

¼ teaspoon dried thyme

½ teaspoon salt

½ teaspoon ground black pepper

¼ cup chopped chives

1. Heat oil in large skillet over medium heat. Add onion and bell pepper and sauté 5 minutes. Add garlic and cook 30 seconds.

2. Add remaining ingredients, except chives, reduce heat to medium-low, and simmer 15 minutes. Top with chives and serve warm.

Dairy-Free Turkey Soup with Coconut and Lime

Diced chicken works just as well as shredded in this soup, or you can use leftover turkey if you have that on hand instead. If you like your soup a little spicier, try adding ¼ teaspoon green Tabasco sauce.

1 teaspoon olive oil

½ cup chopped yellow onion

2 cloves garlic, peeled and chopped

2½ cups low-sodium chicken broth

1 teaspoon ground ginger

3 tablespoons fresh lime juice

1½ tablespoons low-sodium soy sauce

1 (13.5-ounce) can full-fat coconut milk

8 ounces shredded cooked turkey

¼ cup chopped fresh cilantro

¼ teaspoon ground cinnamon

¼ teaspoon paprika

¼ teaspoon chili powder

¼ teaspoon salt

¼ teaspoon ground black pepper

2 cups cooked white rice

½ cup chopped scallions

1 Heat oil in a large soup pot over medium heat. Add onion and sauté about 5 minutes until soft and translucent. Add garlic and cook another 30 seconds.

2 Add broth, ginger, lime juice, and soy sauce. Simmer 15 minutes.

3 Add coconut milk, turkey, cilantro, cinnamon, paprika, chili powder, salt, and pepper and reduce heat to low. Simmer 10 minutes, making sure mixture does not come to a boil.

4 Stir in white rice and garnish with scallions. Serve immediately.

SERVES 4

Per Serving:	
Calories	437
Fat	19g
Protein	23g
Sodium	635mg
Fiber	2g
Carbohydrates	37g
Sugar	6g
Net Carbs	35g

DRY RICE PROBLEMS

Find that your rice is turning out dry, even though you're using the same amount of water as usual? Check the date on the bag. Like flour, rice dries out as it ages. Try adding a bit more water during cooking, and it should help to moisten it up.

Keto Bacon Cheeseburger Casserole

SERVES 4

Per Serving:

Calories	777
Fat	55g
Protein	56g
Sodium	2,063mg
Fiber	4g
Carbohydrates	10g
Sugar	2g
Net Carbs	6g

GETTING RID OF BACON GREASE

Never pour bacon grease down your sink—it will harden and clog the drain. Instead, pour the grease into a mug or empty coffee can and let it sit overnight. This will allow it to harden, and you can throw it in the trash later without making a mess.

This low-carb Keto Bacon Cheeseburger Casserole will win over every burger lover. Leftover ground beef works perfectly, but if you don't have any, just brown up some fresh ground beef after you cook the bacon. Serve this with hot sauce for a little extra spice.

½ pound bacon

½ cup chopped red onion

1 pound cooked 85% lean ground beef

4 tablespoons cream cheese

2 tablespoons sugar-free ketchup

1 tablespoon Worcestershire sauce

1 teaspoon garlic powder

½ teaspoon salt

½ teaspoon ground black pepper

1 cup shredded Cheddar cheese

1 medium avocado, peeled, pitted, and sliced

4 dill pickle spears

1 Preheat oven to 350°F and grease an 8" × 8" baking dish.

2 Heat large frying pan over medium-high heat. Add bacon and cook 4–5 minutes. Using a fork, flip bacon and cook another 2–3 minutes until crispy. Remove bacon and chop into bite-sized pieces.

3 Drain grease from frying pan and reduce heat to medium-low. Add onion, ground beef, cream cheese, ketchup, Worcestershire sauce, garlic powder, salt, and pepper to the pan. Cook until heated through, about 10 minutes.

4 Pour beef mixture into prepared baking dish and top with bacon and Cheddar cheese. Bake 30 minutes or until cheese is golden brown. Serve casserole topped with avocado slices and pickles.

CHAPTER 7

Bowl Meals

Turkey Chili

(GF)

SERVES 4

Per Serving:

Calories	510
Fat	25g
Protein	40g
Sodium	1,284mg
Fiber	13g
Carbohydrates	37g
Sugar	3g
Net Carbs	24g

This filling meal is a healthier version of your typical ground beef and tomato-style chili. It's a bit spicy, so take out the jalapeños if you prefer a milder chili. Serve this with some warm corn bread or toasted sourdough slices.

2 tablespoons olive oil

½ medium yellow onion, peeled and diced

2 cloves garlic, peeled and minced

1 pound lean ground turkey

4 cups low-sodium chicken broth

1 (15-ounce) can white beans, drained and rinsed

1 (15-ounce) can chickpeas, drained and rinsed

1 teaspoon salt

1 teaspoon ground black pepper

4 teaspoons ground cumin

2 teaspoons chili powder

1 teaspoon dried marjoram

2 tablespoons minced jalapeño pepper

4 tablespoons sour cream

½ cup shredded Cheddar cheese

1 Heat oil in a large soup pot over medium heat. Add onion and sauté about 5 minutes until soft and translucent. Add garlic and cook 30 seconds. Add turkey and sauté, using a large spoon to break up turkey into small chunks. Cook until slightly browned, about 5 minutes.

2 Add broth, beans, chickpeas, salt, black pepper, cumin, chili powder, marjoram, and jalapeño. Bring to a boil and simmer 15 minutes. Ladle into bowls and top with sour cream and cheese. Serve immediately.

One-Pot Meatballs and Vegetables

DF

This recipe is incredibly versatile and can be used as a base for other meatball meals. Use a sweet-and-sour sauce and add the meatballs to a stir-fry mix. Serve them over rice or egg noodles, and you have a complete meal. Or use them in a Meatball and Cheese Sub (see recipe in Chapter 6) for a delicious lunch.

½ pound (about 12) frozen meatballs

1½ cups low-sodium beef broth

⅓ cup frozen corn, thawed

⅓ cup frozen peas, thawed

⅓ cup frozen carrots, thawed

½ cup canned crushed tomatoes, with liquid

1 teaspoon dried basil

¼ teaspoon salt

½ teaspoon ground black pepper

Combine all ingredients in a medium saucepan over medium-high heat and bring to a boil. Reduce heat to medium-low, cover, and simmer 15 minutes or until meatballs are hot. Serve immediately.

SERVES 2	
Per Serving:	
Calories	400
Fat	26g
Protein	22g
Sodium	1,446mg
Fiber	6g
Carbohydrates	24g
Sugar	10g
Net Carbs	18g

Simple Caesar Salad

Toasted baguette chunks or Italian bread cubes make excellent substitutes for the croutons. When you're buying salad dressing, pay attention to nutrition labels! Many brands contain unnecessary added sugars.

¾ head romaine lettuce, chopped

1 cup plain croutons

¼ cup bacon bits

¼ cup grated Parmesan cheese

3 tablespoons Caesar salad dressing

¼ teaspoon salt

¼ teaspoon ground black pepper

Mix together lettuce, croutons, bacon bits, and cheese. Just before serving, toss with dressing and sprinkle with salt and pepper. Serve immediately.

SERVES 1	
Per Serving:	
Calories	577
Fat	41g
Protein	27g
Sodium	2,543mg
Fiber	3g
Carbohydrates	27g
Sugar	2g
Net Carbs	24g

Buttery Parmesan Pasta

SERVES 1

Per Serving:

Calories	759
Fat	17g
Protein	25g
Sodium	263mg
Fiber	5g
Carbohydrates	123g
Sugar	5g
Net Carbs	118g

There are two tricks to making pasta come out right every single time. First, make sure there is enough water for the pasta to move around while cooking. Second, stir and separate the pasta pieces immediately after adding them to the boiling water.

1 tablespoon salt

6 ounces penne

1 tablespoon butter

2 tablespoons grated Parmesan cheese

1 Fill a large saucepan with water and add salt. Bring to a boil.

2 Add penne to the boiling water. Stir with a wooden spoon, separating the noodles. Cook until tender but still firm (al dente), about 8 minutes.

3 Drain penne in a colander, transfer to a serving bowl, and top with butter and cheese. Serve immediately.

Spanish Rice

This quick and easy dish works as a side or in tacos, quesadillas, and burritos. Want to add a little more protein? Add ½ cup drained and rinsed black beans with the tomatoes.

2 teaspoons olive oil

½ medium red onion, peeled and chopped

½ medium green bell pepper, seeded and diced

1 pound 85% lean ground beef

1½ cups canned crushed tomatoes, with liquid

1½ cups water

2 cups cooked white rice

½ teaspoon salt

½ teaspoon ground black pepper

¼ teaspoon ground cumin

¼ teaspoon cayenne pepper

½ teaspoon garlic powder

¼ teaspoon dried oregano

SERVES 4

Per Serving:

Calories	425
Fat	20g
Protein	25g
Sodium	807mg
Fiber	2g
Carbohydrates	36g
Sugar	4g
Net Carbs	34g

1 Heat oil in a medium frying pan over medium heat. Add onion and cook about 5 minutes until soft and translucent. Add bell pepper and cook another 5 minutes.

2 Add ground beef to the pan. Sauté, using a large spoon to break up beef into small chunks. Cook until no longer pink, about 5 minutes. Drain excess oil and return pan to the burner.

3 Add tomatoes, water, and rice to ground beef mixture. Stir in salt, black pepper, cumin, cayenne pepper, garlic powder, and oregano. Bring to a boil over medium-high heat, then reduce heat to low. Cover and simmer 20 minutes or until all liquid is absorbed. Serve hot.

Healthy Burrito Bowl

The Greek yogurt replaces the sour cream usually found in a traditional burrito bowl for a little extra-healthy protein. If you prefer, use steak, pork, tofu, or shrimp in this recipe.

1 teaspoon olive oil

1 (4-ounce) boneless, skinless chicken breast, diced

¼ teaspoon chili powder

¼ teaspoon garlic powder

¼ teaspoon paprika

¼ teaspoon dried oregano

¼ teaspoon salt

¼ teaspoon ground black pepper

½ cup cooked white rice

¼ cup chopped red onion

¼ cup mild salsa

¼ cup corn kernels (fresh, frozen, or canned)

1 tablespoon lime juice

¼ cup plain low-fat Greek yogurt

1 tablespoon chopped fresh cilantro

¼ cup shredded Monterey jack cheese

1 Heat oil in a medium frying pan over medium heat. Add chicken and sauté 15 minutes, stirring occasionally.

2 Add chili powder, garlic powder, paprika, oregano, salt, and pepper to chicken and cook 10 minutes. Remove from heat.

3 In a large serving bowl, combine rice, chicken, onion, salsa, corn, and lime juice. Top with yogurt, cilantro, and cheese. Serve immediately.

SERVES 1

Per Serving:

Calories	496
Fat	18g
Protein	40g
Sodium	1,595mg
Fiber	3g
Carbohydrates	49g
Sugar	7g
Net Carbs	46g

WHAT MAKES A BOWL MEAL?

The short answer is anything that fits in a bowl! Bowl meals can be soups, salads, stir-fries, rice mixtures, vegetable mixtures, meat combinations, etc. The one rule is that it has to be a meal, so you can't just throw fruit in a bowl and call it a day. It has to be filling enough for lunch or dinner.

Beef and Bok Choy Stir-Fry

SERVES 2

Per Serving:

Calories	374
Fat	22g
Protein	35g
Sodium	473mg
Fiber	1g
Carbohydrates	10g
Sugar	7g
Net Carbs	9g

If you're short on time, you can purchase premade stir-fry sauce to use instead of the first five ingredients.

½ **teaspoon sesame oil**

2 **teaspoons honey**

½ **teaspoon rice vinegar**

½ **teaspoon ground ginger**

¼ **cup low-sodium beef broth**

3 **teaspoons olive oil, divided**

1 **clove garlic, peeled and minced**

2 **medium stalks bok choy, thinly sliced**

1 **tablespoon low-sodium soy sauce**

½ **pound top round steak, sliced into 2" strips**

1 In a small bowl, stir together sesame oil, honey, vinegar, ginger, and broth. Set sauce aside.

2 Heat 1 teaspoon olive oil in a medium frying pan over medium heat. Add garlic and cook 30 seconds, then add bok choy. Pour in soy sauce and cook until tender, about 5 minutes.

3 Push bok choy mixture to the sides of the pan, then add remaining 2 teaspoons olive oil. Add beef and stir-fry until browned, about 10 minutes. Stir bok choy and beef together, then add reserved sauce. Stir-fry until heated through, about 2 minutes. Serve hot.

Gluten-Free Sweet Potato and Black Bean Bowl

This grain-free, nutrient-packed meal is just what you'll need after a long day of classes. If you have any leftover chicken or turkey, toss it in for some extra protein. You can also add bell peppers or corn for more crunch.

2 large sweet potatoes, peeled and diced

1 tablespoon olive oil

1 teaspoon paprika

2 teaspoons garlic powder, divided

1 teaspoon onion powder

½ teaspoon chili powder

½ teaspoon salt, divided

½ teaspoon ground black pepper

2 tablespoons chopped fresh cilantro

⅓ cup plain low-fat Greek yogurt

½ medium cucumber, peeled and chopped

1 tablespoon honey

1 cup canned black beans, drained and rinsed

¼ cup chopped red onion

1 medium avocado, peeled, pitted, and sliced

SERVES 2

Per Serving:

Calories	563
Fat	20g
Protein	19g
Sodium	955mg
Fiber	19g
Carbohydrates	85g
Sugar	23g
Net Carbs	66g

1 Preheat oven to 400°F and line a baking sheet with parchment paper.

2 Place sweet potatoes on prepared baking sheet and toss with oil. Season with paprika, 1 teaspoon garlic powder, onion powder, chili powder, ¼ teaspoon salt, and pepper. Bake 25 minutes or until soft and cooked through.

3 In a blender, combine cilantro, yogurt, cucumber, honey, remaining ¼ teaspoon salt, and remaining 1 teaspoon garlic powder. Blend until smooth.

4 Divide sweet potatoes, beans, onion, and avocado between two large serving bowls. Drizzle with yogurt mixture. Serve immediately.

White Chicken Chili

SERVES 6

Per Serving:

Calories	403
Fat	12g
Protein	35g
Sodium	1,070mg
Fiber	8g
Carbohydrates	37g
Sugar	7g
Net Carbs	29g

This recipe is perfect for freezing and reheating. Freeze individual portions in plastic containers or zip-top bags to microwave on busy evenings. You can use leftover shredded chicken or buy a whole rotisserie chicken to shred.

1 tablespoon olive oil

1 large yellow onion, peeled and diced

2 cloves garlic, peeled and minced

4 cups low-sodium chicken broth

1 (7-ounce) can diced green chilies

1 tablespoon ground cumin

1 teaspoon dried oregano

1 teaspoon salt

1 teaspoon ground black pepper

2 (15-ounce) cans cannellini beans, drained and rinsed

1 cup frozen corn kernels

2½ cups shredded cooked chicken

1 tablespoon fresh lime juice

½ cup chopped fresh cilantro, divided

¼ cup sour cream

1 cup shredded Monterey jack cheese

1 Heat oil in a large saucepan over medium heat. Add onion and sauté about 5 minutes until soft and translucent. Add garlic and sauté another 30 seconds.

2 Add broth, chilies, cumin, oregano, salt, and pepper. Bring to a boil then reduce heat to medium-low and simmer 10 minutes. In a small bowl, mash half of the cannellini beans, then add to soup along with remaining beans and corn. Simmer another 5 minutes.

3 Stir in chicken, lime juice, and ¼ cup cilantro. Cook until chicken is warm, about 10 minutes. Serve soup topped with sour cream, cheese, and remaining ¼ cup cilantro.

Burger Bowl

If you don't have Worcestershire sauce, use soy sauce instead. Toss in your favorite burger toppings to make this bowl your own!

¼ cup mayonnaise

1 tablespoon ketchup

2 teaspoons Worcestershire sauce

1 teaspoon light brown sugar

½ teaspoon salt

½ teaspoon onion powder

1 tablespoon dill pickle brine

½ pound 85% lean ground beef

2 teaspoons garlic powder

4 slices bacon

1 head romaine lettuce, shredded

½ cup cherry tomatoes

½ cup diced red onion

⅓ cup dill pickle slices

1 medium avocado, peeled, pitted, and sliced

SERVES 2

Per Serving:

Calories	706
Fat	56g
Protein	29g
Sodium	1,892mg
Fiber	7g
Carbohydrates	22g
Sugar	9g
Net Carbs	15g

1 In a small bowl, combine mayonnaise, ketchup, Worcestershire sauce, sugar, salt, onion powder, and pickle brine. Set aside.

2 Heat a medium frying pan over medium heat, then add beef. Sauté, using a large spoon to break up beef into small chunks. Cook until no longer pink, about 5 minutes. Add garlic powder and cook 1 minute. Remove from pan and drain.

3 Add bacon to the pan and cook 4–5 minutes over medium heat. Using a fork, flip bacon and cook 2–3 minutes until crispy. Roughly chop bacon.

4 Divide lettuce between two large serving bowls, then add beef, tomatoes, onion, pickles, avocado, and bacon. Drizzle with mayonnaise dressing and serve.

Low-Carb Caprese Bowl

SERVES 4

Per Serving:	
Calories	246
Fat	15g
Protein	22g
Sodium	496mg
Fiber	1g
Carbohydrates	6g
Sugar	3g
Net Carbs	5g

TYPES OF MOZZARELLA

There is a wide variety of mozzarellas, from the milder *fior di latte* mozzarella made from cow's milk to *mozzarella di bufala*, which is made from buffalo's milk, giving it a very rich flavor. *Bocconcini*, *ciliegine*, and *perlini* are different sized balls of mozzarella best for caprese bowls and salads.

If your grocery store doesn't have mozzarella cheese balls packed in water, you can just buy a large chunk of fresh mozzarella and slice it into bite-sized pieces. Leftover chicken works well here, or you can buy a rotisserie chicken and shred the breast meat. Feel free to add a handful of spinach for extra greens!

1 (8-ounce) container small fresh mozzarella cheese balls

1 pint cherry tomatoes, halved

1 cup shredded cooked chicken breast

1 tablespoon olive oil

1 tablespoon balsamic vinegar

1 teaspoon dried basil

1 teaspoon dried oregano

½ teaspoon salt

½ teaspoon ground black pepper

Combine all ingredients in a large bowl. Mix well, then divide mixture between four serving bowls. Serve immediately.

Cuban Bowl

SERVES 2

Per Serving:

Calories	745
Fat	24g
Protein	38g
Sodium	1,307mg
Fiber	14g
Carbohydrates	99g
Sugar	6g
Net Carbs	85g

Here's a little bowl of Cuba. Plantain chips make a great addition to this Caribbean bowl. Peel and slice a couple of plantains, toss the slices in olive oil, and bake them at 400°F for about 15 minutes.

1 tablespoon olive oil

½ cup chopped yellow onion

2 (4-ounce) boneless, skinless chicken breasts, cubed

2 tablespoons ground cumin

1 tablespoon dried oregano

1 teaspoon paprika

2 teaspoons garlic powder

½ teaspoon salt

½ teaspoon ground black pepper

¼ cup low-sodium chicken broth

1 cup canned black beans, drained and rinsed

2 tablespoons fresh lime juice, divided

2 cups cooked white rice

2 tablespoons chopped fresh cilantro

¼ cup mild salsa

¼ cup chopped fresh pineapple

1 medium avocado, peeled, pitted, and sliced

1 Heat oil in a large frying pan over medium heat. Add onion and cook about 5 minutes until soft and translucent. Add chicken, cumin, oregano, paprika, garlic powder, salt, pepper, and broth and cook until chicken is no longer pink, about 10 minutes.

2 Add beans and 1 tablespoon lime juice and cook another 5 minutes. Remove from heat and set aside.

3 In a medium bowl, combine rice, cilantro, and remaining 1 tablespoon lime juice. Mix well.

4 Spoon rice mixture into two large serving bowls, then add chicken, salsa, and pineapple. Top with avocado slices and serve.

Steak and Rice Bowl

Steak dinners don't have to break the bank. Flank steak is usually very affordable, but you can also try boneless short rib or top round.

2 tablespoons olive oil, divided

1 teaspoon garlic powder

¼ teaspoon ground cumin

¼ teaspoon salt

¼ teaspoon ground black pepper

2 tablespoons fresh lime juice, divided

1 (1-pound) flank steak

1 medium red bell pepper, seeded and sliced into wedges

1 medium yellow bell pepper, seeded and sliced into wedges

¼ medium red onion, peeled and thinly sliced

2 teaspoons Italian seasoning

2 cups cooked white rice

1 In a small bowl, combine 1 tablespoon oil, garlic powder, cumin, salt, pepper, and 1 tablespoon lime juice. Transfer to a plastic bag, then add steak. Marinate for at least 30 minutes in the refrigerator.

2 Heat remaining 1 tablespoon oil in a medium frying pan over medium heat. Add bell peppers, onion, and Italian seasoning. Cook about 15 minutes until onion is soft and translucent.

3 Add rice and mix well. Cook, stirring occasionally, for 5 minutes, then remove from heat and set aside.

4 Heat a separate large frying pan over medium-high heat. Add steak and cook 3–5 minutes on each side or until browned. Transfer to a cutting board and let rest 5 minutes before slicing.

5 Spoon rice mixture into bowls, then top with steak and remaining 1 tablespoon lime juice. Serve warm.

SERVES 4

Per Serving:

Calories	493
Fat	22g
Protein	39g
Sodium	197mg
Fiber	4g
Carbohydrates	36g
Sugar	3g
Net Carbs	32g

COOKING STEAK

Make sure to check the internal temperature of your steak before serving. Medium is at least 145°F, medium well is 150°F, and well done is 160°F. Anything below 145°F is considered rare. Stay at or above medium to avoid the risk of food poisoning.

Breakfast Bowl

SERVES 2

Per Serving:

Calories	324
Fat	23g
Protein	21g
Sodium	1,144mg
Fiber	1g
Carbohydrates	8g
Sugar	3g
Net Carbs	7g

Breakfast for dinner? You bet! This keto-friendly Breakfast Bowl will make you want to have breakfast for dinner every single night.

4 large eggs

¼ cup chopped red onion

¼ cup chopped green bell pepper

¼ cup shredded Cheddar cheese

½ teaspoon salt

1 teaspoon ground black pepper

⅛ teaspoon garlic powder

4 slices bacon, cooked and crumbled

1 teaspoon unsalted butter

1 Beat eggs in a medium bowl. Add onion, bell pepper, cheese, salt, black pepper, garlic powder, and bacon and stir to combine.

2 Heat butter in a medium frying pan over medium heat. Add egg mixture. Cook, using a spatula to stir egg from time to time. Remove scrambled eggs from pan when they are firm but still a bit moist, about 3–4 minutes. Serve immediately.

Shrimp and Noodle Bowl

SERVES 2

Per Serving:

Calories	404
Fat	10g
Protein	32g
Sodium	306mg
Fiber	3g
Carbohydrates	45g
Sugar	3g
Net Carbs	42g

No need to run down to your local Chinese restaurant—you can make your own dish! If you like your shrimp and noodles to have a bit of a kick, add ⅛ teaspoon of red pepper flakes.

4 ounces cooked angel hair pasta

1 tablespoon lime juice

1 tablespoon low-sodium soy sauce

½ teaspoon sesame oil

2 teaspoons ground ginger

1 tablespoon olive oil

½ pound peeled and deveined large shrimp

¼ cup chopped scallions

1 In a large bowl, combine pasta, lime juice, soy sauce, sesame oil, and ginger. Mix well.

2 Heat olive oil in a large frying pan over medium-high heat. Add shrimp and cook 5 minutes or until pink. Add shrimp to pasta mixture, toss to combine, and transfer to two serving bowls. Garnish with scallions and serve.

Greek Meatballs with Tzatziki Sauce

You can serve these delicious, saucy meatballs with rice or on their own. To make gluten-free meatballs, use gluten-free bread crumbs.

½ medium cucumber, peeled and chopped

¾ cup plain low-fat Greek yogurt

1 teaspoon honey

1 tablespoon chopped dill

2½ teaspoons garlic powder, divided

½ teaspoon salt, divided

½ teaspoon ground black pepper, divided

½ cup dried bread crumbs

½ medium yellow onion, peeled and grated

3 tablespoons chopped fresh parsley

3 tablespoons chopped fresh mint

1 large egg

¼ teaspoon ground cumin

1 tablespoon fresh lemon juice

1 tablespoon grated lemon zest

½ pound 85% lean ground beef

SERVES 2	
Per Serving:	
Calories	525
Fat	25g
Protein	38g
Sodium	968mg
Fiber	3g
Carbohydrates	36g
Sugar	9g
Net Carbs	33g

1 In a blender, combine cucumber, yogurt, honey, dill, ½ teaspoon garlic powder, ¼ teaspoon salt, and ¼ teaspoon pepper. Blend until smooth. Set aside.

2 Preheat oven to 450°F and line a large baking sheet with foil. Spray foil with nonstick cooking spray.

3 In a large bowl, mix together bread crumbs, onion, parsley, mint, egg, remaining 2 teaspoons garlic powder, cumin, lemon juice, lemon zest, and remaining ¼ teaspoon each salt and pepper. Mix well, then add ground beef and mix together using your hands.

4 Form mixture into 1" balls and place on prepared baking sheet, leaving about 1" between meatballs. Cook 12–15 minutes until golden brown.

5 Transfer cooked meatballs to two serving bowls and drizzle with yogurt sauce. Serve warm.

Quinoa Nourish Bowl

SERVES 2

Per Serving:

Calories	709
Fat	29g
Protein	29g
Sodium	770mg
Fiber	26g
Carbohydrates	98g
Sugar	13g
Net Carbs	72g

WHY GO ORGANIC?

Organic foods are processed without any pesticides and other harmful chemicals, but they do tend to break the budget. Buy organic only when you can, and focus on buying organic meat, eggs, and dairy. With vegetables, it's a little easier to remove the excess chemicals with thorough washing.

Don't like spinach? Absolutely love asparagus? For this versatile bowl, you can toss in pretty much any vegetable you want. Top it off with a little bit of flavored hummus to add an extra kick of flavor.

2 medium sweet potatoes, peeled and diced

1 (15-ounce) can chickpeas, drained and rinsed

1½ tablespoons olive oil, divided

2 teaspoons paprika

¼ teaspoon salt

½ teaspoon ground black pepper

½ cup chopped yellow onion

4 cups baby spinach leaves

1 cup cooked quinoa

1 medium avocado, peeled, pitted, and sliced

1 tablespoon lemon juice

1 teaspoon garlic powder

¾ cup plain low-fat Greek yogurt

½ medium cucumber, peeled and chopped

1 Preheat oven to 375°F and line a large baking sheet with parchment paper.

2 In a large bowl, toss potatoes and chickpeas with 1 tablespoon olive oil, paprika, salt, and pepper. Transfer to prepared baking sheet and bake 25 minutes.

3 Heat remaining ½ tablespoon oil in a medium frying pan over medium heat. Add onion and cook about 5 minutes until soft and translucent. Add spinach and cook 3–4 minutes until just wilted.

4 Spoon quinoa into two large serving bowls. Top with sweet potato mixture and spinach mixture.

5 In a blender, combine avocado, lemon juice, garlic powder, yogurt, and cucumber. Blend until smooth. Drizzle sauce over quinoa bowls and serve immediately.

Tofu Fried Rice Bowl

This soy-based bowl is the perfect healthy meal. To make it vegan, just remove the eggs.

3 tablespoons low-sodium soy sauce, divided

½ teaspoon garlic powder

2 teaspoons sesame oil

2 teaspoons light brown sugar

7 ounces firm tofu

1 teaspoon olive oil

1 cup cooked white rice

2 large eggs, beaten

½ cup chopped scallions

½ cup frozen peas

½ cup shredded carrots

SERVES 2

Per Serving:

Calories	417
Fat	17g
Protein	20g
Sodium	1,134mg
Fiber	6g
Carbohydrates	45g
Sugar	9g
Net Carbs	39g

1 Combine 2 tablespoons soy sauce, garlic powder, sesame oil, and sugar in a small bowl. Set aside.

2 Place tofu on a paper towel–lined flat plate. Cover with another plate, and put a heavy object on top to press excess liquid from tofu. Let sit 30 minutes.

3 Cut tofu into small cubes, then place in a zip-top plastic bag. Add soy sauce mixture, seal bag, and marinate in the refrigerator for 20 minutes. Remove from marinade and discard marinade.

4 Heat olive oil in a large frying pan over medium heat. Add tofu and cook about 7 minutes or until browned, flip and cook additional 7 minutes.

5 Turn heat down to medium-low, then add rice and remaining 1 tablespoon soy sauce. Mix well, and push rice mixture to the side of the pan. Add eggs to the middle of the pan. Cook eggs, stirring often, until almost set (about 3 minutes). Combine eggs with rice mixture. Add scallions, peas, and carrots and mix well. Cook, stirring, until peas are fully cooked through, about 5 minutes. Divide mixture between two serving bowls and serve immediately.

TOFU FACTS

Tofu is made from soy milk and undergoes a process similar to cheese-making. While you're shopping, try to find a tofu brand with a short ingredient list. Tofu should be thoroughly rinsed before using and can be kept in the refrigerator for one week, as long as it's covered with water.

Dairy-Free Vegetable Bowl

This vegetable bowl is packed with healthy micronutrients and vitamins. The simple flavors of the vegetables combine to make a wonderful salad in bright colors.

1 medium sweet potato, peeled and diced

1 cup peeled and diced butternut squash

2 tablespoons olive oil, divided

½ teaspoon salt, divided

½ teaspoon ground black pepper, divided

1 teaspoon garlic powder, divided

1 teaspoon paprika

1 medium green bell pepper, seeded and sliced

1 medium carrot, peeled and sliced

¼ medium red onion, peeled and chopped

1 medium zucchini, sliced into half moons

1 cup green beans

1 teaspoon Italian seasoning

1 cup cooked white rice

1. Preheat oven to 400°F and line a large baking sheet with parchment paper.

2. In a large bowl, combine sweet potato and squash with 1 tablespoon olive oil, ¼ teaspoon salt, ¼ teaspoon black pepper, ½ teaspoon garlic powder, and paprika. Toss to coat. Transfer to prepared baking sheet and bake 10 minutes.

3. In the same bowl, combine bell pepper, carrot, onion, zucchini, and green beans. Add Italian seasoning and remaining 1 tablespoon olive oil, ¼ teaspoon salt, ¼ teaspoon black pepper, and ½ teaspoon garlic powder.

4. Remove baking sheet from the oven, stir sweet potato and squash and push to one half of baking sheet. Transfer bell pepper mixture to the other half of baking sheet. Return to oven and bake 20 minutes. Remove from oven and toss vegetables together.

5. Spoon rice into two large serving bowls. Top with roasted vegetables. Serve immediately.

SERVES 2

Per Serving:	
Calories	389
Fat	14g
Protein	7g
Sodium	655mg
Fiber	7g
Carbohydrates	60g
Sugar	10g
Net Carbs	53g

MAKE YOUR OWN ITALIAN SEASONING

Don't have Italian seasoning? No worries! Combine 2 teaspoons dried basil, 2 teaspoons dried oregano, 1 teaspoon dried rosemary, 2 teaspoons dried parsley, 1 teaspoon dried thyme, 1 teaspoon red pepper flakes, and ⅓ teaspoon garlic powder.

Gluten-Free Barbecue Bowl

SERVES 2

Per Serving:

Calories	561
Fat	12g
Protein	41g
Sodium	1,106mg
Fiber	5g
Carbohydrates	76g
Sugar	23g
Net Carbs	71g

Make sure to check the nutrition label on the barbecue sauce. Most barbecue sauces don't include gluten, but better safe than sorry.

2 (6-ounce) boneless, skinless chicken breasts, cooked and shredded

½ cup gluten-free barbecue sauce

½ cup frozen corn kernels

½ cup canned black beans, drained and rinsed

1 cup cooked white rice

2 tablespoons fresh lime juice

¼ cup chopped scallions

¼ cup sour cream

1 Heat a large frying pan over medium heat. Add chicken, barbecue sauce, corn, and black beans and mix well. Cook until sauce is heated through, about 7 minutes.

2 Add rice to two serving bowls and top with chicken mixture. Sprinkle with lime juice and garnish with scallions and sour cream. Serve immediately.

Couscous and Sausage Bowl

SERVES 2

Per Serving:

Calories	348
Fat	15g
Protein	15g
Sodium	443mg
Fiber	6g
Carbohydrates	36g
Sugar	10g
Net Carbs	30g

Sausage and peppers are a classic combination, and the couscous adds some depth to the dish.

1 teaspoon olive oil

1 medium green bell pepper, seeded and sliced

1 medium yellow bell pepper, seeded and sliced

1 medium red bell pepper, seeded and sliced

4 ounces sweet Italian pork sausage, sliced

½ teaspoon ground black pepper

1 cup cooked couscous

1 Heat oil in a large frying pan over medium heat. Add bell peppers and cook 5 minutes, then add sausage and black pepper. Cook about 10–15 minutes until sausage is no longer pink.

2 Add couscous to two large serving bowls and top with sausage mixture. Serve immediately.

Chicken and Avocado Salad

The flavors in this salad pair wonderfully together. The zing in the lime helps bring out the freshness of the avocado, while the sharpness of the onion works well with the milder flavor of the cucumber. If you want to add some more spice, try ¼ teaspoon ground cumin in the salad dressing.

2 tablespoons olive oil

2 tablespoons lime juice

2 tablespoons honey

½ teaspoon salt

½ teaspoon ground black pepper

2 (6-ounce) boneless, skinless chicken breasts, cooked and shredded

2 large avocadoes, peeled, pitted, and cubed

1 cup halved cherry tomatoes

½ cup fresh corn kernels

½ medium cucumber, peeled and sliced into half moons

½ cup chopped red onion

¼ cup chopped fresh cilantro

1 In a small bowl, combine olive oil, lime juice, honey, salt, and pepper.

2 In a large bowl, combine chicken, avocadoes, tomatoes, corn, cucumber, onion, and cilantro. Drizzle with olive oil dressing and mix well. Serve immediately.

SERVES 4

Per Serving:

Calories	374
Fat	24g
Protein	20g
Sodium	544mg
Fiber	8g
Carbohydrates	26g
Sugar	13g
Net Carbs	18g

Fish Taco Bowl

GF

SERVES 2

Per Serving:

Calories	701
Fat	33g
Protein	48g
Sodium	1,722mg
Fiber	10g
Carbohydrates	55g
Sugar	17g
Net Carbs	45g

SOMETHING SMELLS FISHY

Before you serve your fish, check its internal temperature with a meat thermometer—it should be at least 145°F. The fish should be opaque and flaky enough to easily break apart with a fork. If you're serving raw fish, like ahi tuna or salmon, make sure you buy sushi-grade and don't use any that is past its expiration date.

These Fish Taco Bowls make you feel like you're on the boardwalk at the beach—only without the sand, the seagulls, or the crowds! After you've fried the fish it should easily crumble into your bowl.

½ teaspoon garlic powder

½ teaspoon onion powder

½ teaspoon salt

¼ teaspoon paprika

¼ teaspoon cayenne pepper

¼ teaspoon ground black pepper

2 tablespoons olive oil, divided

¾ pound fresh cod

4 cups shredded cabbage

1 medium avocado, peeled, pitted, and cubed

1 tablespoon fresh lime juice

½ cup plain low-fat Greek yogurt

1 tablespoon honey

1 cup cooked white rice

½ cup mild salsa

2 tablespoons chopped fresh cilantro

1   In a large bowl, combine garlic powder, onion powder, salt, paprika, cayenne pepper, black pepper, and 1 tablespoon oil. Mix well, then add cod, tossing to coat in seasoning. Cover and refrigerate for 30 minutes.

2   Combine cabbage, avocado, lime juice, yogurt, and honey in a large bowl. Mix well and mash together until avocado is no longer chunky. Set aside.

3   Heat remaining 1 tablespoon oil in a large frying pan over medium heat. Add fish and cook 4 minutes, then flip and cook another 4 minutes.

4   Divide rice, cabbage mixture, fish, salsa, and cilantro between two serving bowls. Serve immediately.

Chicken and Kale Power Bowl

This power bowl is the ultimate healthy meal. You've got nutrient-packed greens and loads of protein with the chicken and the eggs.

2 teaspoons olive oil

½ cup chopped onion

2 (6-ounce) boneless, skinless chicken breasts, cubed

½ cup low-sodium chicken broth

2 tablespoons lemon juice

2 teaspoons Italian seasoning

1 teaspoon salt

1 teaspoon ground black pepper

4 cups chopped kale

2 large eggs

1 cup cooked quinoa

SERVES 2	
Per Serving:	
Calories	486
Fat	16g
Protein	49g
Sodium	1,690mg
Fiber	9g
Carbohydrates	40g
Sugar	3g
Net Carbs	31g

1 Heat oil in a large frying pan over medium heat. Add onion and sauté 5 minutes. Add chicken, broth, lemon juice, Italian seasoning, salt, and pepper and cook about 10 minutes or until chicken is no longer pink.

2 Add kale and cook until wilted, about 3 minutes. Move chicken mixture to the side of the pan and add eggs to the middle of the pan. Fry eggs about 5 minutes or until yolk is cooked through. Remove from heat.

3 Add quinoa to two large serving bowls, then add chicken and kale and top with eggs. Serve immediately.

Spring Roll Bowl

Top this tasty bowl off with some sliced scallions and you have a delicious and healthy meal.

SERVES 2

Per Serving:

Calories	194
Fat	2g
Protein	4g
Sodium	327mg
Fiber	4g
Carbohydrates	42g
Sugar	11g
Net Carbs	38g

7 ounces cooked rice noodles

½ medium cucumber, peeled and sliced

1 large carrot, peeled and shredded

½ cup shredded purple cabbage

1 medium red bell pepper, seeded and sliced

1 tablespoon low-sodium soy sauce

½ teaspoon sesame oil

2 teaspoons maple syrup

1 tablespoon lime juice

1 teaspoon sriracha

½ teaspoon garlic powder

1 Place noodles in two large serving bowls. Top with cucumber, carrot, cabbage, and pepper.

2 In a small bowl, combine soy sauce, oil, maple syrup, lime juice, sriracha, and garlic powder. Mix well and drizzle over noodles. Serve immediately.

Greek Vegetable Bowl

For an extra-fresh flavor, top this bowl off with a ¼ cup chopped mint. You'll be pleasantly surprised at how delicious it tastes.

SERVES 2

Per Serving:

Calories	555
Fat	29g
Protein	24g
Sodium	2,093mg
Fiber	10g
Carbohydrates	52g
Sugar	7g
Net Carbs	42g

1 cup cooked quinoa

2 cups baby spinach leaves

½ cup halved cherry tomatoes

½ medium cucumber, peeled and sliced

½ cup chopped red onion

½ cup chopped yellow bell pepper

½ cup crumbled feta cheese

1 tablespoon olive oil

½ teaspoon salt

½ teaspoon ground black pepper

½ cup hummus

¼ cup sliced Kalamata olives

In a large bowl, combine quinoa, spinach, tomatoes, cucumber, onion, bell pepper, cheese, oil, salt, and pepper. Divide between two serving bowls and top with hummus and olives. Serve immediately.

CHAPTER 8

Party Food

Deviled Eggs

SERVES 8

Per Serving:

Calories	120
Fat	10g
Protein	6g
Sodium	158mg
Fiber	0g
Carbohydrates	1g
Sugar	1g
Net Carbs	1g

The trick to this recipe is to carefully remove the egg yolks without damaging the whites, and then mashing the yolk until it's fluffy. Feel free to toss some chopped pickles, celery, or paprika into the yolk mixture.

8 Hard-Boiled Eggs (see recipe in Chapter 2), peeled

4 tablespoons mayonnaise

2 tablespoons Worcestershire sauce

½ teaspoon curry powder

1 Cut each egg in half lengthwise and place yolks in a small bowl. Set egg whites aside.

2 Combine yolks, mayonnaise, Worcestershire sauce, and curry powder in a small bowl. Mash together with a fork until there are no large egg pieces. Carefully fill each egg half with a tablespoon of mashed yolk mixture. Store in the refrigerator until ready to serve.

Phenomenal Pretzels

SERVES 15

Per Serving:

Calories	214
Fat	11g
Protein	3g
Sodium	357mg
Fiber	1g
Carbohydrates	26g
Sugar	1g
Net Carbs	25g

You can use canola oil if you don't have olive oil. If you want an extra kick of heat, sprinkle in an extra ½ teaspoon of the cayenne.

¾ cup olive oil

1 (16-ounce) bag mini pretzels

1 (1-ounce) package Hidden Valley ranch dressing mix

¾ teaspoon garlic powder

½ teaspoon cayenne pepper

1 Preheat oven to 200°F and line two large baking sheets with parchment paper.

2 Add oil, pretzels, ranch dressing mix, garlic powder, and cayenne pepper to a large bowl. Mix well until pretzels are fully coated.

3 Evenly spread pretzels onto prepared baking sheets and bake 1 hour, stirring and flipping every 15 minutes. Cool completely before serving.

Chicken Fingers

These are the perfect healthy alternative to the fried chicken fingers you'll usually find at the dining hall. You can serve these on their own or with any of the traditional dipping sauce accompaniments for chicken wings, including honey mustard, soy sauce, or ketchup.

¾ **cup salted butter, melted**

½ **teaspoon dried oregano**

¾ **teaspoon dried basil**

¼ **teaspoon garlic powder**

¼ **teaspoon onion powder**

1½ **pounds boneless, skinless chicken breast tenders**

½ **(11-ounce) bag tortilla chips, crushed**

1 Preheat oven to 400°F and line a baking sheet with parchment paper. Spray with nonstick cooking spray.

2 In a small bowl, combine butter, oregano, basil, garlic powder, and onion powder.

3 Dip chicken into butter mixture, then coat with crushed chips. Lay out on prepared baking sheet.

4 Bake chicken 20–25 minutes. Flip and cook another 20 minutes until cooked through and golden brown. Serve immediately.

SERVES 4

Per Serving:

Calories	484
Fat	21g
Protein	56g
Sodium	371mg
Fiber	3g
Carbohydrates	27g
Sugar	0g
Net Carbs	24g

FRIED VERSUS BAKED

Which one is healthier? Frying means dipping food in oil to cook, so you get a lot of extra fat in your meal. It's part of the reason why fried food tastes so good! Baking, on the other hand, involves much less oil, which means it's usually better for you.

Stovetop Italian Meatballs

MAKES 30 MEATBALLS

Per Serving (3 meatballs):

Calories	112
Fat	8g
Protein	7g
Sodium	80mg
Fiber	0g
Carbohydrates	3g
Sugar	0g
Net Carbs	3g

GOT BEEF?

When you're purchasing ground beef, you'll notice the packaging has either an 80/20, 85/15, or 90/10 label. The first number means the amount of lean meat, and the second number means the amount of fat. If a recipe calls for lean ground beef, you'll want to choose either 85/15 or 90/10.

Getting meatballs to cook through evenly in the frying pan can be a challenge. One trick is to shake the pan during cooking to help the meatballs retain their round shape. If that doesn't work, finish the meatballs off by simmering them in beef broth.

1¾ pounds 85% lean ground beef
¾ cup crushed saltine crackers
½ teaspoon dried oregano
¼ teaspoon dried parsley
3 tablespoons grated Parmesan cheese
1 clove garlic, peeled and finely chopped
5 teaspoons water
4 teaspoons olive oil, divided

1 In a large bowl, mix together beef, crackers, oregano, parsley, cheese, and garlic. Mix in 3 teaspoons water. Continue adding water 1 teaspoon at a time as needed until mixture is lightly moistened, then form mixture into balls approximately 1½" in diameter.

2 Heat 2 teaspoons oil in a medium frying pan over medium heat. Add half the meatballs and cook about 15 minutes, turning occasionally, until meatballs are cooked through. Remove meatballs with a slotted spoon and place on paper towels to drain.

3 Clean out frying pan, add remaining 2 teaspoons olive oil, and cook remaining meatballs.

Marinated Chicken Quesadillas

Marinating the chicken before cooking gives it extra flavor. If you don't have time for marinating, try tossing the chicken with ½ teaspoon hot chili powder before frying.

⅓ cup low-sodium soy sauce

1 clove garlic, peeled and finely chopped

2 thin slices fresh ginger, peeled

1½ tablespoons light brown sugar

2 (6-ounce) boneless, skinless chicken breasts

1 tablespoon olive oil

2 tablespoons unsalted butter, divided

4 (10") flour tortillas

2 cups shredded Monterey jack cheese, divided

4 large fresh button mushrooms, sliced and divided

2 scallions, sliced and divided

6 whole black olives, chopped and divided

1 Combine soy sauce, garlic, ginger, and brown sugar in a small bowl. Pour marinade into a large resealable plastic bag, add chicken, and seal the bag. Marinate in the refrigerator for 1 hour.

2 Heat oil in a medium frying pan over medium heat, add chicken and sauté until cooked through, about 5 minutes per side. Remove from frying pan and cut into thin strips.

3 Melt 1 tablespoon butter in a medium frying pan over medium heat. Add 1 tortilla, then sprinkle ½ cup cheese over tortilla. Let cheese melt, then add half the mushrooms, scallions, olives, and chicken.

4 Lay a second tortilla on top of first tortilla. Cook until first tortilla is browned on the bottom, about 2 minutes, then flip and cook an additional 4 minutes. Sprinkle ½ cup cheese over top and cook an additional minute. Remove from pan and repeat with remaining ingredients.

SERVES 12

Per Serving:

Calories	189
Fat	10g
Protein	12g
Sodium	524mg
Fiber	1g
Carbohydrates	12g
Sugar	3g
Net Carbs	11g

HOW TO DOUBLE A RECIPE

Whenever you're feeding a crowd, always check the recipe to see how many servings it yields. If you need more, you can double or even triple the recipe. Just multiply each ingredient amount by 2 or 3, depending on how much more you need. It helps to write down your calculations so you won't forget!

Guacamole with Tortilla Chips

Turn the heat up or down by using hot or mild salsa. For best results, homemade guacamole should be served the same day it's made.

MAKES 3½ CUPS

Per Serving (¼ cup):

Calories	254
Fat	15g
Protein	4g
Sodium	345mg
Fiber	5g
Carbohydrates	29g
Sugar	0g
Net Carbs	24g

4 medium avocados, peeled, pitted, and mashed

1 small red onion, peeled and chopped

2 cloves garlic, peeled and finely chopped

3 tablespoons lime juice

¼ cup medium salsa

½ teaspoon ground cumin

1 teaspoon salt

1 (18-ounce) bag tortilla chips

Mix avocados, onion, garlic, lime juice, salsa, cumin, and salt in a medium bowl. Refrigerate for about 15 minutes to give flavors time to blend, and serve with tortilla chips.

LEAVE THE PIT IN

If you use only half an avocado, leave the pit in the other half. The avocado has an enzyme that reacts with oxygen to turn it brown. Leaving the pit in will help protect part of the avocado, leaving it fresh and green.

Stuffed Potatoes with Spinach

SERVES 8

Per Serving:

Calories	497
Fat	21g
Protein	11g
Sodium	701mg
Fiber	5g
Carbohydrates	70g
Sugar	4g
Net Carbs	65g

These flavorful potatoes can be prepared a few hours in advance. Cover tightly with plastic wrap and store in the refrigerator until you're ready to cook them.

8 large russet potatoes

2 teaspoons olive oil

4 cups chopped fresh baby spinach leaves

1 cup sour cream

½ cup unsalted butter

2 teaspoons garlic powder

2 teaspoons salt

1 teaspoon ground black pepper

½ cup shredded Monterey jack cheese

1 Preheat oven to 400°F.

2 Pierce potatoes four times with a fork and bake 45 minutes or until done. To make sure they're done, a fork stuck into the center should go through easily.

3 Heat oil in a medium frying pan over medium heat. Sauté spinach until bright green, about 1 minute, then set aside.

4 Slice potatoes open lengthwise. Carefully scoop out most of the potatoes, leaving about ¼" around the skins. Place potato pulp in a large bowl and mash. Mix in spinach, sour cream, butter, garlic powder, salt, and pepper.

5 Place potato skins on an ungreased baking sheet. Spoon an even amount of spinach mixture into each skin. Sprinkle each potato with 1 tablespoon cheese, then place in the oven and bake 15 minutes or until cheese is melted.

Picnic Potato Salad

This simple potato salad is perfect for a hot summer picnic or backyard barbecue.

2 pounds russet potatoes, peeled and cubed

3 Hard-Boiled Eggs (see recipe in Chapter 2), chopped

1 medium celery stalk, sliced

⅔ cup mayonnaise

¼ cup red wine vinegar

½ medium red onion, peeled and chopped

½ teaspoon salt

½ teaspoon ground black pepper

SERVES 4	
Per Serving:	
Calories	399
Fat	30g
Protein	8g
Sodium	598mg
Fiber	2g
Carbohydrates	28g
Sugar	2g
Net Carbs	26g

1 Fill a large pot with enough salted water to cover potatoes. Add potatoes and bring water to a boil over medium-high heat. Reduce heat to low, cover, and simmer until tender, about 10 minutes.

2 Place potatoes and remaining ingredients in a large bowl and mix well. Refrigerate for 1 hour and serve cold.

Summer Coleslaw

The exact amount of dressing needed will depend on the size of the cabbage and how finely it's shredded. If you like your coleslaw to be creamier, add a little extra dressing. It's up to you.

1 large head green cabbage, shredded

2 large carrots, peeled and shredded

2 medium red bell peppers, seeded and diced

¼ cup mayonnaise

1 tablespoon Dijon mustard

½ cup apple cider vinegar

SERVES 6	
Per Serving:	
Calories	133
Fat	7g
Protein	3g
Sodium	155mg
Fiber	6g
Carbohydrates	16g
Sugar	8g
Net Carbs	10g

1 In a large bowl, combine cabbage, carrots, and bell peppers and toss to mix.

2 In a small bowl, whisk mayonnaise, mustard, and vinegar until combined. Pour dressing over vegetable mixture and toss to mix thoroughly. Refrigerate in a sealed container until ready to serve.

Game Day Nachos

SERVES 6

Per Serving:

Calories	783
Fat	47g
Protein	36g
Sodium	977mg
Fiber	5g
Carbohydrates	52g
Sugar	2g
Net Carbs	47g

To spice up this dish, you can add some canned jalapeño peppers in with the shredded cheese before you bake the nachos. Serve with sour cream, guacamole, and your favorite salsa.

2 teaspoons olive oil

½ cup chopped red onion

1½ pounds 85% lean ground beef

1 (1-ounce) packet taco seasoning

1 (13.5-ounce) bag tortilla chips

2½ cups shredded Monterey jack cheese

2 large tomatoes, chopped

½ cup sliced black olives

1 Preheat oven to 350°F.

2 Heat oil in a medium frying pan over medium-low heat, then add onion and cook for about 5 minutes or until soft and translucent. Add ground beef and stir in taco seasoning. Sauté, using a large spoon to break up beef into small chunks. Cook until no longer pink, around 5 minutes. Drain off excess liquid.

3 Spread out half the tortilla chips in the bottom of a 9" × 13" glass baking dish. Spoon beef over chips, then sprinkle 1 cup cheese over beef. Cover with remaining chips and 1 cup cheese. Sprinkle tomatoes and olives on top, then top with remaining ½ cup cheese. Bake 5 minutes or until cheese is melted. Serve hot.

Texas Chili

Instead of the beef cubes, you can use 85% lean ground beef. If you make this substitution, reduce the amount of olive oil to 2 tablespoons, as the liquid from the ground beef will add more moisture.

¼ cup olive oil

1 (3-pound) boneless beef round or chuck, cut into 1" cubes

2 medium green bell peppers, seeded and chopped

1 medium yellow onion, peeled and chopped

4 cloves garlic, peeled and chopped

2 jalapeño peppers, seeded and chopped

6 cups tomato sauce

1 cup tomato paste

2 tablespoons chili powder

1 tablespoon dried oregano

½ teaspoon salt

½ teaspoon ground black pepper

2 (13.5-ounce) bags tortilla chips

SERVES 6

Per Serving:

Calories	996
Fat	50g
Protein	58g
Sodium	2,043mg
Fiber	13g
Carbohydrates	77g
Sugar	18g
Net Carbs	64g

1 Heat oil in a large saucepan over medium-high heat. Add half the beef cubes and cook until brown, about 5 minutes per side. Remove beef from saucepan and drain on paper towels. Repeat with remaining beef.

2 Reduce heat to medium and add bell peppers, onion, garlic, and jalapeños to the saucepan. Cook for about 5 minutes or until onion is soft and translucent. Add tomato sauce, tomato paste, chili powder, oregano, salt, and black pepper.

3 Bring chili to a boil. Reduce heat to medium-low, cover, and simmer for 90 minutes or until beef is tender. Serve with tortilla chips.

Sloppy Joes

This Sloppy Joe recipe is perfect for when you're serving a crowd but don't have much time. You can top these off with shredded Cheddar or Monterey jack cheese for some extra flavor. If you want to kick the heat up a notch, add some canned jalapeno peppers for extra spice.

SERVES 6

Per Serving:

Calories	623
Fat	27g
Protein	41g
Sodium	955mg
Fiber	11g
Carbohydrates	55g
Sugar	13g
Net Carbs	44g

2 teaspoons unsalted butter

1 medium yellow onion, peeled and chopped

2 medium red bell peppers, seeded and sliced

2 pounds 85% lean ground beef

2 cups canned kidney beans, drained and rinsed

2 cups tomato sauce

4 tablespoons tomato paste

1 cup water

1 teaspoon ground cumin

½ teaspoon chili powder

¼ teaspoon Worcestershire sauce

½ teaspoon garlic powder

¼ teaspoon ground black pepper

6 whole-wheat hamburger buns

1 Heat butter in a large frying pan over medium heat. Add onion and cook 1 minute, then add bell peppers and cook another minute.

2 Add ground beef and sauté, using a large spoon to break up beef into small chunks. Cook until no longer pink, around 5 minutes, then drain off excess liquid.

3 Add beans, tomato sauce, tomato paste, water, cumin, chili powder, Worcestershire sauce, garlic powder, and black pepper and mix thoroughly.

4 Bring to a boil. Cover and simmer for 20–25 minutes or until heated thoroughly. Spoon meat mixture over hamburger buns and serve.

Spiced Nuts

Feel free to incorporate a little bit of variety by using raw pecans, almonds, or cashews. For an extra bit of spice, coat your nuts in 1 teaspoon of cinnamon while they're cooling.

1½ cups raw walnut halves

½ cup raw pumpkin seeds

6 tablespoons unsalted butter

6 tablespoons granulated sugar

2 teaspoons five-spice powder

1 teaspoon salt

1 Preheat oven to 350°F.

2 Place walnuts and pumpkin seeds on an ungreased baking sheet and toast for 8–10 minutes, checking frequently to make sure they don't burn. Remove from oven and set aside. Once cool, line baking sheet with parchment paper.

3 Melt butter in a medium frying pan over low heat. Add sugar, stirring to dissolve, then stir in five-spice powder and salt.

4 Add toasted nuts and stir to coat. Cook until liquid is nearly absorbed, about 2 minutes, then pour nuts onto baking sheet. Separate using a spatula and let cool before serving.

MAKES 2 CUPS

Per Serving (½ cup):

Calories	247
Fat	22g
Protein	3g
Sodium .	295mg
Fiber	2g
Carbohydrates	13g
Sugar	10g
Net Carbs	11g

Barbecue Chicken Sliders

You can use American or pepper jack cheese slices instead of shredded Cheddar, and Hawaiian dinner rolls instead of plain. Add a bit of crunch with some sliced bell peppers in the barbecue mixture and a little extra flavor with some chopped parsley in the melted butter.

1 tablespoon olive oil

1 small red onion, peeled and sliced

3 cloves garlic, peeled and minced

2½ cups shredded cooked chicken

1 cup barbecue sauce

½ teaspoon salt

½ teaspoon ground black pepper

12 dinner rolls, halved horizontally

2 cups shredded Cheddar cheese

¼ cup unsalted butter, melted

1　Preheat oven to 350°F and grease a 9" × 13" baking dish with nonstick cooking spray.

2　Heat oil in a large frying pan over medium heat. Add onion and cook for about 5 minutes or until onion is soft and translucent. Add garlic and cook another 30 seconds, then add chicken, barbecue sauce, salt, and pepper. Mix well and cook 5 minutes or until heated through.

3　Lay bottom halves of rolls in prepared baking dish, top with barbecue chicken mixture, then layer on cheese. Close rolls with top halves, then brush with butter. Bake 10–15 minutes, until cheese is completely melted and rolls are heated through.

SERVES 12

Per Serving:	
Calories	306
Fat	13g
Protein	17g
Sodium	598mg
Fiber	1g
Carbohydrates	29g
Sugar	9g
Net Carbs	28g

BARBECUE SAUCE WARS

Different regions across the southern United States each have their own unique style of barbecue sauce, ranging from the vinegar-flavored Eastern Carolina sauce to Alabama's unique white sauce.

Perfect Hamburgers

There's nothing better on a hot summer day than a perfectly cooked hamburger with nicely toasted burger buns. Don't forget to make sure the patties are 160°F so they're fully cooked.

SERVES 6	
Per Serving:	
Calories	397
Fat	17g
Protein	21g
Sodium	721mg
Fiber	2g
Carbohydrates	37g
Sugar	6g
Net Carbs	35g

½ teaspoon salt

½ teaspoon ground black pepper

1 pound 85% lean ground beef

¼ cup finely chopped yellow onion

1 cup dried bread crumbs

¼ cup Worcestershire sauce

2 tablespoons unsalted butter

6 hamburger buns

1 Mix together salt, pepper, beef, onion, bread crumbs, and Worcestershire sauce in a large bowl. Form mixture into six patties.

2 Melt butter in a large frying pan over medium heat. Add patties and cook for 3–4 minutes per side or until browned and cooked through. Place patties on buns and serve immediately.

Festive Fruit Salad

Feel free to experiment by using different seasonal fresh fruits, such as mangoes, watermelon, kiwi, and cantaloupe. For an extra-special treat, add in some mint leaves and a drizzle of honey.

SERVES 4	
Per Serving:	
Calories	347
Fat	3g
Protein	4g
Sodium	17mg
Fiber	15g
Carbohydrates	83g
Sugar	59g
Net Carbs	68g

4 medium green apples, peeled and sliced

3 medium bananas, peeled and sliced

2 medium oranges, peeled and sliced

2 cups canned pineapple chunks, with juice

3 cups sliced strawberries

2 cups blueberries

4 tablespoons sweetened coconut flakes

Combine apples, bananas, oranges, pineapple, strawberries, and blueberries into a large bowl and mix well. Cover and refrigerate until ready to serve, then sprinkle with coconut flakes.

Ginger Pork Chops

Before frying the pork chops, make sure to trim off any excess fat. Finish this meal off with some buttery mashed potatoes and steamed vegetables for a delicious—and healthy—meal.

1 teaspoon curry powder

4 (8-ounce) boneless center-cut pork loin chops

1 tablespoon olive oil

2 slices fresh ginger, peeled

1 (10.75-ounce) can condensed tomato soup

1⅓ cups water

4 teaspoons Worcestershire sauce

½ medium white onion, peeled and chopped

1 Preheat oven to 350°F.

2 Rub curry powder lightly over both sides of pork chops. Heat oil in a large frying pan over medium heat and add pork chops. Cook for 7–8 minutes until browned, then flip and cook another 7–8 minutes. Add ginger slices and cook for another minute. Transfer pork to a 9" × 13" casserole dish, removing ginger.

3 In a small bowl, combine soup, water, Worcestershire sauce, and onion and pour soup mixture over the pork. Bake 1 hour or until pork chops are tender and cooked through.

SERVES 4

Per Serving:

Calories	355
Fat	13g
Protein	47g
Sodium	765mg
Fiber	1g
Carbohydrates	15g
Sugar	8g
Net Carbs	14g

Middle Eastern Party Platter

THE MIDDLE EASTERN DIET

You may have heard of the Mediterranean diet, but what about the Middle Eastern diet? They both refer to the same types of foods: lean protein, healthy fats, whole grains, fruit, and vegetables—not to mention amazing spices you won't find in other diets.

If you like crispier pita slices, toast them at 350°F for 8–10 minutes before serving. You can save some time by using prepared pita chips instead of toasting your own.

1½ cups halved cherry tomatoes

1 teaspoon dried basil

¼ teaspoon salt

¼ teaspoon ground black pepper

1 (19-ounce) can chickpeas, with liquid

3 cloves garlic, peeled and chopped

2 tablespoons plus 1 teaspoon lemon juice

2 tablespoons tahini

¼ teaspoon ground cumin

2 (8") pita breads

1 medium cucumber, peeled and chopped into half moons

1 cup sugar snap peas

1 cup crumbled feta cheese

½ cup whole green olives

½ cup whole black olives

1 In a small bowl, toss tomatoes with basil, salt, and pepper, then set aside.

2 Drain chickpeas, reserving 4 tablespoons liquid. Rinse chickpeas and drain again. Transfer chickpeas to a blender. Pulse two or three times, then add garlic, lemon juice, tahini, cumin, and reserved chickpea liquid. Blend until smooth to form a hummus, then transfer to serving bowl.

3 Cut each pita into eight equal wedges. Serve with tomatoes, hummus, cucumbers, peas, cheese, and olives.

Pan-Fried Bacon French Fries

If you're not a fan of bacon, heat 2 tablespoons olive oil in the frying pan before adding the potato slices. Feel free to use sweet potatoes instead of baking potatoes for a sweet-and-savory flavor combination.

12 slices bacon

6 medium baking potatoes, peeled and sliced lengthwise into ¼" thick pieces

⅔ cup olive oil

2 teaspoons salt

1 teaspoon ground black pepper

1 Heat a large frying pan over medium-high heat. Add bacon and cook 4–5 minutes. Using a fork, flip bacon and cook for another 2–3 minutes or until crispy. Drain bacon on paper towels until cool, then crumble and set aside.

2 In a medium bowl, coat potatoes with olive oil and toss until slices are completely coated.

3 Heat the same large frying pan over medium heat. Add potatoes so that none are stacked on top of each other, working in batches if necessary. Reserve any oil left in the bowl. Cook 10 minutes or until browned on one side. Turn over and add reserved olive oil. Cook another 10 minutes or until browned. Remove fries and drain on paper towels. Sprinkle with salt and pepper before serving. Serve with bacon bits.

SERVES 6

Per Serving:

Calories	355
Fat	19g
Protein	10g
Sodium	1,118mg
Fiber	4g
Carbohydrates	39g
Sugar	2g
Net Carbs	35g

THE BEST BACON

There are quite a few options when it comes to buying bacon. A good rule of thumb is to stick with the brands with no added nitrites or nitrates, which are chemicals used in the preserving process. As far as thick or thin cut, it all depends on your preference!

Baked Honey Wings

HONEY PROPERTIES

Honey isn't just a delicious sweetening agent. It's been shown to soothe sore throats, boost antioxidant levels, and even work as an antibacterial agent.

You can top these bad boys off with some chopped fresh cilantro and scallion if you'd like. This is another great recipe for those game-day tailgates! Serve them on their own or with sides like Picnic Potato Salad, Summer Coleslaw, or Pan-Fried Bacon French Fries (see recipes in this chapter).

4 pounds chicken wings

2 teaspoons olive oil

2 teaspoons salt

½ teaspoon ground black pepper

2 cups honey

¾ cup low-sodium soy sauce

¾ teaspoon garlic powder

1 Preheat oven to 400°F and line a large baking sheet with parchment paper.

2 Add chicken, oil, salt, and pepper to a large bowl and mix well, until wings are completely covered in oil and seasoning. Transfer wings to prepared baking sheet, making sure they don't stack. Bake 20–25 minutes, then flip them over. Bake another 20 minutes or until golden.

3 Heat a medium saucepan over medium-high heat, then add honey, soy sauce, and garlic powder. Bring to a boil, then reduce heat to medium-low and simmer 3 minutes, stirring occasionally. Remove from heat and set aside.

4 Place cooked wings in a large bowl, then add honey sauce. Mix well until all wings are completely coated. Serve.

Grilled Honey and Garlic Spareribs

SERVES 8

Per Serving:

Calories	607
Fat	40g
Protein	39g
Sodium	206mg
Fiber	1g
Carbohydrates	21g
Sugar	19g
Net Carbs	20g

Don't have a grill? These ribs can also be baked at 350°F for 1½ hours or until tender. Baste the spareribs frequently with the honey and garlic marinade during the final 30 minutes of cooking.

6 pounds pork spareribs, cut in half

4 cloves garlic, peeled and finely chopped

¼ cup molasses

¼ cup ketchup

¼ cup honey

2 teaspoons ground black pepper

1 cup sliced scallion

1 Preheat grill to medium heat.

2 Bring a large pot of water to a boil. Add ribs, cover, and simmer for 30 minutes or until ribs are tender, then drain.

3 In a small bowl, combine garlic, molasses, ketchup, honey, and pepper.

4 Brush ribs on all sides with honey-garlic mixture, then place on the grill and cook for 20–25 minutes or until heated through, turning the ribs every 6 minutes and brushing with marinade. Garnish with scallions and serve.

Mini Cheddar Bacon Quiches

If you have leftovers after a party, these Cheddar bacon quiches make for an easy breakfast, a light lunch, or a great midday snack. Double the recipe if you're serving a larger crowd. These go quick!

1 (14.1-ounce) package frozen pie dough, thawed

¼ cup shredded Cheddar cheese, divided

2 slices bacon, cooked and crumbled

1 tablespoon sliced scallions

¾ cup whole milk

2 large eggs

¼ teaspoon salt

⅛ teaspoon ground black pepper

SERVES 24	
Per Serving:	
Calories	55
Fat	3g
Protein	2g
Sodium	101mg
Fiber	0g
Carbohydrates	4g
Sugar	0g
Net Carbs	4g

1   Preheat oven to 350°F and spray a 24-cup mini muffin tin with nonstick cooking spray.

2   Spread dough on a work surface, then cut twenty-four equal circles using a 2½"–3"-diameter cup rim. Fill each muffin well with a circle of dough, making sure to push it into the bottom and up the sides of each tin. Sprinkle ⅛ cup cheese on top of dough, then top with equal amounts bacon and scallion.

3   In a medium bowl, whisk together milk, eggs, salt, and pepper. Pour equal amounts egg mixture into each well, then top with remaining ⅛ cup cheese. Bake 20–25 minutes or until cheese is melted. Let cool before serving.

Pineapple Jalapeño Salsa

MAKES 3 CUPS

Per Serving (1 cup):

Calories	67
Fat	0g
Protein	2g
Sodium	203mg
Fiber	2g
Carbohydrates	17g
Sugar	8g
Net Carbs	15g

If you like your salsa a bit spicier, feel free to add a few teaspoons of hot sauce to the mix. If you don't like pineapple, you can always use mango or add an extra cup of tomatoes. Don't forget the tortilla chips!

1 cup chopped fresh pineapple

1 cup finely chopped Roma tomatoes

½ cup chopped red onion

½ cup chopped green bell pepper

1 tablespoon chopped fresh cilantro

1 medium jalapeño pepper, seeded and minced

1 medium lime, juiced

¼ teaspoon salt

Combine all ingredients in a medium bowl and mix until fully combined. Cover and store in the refrigerator for 30 minutes before serving.

Spinach and Artichoke Dip

SERVES 12

Per Serving:

Calories	187
Fat	17g
Protein	5g
Sodium	386mg
Fiber	1g
Carbohydrates	4g
Sugar	2g
Net Carbs	3g

This dip goes perfectly alongside some crunchy bread, crackers, or raw vegetables. Make sure you squeeze all the excess liquid from the spinach.

1 (14-ounce) can artichoke hearts, drained and chopped

½ cup mayonnaise

½ cup sour cream

8 ounces cream cheese, softened

1 clove garlic, peeled and finely chopped

1 cup grated Parmesan cheese

1 (10-ounce) package frozen chopped spinach, thawed and drained

¼ teaspoon salt

¼ teaspoon ground black pepper

¼ teaspoon Italian seasoning

1 Preheat oven to 350°F and grease an 8" × 8" baking dish with nonstick cooking spray.

2 In a large mixing bowl, add all ingredients and mix until combined. Bake 20 minutes or until heated through.

Charcuterie Platter

A basic charcuterie platter has three main ingredients: cheese, savories, and sweets. Ideally, you want a good variety of flavors on the platter to allow for many different combinations of cracker, cheese, and topping.

1 (8-ounce) block Cheddar cheese, sliced

1 (8-ounce) block Havarti cheese, sliced

1 (8-ounce) block Parmesan cheese, sliced

2 medium bunches red grapes

2 cups Wheat Thins crackers

1 (8-ounce) package hard salami

¼ cup honey

¾ cup whole black olives

Evenly spread all ingredients on a large cheese plate or serving plate.

SERVES 12	
Per Serving:	
Calories	351
Fat	24g
Protein	19g
Sodium	679mg
Fiber	1g
Carbohydrates	13g
Sugar	9g
Net Carbs	12g

Homemade Cheese Pizzas

The best part of pizza? You can personalize your own. Add as many different toppings as you'd like, such as pepperoni, green pepper, mushrooms, ham, pineapple, or red onion.

6 (6") pita breads

1 (6.5-ounce) can tomato sauce

4 small tomatoes, sliced

½ cup fresh basil leaves

½ cup shredded mozzarella cheese

1 teaspoon salt

½ teaspoon ground black pepper

SERVES 6	
Per Serving:	
Calories	169
Fat	3g
Protein	7g
Sodium	855mg
Fiber	2g
Carbohydrates	29g
Sugar	3g
Net Carbs	27g

1 Preheat oven to 375°F and line a large baking sheet with aluminum foil.

2 Place pita breads on prepared sheet and top each with even amounts of tomato sauce, tomatoes, basil, cheese, salt, and pepper. Bake for 5 minutes or until cheese is completely melted.

Baked Brie with Raspberry Jam

SERVES 8	
Per Serving:	
Calories	222
Fat	11g
Protein	6g
Sodium	346mg
Fiber	0g
Carbohydrates	25g
Sugar	16g
Net Carbs	25g

You can mix up the flavors by using either apricot or grape jelly. Drizzle honey over the top before serving and set some crackers or green apples slices beside it.

1 (8-ounce) tube crescent roll dough

½ cup raspberry jam

1 (6-ounce) block Brie cheese

1 Preheat oven to 375°F.

2 Gently roll out dough on a large baking sheet, making sure to merge the seams in the dough together to form one large rectangular sheet. Spread jam over dough, then place Brie in the middle.

3 Fold corners and edges of the dough over Brie in a star pattern, wrapping it until cheese is covered. Bake 15 minutes or until dough turns golden brown. Serve warm.

Buffalo Chicken Sandwiches

SERVES 8	
Per Serving:	
Calories	370
Fat	14g
Protein	25g
Sodium	1,904mg
Fiber	1g
Carbohydrates	35g
Sugar	5g
Net Carbs	34g

Gearing up for game day? Here's the perfect recipe for your tailgate! The classic combination of buffalo sauce and ranch dressing will have everyone celebrating like the home team just scored! Feel free to use Hawaiian rolls instead of sandwich buns for a little extra sweetness.

3 cups cooked shredded chicken

1½ cups buffalo sauce

2 tablespoons unsalted butter

8 sandwich buns, toasted

½ cup ranch dressing

1 In a large frying pan over medium heat, combine chicken, buffalo sauce, and butter. Stir until combined and cook about 5 minutes or until completely heated through.

2 Evenly spread equal amounts of chicken mixture onto each sandwich bun bottom, top with ranch dressing, close bun, and serve.

CHAPTER 9

Vegan and Vegetarian

Vegan Cabbage Rolls

If you like your cabbage rolls a little sweeter, feel free to add 2 teaspoons maple syrup or granulated sugar to the tomato sauce mixture.

SERVES 8

Per Serving:

Calories	63
Fat	2g
Protein	3g
Sodium	221mg
Fiber	3g
Carbohydrates	8g
Sugar	4g
Net Carbs	5g

HOW TO BOIL CABBAGE LEAVES

Fill a large pot with water up to its halfway mark. Bring to a boil, then pierce cabbage with a fork several times. Drop cabbage in the water, cook for 2 minutes, then take it out to remove the outer leaves. Drop it back in and cook until the inner leaves are soft, another 2–3 minutes.

2 teaspoons olive oil

1 clove garlic, peeled and chopped

½ small red onion, peeled and diced

6 ounces firm tofu, drained and diced

1 cup crushed tomatoes, with liquid

½ medium green bell pepper, seeded and diced

½ teaspoon ground cumin

⅛ teaspoon paprika

8 large cabbage leaves, boiled

¾ cup tomato sauce

⅓ cup water

2 tablespoons white vinegar

1 Preheat oven to 350°F and spray a 9" × 9" baking dish with non-stick cooking spray.

2 Heat oil in a medium frying pan over medium heat, then add garlic and onion. Cook for about 5 minutes or until onion is soft and translucent. Crumble tofu into frying pan, then add tomatoes and peppers, mashing tomatoes with a spatula to break them up slightly. Stir in cumin and paprika.

3 Lay a cabbage leaf flat on the counter. Spoon tofu mixture onto leaf, spreading outward, making sure to leave 1" of room around the edges. Roll leaf tightly, then place in prepared baking dish seam-side down. Repeat for remaining cabbage leaves.

4 In a small bowl, combine tomato sauce, water, and vinegar. Pour over cabbage rolls, then bake 40–45 minutes.

Vegetarian Chili

A bowl of chili wouldn't be complete without something to dip in it. Tortilla chips, crackers, and crusty French bread are all great choices. You could also serve the chili on hamburger buns to create your own version of vegetarian Sloppy Joes.

1 teaspoon olive oil

½ medium yellow onion, peeled and diced

4 medium russet potatoes, peeled and cubed

2 cups baby carrots, chopped

4 cups canned pinto beans, drained

2 cups canned chickpeas, drained

3 cups canned green beans, drained

5 cups tomato sauce

1 cup low-sodium vegetable broth

5 teaspoons chili powder

2 teaspoons ground cumin

½ teaspoon salt

½ cup shredded Cheddar cheese

½ cup sour cream

SERVES 6

Per Serving:

Calories	444
Fat	9g
Protein	20g
Sodium	2,248mg
Fiber	20g
Carbohydrates	73g
Sugar	14g
Net Carbs	53g

1 Heat oil in a large saucepan over medium heat. Add onion and cook for about 5 minutes or until soft and translucent.

2 Add potatoes, carrots, pinto beans, chickpeas, green beans, tomato sauce, and broth. Mix well, then stir in chili powder, cumin, and salt.

3 Bring to a boil, then reduce heat to low, cover, and simmer for approximately 1 hour or until vegetables are tender. Serve warm and top with cheese and sour cream.

Vegan Stew

SERVES 4

Per Serving:

Calories	178
Fat	3g
Protein	9g
Sodium	986mg
Fiber	11g
Carbohydrates	36g
Sugar	7g
Net Carbs	25g

This stew is a great dish for cold winter days when you're in a hurry for a hot meal. Feel free to substitute your favorite type of beans.

2 teaspoons olive oil

½ medium yellow onion, peeled and chopped

1 clove garlic, peeled and chopped

2 medium russet potatoes, peeled and cubed

2 medium carrots, peeled and chopped

1 cup canned kidney beans, drained and rinsed

½ cup Italian green beans

½ cup canned chickpeas, drained and rinsed

6 cups low-sodium vegetable broth

1 teaspoon ground cumin

½ teaspoon lemon juice

1 teaspoon paprika

1 teaspoon salt

1 Heat oil in a large saucepan over medium-low heat. Add onion and garlic and cook for about 5 minutes, until onion is soft and translucent.

2 Stir in remaining ingredients. Bring to a boil, cover, and simmer for 30 minutes. Serve warm.

Pink Bean Soup

If you don't have onion powder, feel free to use 1 small yellow onion, chopped and sautéed in 1 teaspoon olive oil before adding the soaked beans.

1 pound dried pink beans, rinsed, soaked, and drained

7 cups water, divided

½ teaspoon garlic powder

½ teaspoon onion powder

2 teaspoons salt

¼ teaspoon dried thyme

¼ teaspoon dried marjoram

1¼ cups low-sodium vegetable broth

1 (16-ounce) can chopped tomatoes, with liquid

1 tablespoon chili powder

SERVES 6	
Per Serving:	
Calories	176
Fat	0g
Protein	19g
Sodium	850mg
Fiber	9g
Carbohydrates	53g
Sugar	5g
Net Carbs	44g

1 In a large pot over medium-high heat, add beans, 6 cups water, garlic powder, onion powder, salt, thyme, and marjoram. Bring to a boil, reduce heat to low, and cover. Simmer for 2½–3 hours or until beans are tender.

2 Remove 1 cup beans and about ½ cup liquid from the pot. Using a potato masher or a fork, mash beans and liquid thoroughly. Return to pot and add broth, tomatoes, chili powder, and remaining 1 cup water. Stir well and heat 10 minutes. Ladle into soup bowls and serve immediately.

Rainbow Salad with Fennel

SERVES 1

Per Serving:

Calories	489
Fat	27g
Protein	7g
Sodium	449mg
Fiber	16g
Carbohydrates	54g
Sugar	41g
Net Carbs	38g

This colorful salad goes with anything! If you can't find fennel, parsley works well too. Add a little salt, pepper, and cilantro for some extra bursts of flavor.

1 medium carrot, peeled and grated

1 medium red bell pepper, seeded and sliced

2 cups shredded red cabbage

2 tablespoons plus 2 teaspoons mayonnaise

3 teaspoons honey

1 medium fennel bulb, cored and sliced

Mix carrot, bell pepper, and cabbage in a small bowl, then add mayonnaise and honey. Toss until combined, making sure mayonnaise and honey completely coat vegetables. Top with fennel.

Ten-Minute Vegan Chili

SERVES 4

Per Serving:

Calories	399
Fat	2g
Protein	32g
Sodium	1,363mg
Fiber	19g
Carbohydrates	63g
Sugar	12g
Net Carbs	44g

No time? No problem! This is a quick and easy way to get some veggies and protein on the table with no hassle.

1 (12-ounce) jar mild salsa

1 (14.5-ounce) can diced tomatoes

2 (14-ounce) cans kidney beans, drained

½ cup frozen peas

½ cup frozen corn kernels

½ cup frozen carrots

4 (4-ounce) vegan burgers, crumbled

2 tablespoons chili powder

1 teaspoon ground cumin

½ cup water

In a large pot, combine all ingredients together. Simmer for 10 minutes, stirring frequently.

Roasted Pepper, Chickpea, and Spinach Medley

Letting the roasted pepper sit for several hours drains off the excess moisture. For extra flavor, toss in ½ cup sliced red onions, ¼ teaspoon paprika, ¼ teaspoon salt, and ⅛ teaspoon ground black pepper when your medley is complete.

1 medium red bell pepper

1 medium orange bell pepper

1 cup canned chickpeas, drained and rinsed

4 tablespoons red wine vinegar

2 teaspoons lemon juice

1 teaspoon extra-virgin olive oil

⅛ teaspoon garlic powder

3 packed cups fresh baby spinach leaves

2 medium tomatoes, sliced

SERVES 2

Per Serving:	
Calories	210
Fat	4g
Protein	9g
Sodium	228mg
Fiber	10g
Carbohydrates	32g
Sugar	9g
Net Carbs	22g

1. Preheat oven broiler. Line an 8" × 8" roasting pan with aluminum foil, then broil bell peppers for 5 minutes or until skins are blackened. Turn peppers over and broil another 5 minutes, so that both sides blacken. Remove from oven, place in a plastic bag, and seal. Leave peppers in the bag for at least 10 minutes.

2. Remove skin from peppers, cut in half, and remove seeds. Slice peppers into long strips and let sit for 2–3 hours. Wipe strips dry and dice.

3. In a large bowl, toss chickpeas with vinegar, lemon juice, oil, and garlic powder. Add peppers, spinach, and tomatoes and mix. Serve immediately.

Three-Bean Cassoulet

SERVES 2

Per Serving:

Calories	270
Fat	1g
Protein	16g
Sodium	1,387mg
Fiber	9g
Carbohydrates	52g
Sugar	11g
Net Carbs	43g

This recipe is perfect for when you're studying for a big test all afternoon. Just throw everything in a casserole dish and let it bake for 2 hours or so. It will fill you up, has great flavor, and you'll probably have leftovers for lunch or dinner the next day.

4 ounces fresh green beans, ends trimmed

1 clove garlic, peeled and chopped

1 medium zucchini, sliced

⅓ cup chopped yellow onion

1 cup Romano beans

¾ cup black-eyed peas

1 cup tomato sauce

1 cup low-sodium vegetable broth

1 teaspoon dried parsley flakes

½ teaspoon dried basil

¼ teaspoon onion powder

⅛ teaspoon salt

⅛ teaspoon ground black pepper

1 Preheat oven to 350°F.

2 In a small pot, boil water. Blanch green beans for 3 minutes or until they turn bright green.

3 Combine green beans, garlic, zucchini, onion, Romano beans, black-eyed peas, tomato sauce, and broth in a 1½–2-quart casserole dish. Stir in parsley, basil, onion powder, salt, and pepper, mixing until fully combined with bean mixture.

4 Bake 2–2½ hours, stirring occasionally, until vegetables are tender and cassoulet has thickened.

Spring Roll Salad

Many of the ingredients that are traditionally found in spring rolls make for an amazing salad. If you don't feel like making the dressing, you can always use a jar of yum yum sauce!

1 cup mung bean sprouts, drained

1 medium carrot, peeled and sliced into 2" strips

1 medium red bell pepper, seeded and sliced into 2" strips

1 (14-ounce) can baby corn

2 teaspoons olive oil

3 teaspoons low-sodium soy sauce

2 teaspoons red wine vinegar

Add bean sprouts, carrot, pepper, and corn to a small mixing bowl. In a separate small bowl, combine oil, soy sauce, and vinegar. Pour dressing over salad, mix thoroughly, and serve.

SERVES 2

Per Serving:

Calories	202
Fat	5g
Protein	10g
Sodium	873mg
Fiber	10g
Carbohydrates	24g
Sugar	13g
Net Carbs	14g

Vegetarian Stir-Fry

It's hard to go wrong with this simple recipe, since there are a number of good stir-fry sauces on the market. You can substitute soy sauce for the stir-fry sauce if you'd like. Serve by itself or with brown rice.

2 teaspoons olive oil

⅓ cup frozen carrots

⅓ cup frozen peas

⅓ cup frozen broccoli

2 tablespoons vegetarian stir-fry sauce

Heat oil in a medium frying pan over medium heat. Add vegetables and cook, stirring continuously, for at least 5 minutes or until vegetables are brightly colored and tender. Stir in sauce. Mix thoroughly and serve hot.

SERVES 1

Per Serving:

Calories	187
Fat	9g
Protein	6g
Sodium	1,136mg
Fiber	5g
Carbohydrates	20g
Sugar	11g
Net Carbs	15g

Vegetarian Lasagna

This is the perfect recipe for busy weeknights—no noodles to boil, and no beef to brown. You don't even need a proper casserole dish! If you can't find oven-ready lasagna noodles, just boil regular lasagna noodles for 5 minutes. If the noodles don't perfectly fit your casserole dish, you can break them in half.

½ cup crushed tomatoes, with liquid

⅓ cup part-skim ricotta cheese

⅓ cup grated mozzarella cheese

1 tablespoon grated Parmesan cheese

⅛ teaspoon dried oregano

⅛ teaspoon dried basil

6 oven-ready lasagna noodles

1   Add crushed tomatoes to a medium bowl, then stir in ricotta, then mozzarella, and then Parmesan, making sure each cheese is thoroughly mixed in before adding the next. Stir in oregano and basil.

2   Lay out 2 lasagna noodles in a shallow bowl or small (½-quart) microwave-safe casserole dish. Spoon ⅓ of tomato mixture evenly over the top. Repeat twice more with remaining noodles and tomato-cheese mixture.

3   Cover dish with wax paper. Microwave on high heat for 6–8 minutes, until noodles are cooked. Let stand 10 minutes before serving.

SERVES 2

Per Serving:

Calories	242
Fat	8g
Protein	15g
Sodium	330mg
Fiber	3g
Carbohydrates	28g
Sugar	3g
Net Carbs	25g

OVEN-READY RIGHT AWAY

Oven-ready lasagna noodles are precooked at the factory before being dehydrated and shipped off to supermarkets. As the lasagna bakes in the oven, the moisture from the sauce rehydrates the noodles.

Sweet Potato Soup

Think you don't have time to make a creamy and delicious soup? Oh, yeah, you do. Not only will this soup satisfy your hunger after a long day of classes; it's loaded with antioxidants from the turmeric. If you feel like you're getting sick, it's the perfect remedy to get you back on your feet.

SERVES 2

Per Serving:

Calories	421
Fat	13g
Protein	11g
Sodium	252mg
Fiber	9g
Carbohydrates	70g
Sugar	41g
Net Carbs	61g

2 large sweet potatoes, steamed

2 cups unsweetened almond milk

4 tablespoons maple syrup

1 teaspoon ground cinnamon

½ teaspoon ground nutmeg

½ teaspoon ground turmeric

¼ cup pumpkin seeds

Cut sweet potatoes in half and scoop out flesh. Transfer to large blender and add milk, maple syrup, cinnamon, nutmeg, and turmeric. Blend until smooth. Serve warm or cold and garnish with pumpkin seeds.

Vegan Pancakes

Spice up these easy cakes by adding 2 teaspoons of cinnamon to the batter before cooking. If you don't have almond milk, any plant-based milk will work just fine!

MAKES 10 PANCAKES

Per Serving (1 pancake):

Calories	85
Fat	1g
Protein	2g
Sodium	18mg
Fiber	2g
Carbohydrates	17g
Sugar	3g
Net Carbs	15g

2 cups rolled oats

2 medium ripe bananas

1 cup unsweetened almond milk

1 Add oats to a blender and blend until they reach a flour-like consistency, about 1 minute. Add bananas and milk and blend until mixture becomes a batter, about 3 minutes.

2 Spray a medium frying pan with nonstick cooking spray, then heat over medium heat. Add ¼ cup batter to the pan and cook 4 minutes. Flip, then cook another 4 minutes. Repeat with remaining batter.

Vegetarian Taco Soup

You got a lil' bit of spice and a lil' bit of sweet in this vegetarian taco soup recipe. Feel free to serve alongside some tortilla chips and garnish with some red onion and extra cilantro.

2 teaspoons olive oil

½ medium yellow onion, peeled and diced

1 clove garlic, peeled and chopped

1 (1-ounce) packet taco seasoning mix

2 cups low-sodium vegetable broth

1 (14-ounce) can black beans, drained and rinsed

1 (14-ounce) can pinto beans, drained and rinsed

1 (14-ounce) can kidney beans, drained and rinsed

1 (14-ounce) can diced tomatoes, with liquid

1 cup frozen corn kernels

½ teaspoon salt

¼ teaspoon ground black pepper

1 tablespoon fresh lime juice

1 tablespoon chopped fresh cilantro

½ medium tomato, chopped

½ cup shredded Cheddar cheese

¼ cup sour cream

SERVES 4	
Per Serving:	
Calories	495
Fat	10g
Protein	22g
Sodium	1,665mg
Fiber	17g
Carbohydrates	74g
Sugar	9g
Net Carbs	57g

1 Heat oil in a large saucepan over medium heat. Add onion and cook for about 5 minutes or until soft and translucent. Add garlic and taco seasoning and sauté another 30 seconds or until fragrant.

2 Add broth, black beans, pinto beans, kidney beans, and diced tomatoes. Mix well and reduce heat to low. Simmer for 30 minutes. Add corn and cook until heated through, about 3 minutes. Stir in salt, pepper, lime juice, cilantro, and chopped tomato. Garnish with cheese and sour cream and serve.

Lentil Soup

There's nothing like some hearty soup after a tough day of study-ing. You can use brown, red, yellow, or green lentils for this recipe. It changes nothing except the color of your soup! Serve this with some warm, crusty bread for dipping.

LOADED LENTILS

Lentils are small leg-umes, and they're loaded with protein, fiber, folic acid, and potassium. Because of their low fat and high protein content, they're an amazing substi-tute for meat. For best results, soak your lentils in hot water for 30 min-utes, or even overnight, to aid in digestion.

2 tablespoons olive oil

1 medium yellow onion, peeled and chopped

2 medium carrots, peeled and sliced

2 medium celery stalks, sliced

2 cloves garlic, peeled and chopped

2 cups dried lentils, picked over and rinsed

1 (28-ounce) can crushed tomatoes, with liquid

6 cups low-sodium vegetable broth

2 teaspoons ground cumin

½ teaspoon paprika

½ teaspoon dried thyme

2 tablespoons lemon juice

2 tablespoons lemon zest

¼ teaspoon salt

¼ teaspoon ground black pepper

1 Heat oil in a large saucepan over medium heat. Add onion, car-rots, and celery and sauté 5 minutes or until onion is soft and translucent. Add garlic and sauté about 30 seconds or until fra-grant. Add lentils, tomatoes, broth, cumin, paprika, thyme, lemon juice, lemon zest, salt, and pepper.

2 Raise heat to high, mix well, and bring to a boil, then reduce heat to medium-low. Cover and let simmer for 25–30 minutes or until lentils are tender.

Asian Tofu Lettuce Wraps

If you like your wraps a little bit spicier, add ¼ teaspoon red pepper flakes when you add the hoisin sauce mixture to the tofu.

1 (14-ounce) package extra-firm tofu

3 tablespoons hoisin sauce

3 tablespoons low-sodium soy sauce

2 tablespoons rice vinegar

1 teaspoon sesame oil

2 teaspoons canola oil

1 small yellow onion, peeled and chopped

2 cloves garlic, peeled and minced

1 (8-ounce) can water chestnuts, drained

2 teaspoons minced fresh ginger

2 medium scallions, thinly sliced and divided

8 large iceberg lettuce leaves

1   Place tofu on a plate between paper towels, and cover with a heavy object. Let sit for 20 minutes to drain excess liquid.

2   In a small bowl, combine hoisin sauce, soy sauce, vinegar, and sesame oil. Mix well and set aside.

3   Heat canola oil in a large frying pan over medium heat. Add onion and cook for about 5 minutes or until soft and translucent. Add garlic and sauté 30 seconds. Add pressed tofu and crumble it into tiny pieces using a wooden spoon. Cook for 8–10 minutes or until tofu turns golden brown. Stir in water chestnuts, ginger, ¾ of the scallions, and hoisin sauce mixture. Cook until sauce is warmed through, about 1–2 minutes.

4   Put lettuce leaves on a large plate and carefully spoon an even amount of tofu mixture onto each leaf. Garnish with remaining ¼ of the scallions and serve immediately.

SERVES 2

Per Serving:

Calories	423
Fat	16g
Protein	23g
Sodium	1,334mg
Fiber	7g
Carbohydrates	43g
Sugar	19g
Net Carbs	36g

LETTUCE EAT!

When it comes to lettuce wraps, it's best to choose either butterhead or iceberg lettuce because their leaves hold their shape well and don't flop all over the place. They're not the most nutritious, however. If you're looking for healthier greens, go for dark, leafy ones like spinach, romaine, kale, and arugula. Darker leaves usually have a stronger taste and more nutrients.

Spicy Black Bean and Bell Pepper Soup

SERVES 6

Per Serving:

Calories	372
Fat	7g
Protein	18g
Sodium	995mg
Fiber	17g
Carbohydrates	60g
Sugar	5g
Net Carbs	43g

Be careful when blending the soup! It will be very hot, and steam will escape from the top of your blender. Use oven mitts to protect yourself from the heat.

1 tablespoon olive oil

1 large yellow onion, peeled and chopped

1 medium red bell pepper, seeded and chopped

4 cloves garlic, peeled and chopped

4 (15-ounce) cans black beans, drained and rinsed

4 cups low-sodium vegetable broth

4 teaspoons ground cumin

½ teaspoon red pepper flakes

1 teaspoon salt

1 teaspoon ground black pepper

¼ cup chopped fresh cilantro

2 tablespoons fresh lime juice

1 medium avocado, peeled, pitted, and sliced

1 Heat oil in a large saucepan over medium heat. Add onion and bell pepper and cook for about 5 minutes, until onion is soft and translucent. Add garlic and sauté 30 seconds, then stir in beans, broth, cumin, red pepper flakes, salt, and black pepper.

2 Bring to a simmer, then reduce heat to medium-low. Cook 30 minutes or until beans are tender.

3 Transfer 4 cups soup to a blender and blend until smooth. Pour soup back into pot, then stir in cilantro and lime juice. Transfer to serving bowls, top with avocado, and serve immediately.

Split Pea Soup

This hearty soup is loaded with protein, healthy vegetables, and rich flavors.

2 tablespoons olive oil

1 medium yellow onion, peeled and chopped

3 large carrots, peeled and diced

3 medium celery stalks, sliced

2 cloves garlic, peeled and minced

½ teaspoon dried oregano

¼ teaspoon dried basil

1 teaspoon dried parsley flakes

1 teaspoon salt

1 teaspoon ground black pepper

8 cups low-sodium vegetable broth

1 pound dried split green peas, divided

2 medium scallions, sliced

SERVES 6	
Per Serving:	
Calories	303
Fat	5g
Protein	17g
Sodium	617mg
Fiber	19g
Carbohydrates	48g
Sugar	10g
Net Carbs	29g

1. Heat oil in a large pot over medium heat. Add onion, carrots, and celery and cook for about 5 minutes or until onion is soft and translucent. Add garlic, oregano, basil, parsley, salt, and pepper. Sauté until fragrant, about 1 minute.

2. Add broth and ½ pound split peas. Raise heat to high and bring to a boil, then reduce heat to medium-low and simmer uncovered for 40 minutes, making sure to skim foam off the top while cooking.

3. Add remaining ½ pound split peas and cook another 40 minutes or until all peas are soft, stirring frequently.

4. Transfer to serving bowls and garnish with scallions. Serve immediately.

Vegan Mac 'n' Cheese

SERVES 3

Per Serving:

Calories	686
Fat	11g
Protein	27g
Sodium	808mg
Fiber	8g
Carbohydrates	124g
Sugar	8g
Net Carbs	116g

NUTRITIONAL YEAST... CHEESE?

Nutritional yeast is a great way to add a cheesy flavor to your food. It tastes similar to Parmesan, but it has far more health benefits. If you've never tried it, however, go slow with introducing it to your system. It's packed with fiber and may upset your stomach.

This creamy comfort food gives you all of that rich flavor without any animal by-products. The nutritional yeast provides the cheesy flavor, and the blended cashews give the sauce a smooth texture, exactly like traditional mac 'n' cheese.

½ cup raw cashews
1 medium carrot, peeled, chopped, and steamed
¼ cup nutritional yeast
1 teaspoon apple cider vinegar
½ cup water
1 teaspoon salt
¼ teaspoon onion powder
¼ teaspoon garlic powder
1 pound elbow macaroni, cooked

In a small bowl, cover cashews with water and soak 4 hours. Drain, then transfer to blender. Add carrot, yeast, vinegar, water, salt, onion powder, and garlic powder and blend until smooth. Pour blended sauce over macaroni, mix thoroughly until it is completely covered, and serve.

Vegetarian Chickpea Sandwich

SERVES 2

Per Serving:

Calories	390
Fat	15g
Protein	14g
Sodium	1,352mg
Fiber	11g
Carbohydrates	46g
Sugar	12g
Net Carbs	35g

Chickpeas are loaded with protein and other nutrients, making them the perfect substitute for meat in a vegetarian or vegan diet. Add a little color to this sandwich with ⅛ teaspoon turmeric.

1 (15-ounce) can chickpeas, drained and rinsed

¼ cup chopped red onion

¼ cup chopped dill pickles

2 tablespoons mayonnaise

¼ teaspoon sea salt

¼ teaspoon ground black pepper

4 (1-ounce) slices whole-wheat bread, toasted

1 Add chickpeas to a blender. Pulse two or three times. In a small bowl, combine chickpeas, onion, pickles, mayonnaise, salt, and pepper.

2 Place 2 pieces of toast on a work surface. Spread chickpea mixture equally onto each slice. Place remaining slices on top to close sandwiches, cut in half, and serve.

Scrambled Tofu

SERVES 4

Per Serving:

Calories	184
Fat	12g
Protein	13g
Sodium	604mg
Fiber	2g
Carbohydrates	5g
Sugar	0g
Net Carbs	3g

The nutritional yeast gives the tofu a cheesy flavor, and the turmeric gives it the classic yellow color of scrambled eggs.

1 (16-ounce) package extra-firm tofu

2 tablespoons olive oil

3 tablespoons nutritional yeast

1 teaspoon ground turmeric

1 teaspoon salt

½ teaspoon ground black pepper

1 Place tofu on a plate between paper towels, and cover with a heavy object. Let sit for 20 minutes to drain excess liquid.

2 In a large bowl, crumble tofu using a potato masher or fork.

3 Heat oil in a medium frying pan over medium heat. Add tofu and cook 5 minutes. Add yeast, turmeric, salt, and pepper, and cook 2–3 minutes. Serve hot.

Vegan Lasagna

To make this lasagna even cheesier, take it out 20 minutes before it's done and sprinkle vegan mozzarella cheese on top, then place it back in the oven for the remaining 20 minutes.

1 cup raw cashews

1 (12-ounce) package extra-firm tofu

2 cups baby spinach leaves

¼ cup chopped fresh basil leaves

2 cloves garlic, peeled and minced

1 teaspoon salt

¼ cup nutritional yeast

1 teaspoon dried oregano

2 tablespoons fresh lemon juice

3 cups marinara sauce

1 (9-ounce) package oven-ready lasagna noodles

SERVES 9

Per Serving:

Calories	243
Fat	8g
Protein	12g
Sodium	276mg
Fiber	3g
Carbohydrates	30g
Sugar	2g
Net Carbs	27g

1   In a small bowl, cover cashews with water and soak 4 hours. Drain, then transfer to blender. Pat tofu dry with paper towels, then add to blender, along with spinach, basil, garlic, salt, yeast, oregano, and lemon juice. Blend until smooth and set aside.

2   Preheat oven to 350°F.

3   Add 1 cup marinara sauce to a 9" × 13" pan and spread evenly. Add 4 lasagna noodles evenly on top of marinara, then top with half of the cashew mixture, spread evenly. Add another cup marinara sauce, spread evenly, then place another 4 noodles on top of marinara. Spread remaining half of cashew mixture evenly, then top with remaining 4 noodles. Pour remaining 1 cup sauce over noodles, spreading evenly.

4   Cover with aluminum foil and bake 1 hour. Let rest 5 minutes and serve hot.

Black Bean Burgers

SERVES 4

Per Serving:

Calories	222
Fat	7g
Protein	8g
Sodium	714mg
Fiber	7g
Carbohydrates	30g
Sugar	2g
Net Carbs	23g

BEANS: A COLLEGE STUDENT'S DREAM

Beans are absolutely packed with protein and fiber, more than enough to keep you full for hours. They're incredibly versatile too. Add them to some soup, press them into burgers, or use them in a dip. They're perfect for any college student on a budget.

The seasonings in these burgers combine to create a burst of flavor in every bite. Feel free to add some lime zest to the patties for some extra citrus flavor.

2 cups canned black beans, drained and rinsed

¼ cup dried bread crumbs

¼ cup chopped scallions

2 tablespoons lime juice

⅛ teaspoon red pepper flakes

2 teaspoons onion powder

1 teaspoon ground cumin

1 teaspoon garlic powder

½ cup chopped fresh cilantro

¾ teaspoon salt

¼ teaspoon ground black pepper

2 tablespoons olive oil

1 Add beans to a blender. Pulse two or three times. Transfer to a medium bowl, then add bread crumbs, scallions, lime juice, red pepper flakes, cumin, garlic powder, onion powder, cilantro, salt, and black pepper. Mix until fully combined. Cover and refrigerate for 15 minutes.

2 Shape bean mixture into four even balls, then press down with the palm of your hand to form patty shapes.

3 Heat oil in a large frying pan over medium heat. Add patties and cook 5 minutes, then flip and cook additional 5 minutes. Serve immediately.

Vegetable Pot Pie

This Vegetable Pot Pie is perfect for a big gathering. You can add a golden sheen to the crust by brushing it with a beaten egg or vegan egg wash.

1 tablespoon olive oil

1 medium yellow onion, peeled and chopped

1 medium russet potato, peeled and diced

1 teaspoon salt

1 teaspoon ground black pepper

¼ cup all-purpose flour

½ cup low-sodium vegetable broth

¾ cup whole milk

1 cup frozen peas

1 cup frozen corn kernels

1 cup frozen carrots

⅓ cup sliced chives

¼ cup chopped parsley

2 premade frozen vegan pie crusts, thawed

SERVES 6

Per Serving:

Calories	378
Fat	17g
Protein	7g
Sodium	687mg
Fiber	3g
Carbohydrates	51g
Sugar	9g
Net Carbs	48g

HOW TO MAKE A VEGAN EGG WASH

The best way to make a vegan egg wash is to combine 1 tablespoon chia seeds or flaxseed meal with 3 tablespoons water. Stir to combine, then refrigerate for 15 minutes to turn the mixture into silky egg goodness.

1 Preheat oven to 400°F.

2 Heat oil in a large frying pan over medium heat. Add onion and cook about 5 minutes or until soft and translucent. Add potato, salt, and pepper and cook another 5 minutes, stirring to fully coat vegetables in seasoning.

3 Stir in flour and cook another 2 minutes, then add broth and milk. Stirring constantly, bring to a simmer and cook until mixture thickens, about 5–10 minutes.

4 Remove from heat, add peas, corn, carrots, chives, and parsley and stir to combine.

5 Spread one pie crust into an 8" × 8" baking pan or pie plate until the bottom and sides are completely covered. Add in vegetable mixture, then top with second pie crust. Place pan on a baking sheet and bake 25–30 minutes or until crust is golden brown. Serve warm.

Vegan Stuffed Peppers

SERVES 6

Per Serving:

Calories	263
Fat	4g
Protein	9g
Sodium	723mg
Fiber	8g
Carbohydrates	49g
Sugar	9g
Net Carbs	41g

VEGAN RULES

When you're making any vegan dishes, be careful not to use any animal products whatsoever. This includes some things you might not think of, like honey, gelatin, and Worcestershire sauce. Always check ingredient lists on products, even on pasta, candy, and French fries. You may find eggs in pasta, gelatin in candy, and French fries dipped in animal fat.

Feel free to add some shredded vegan cheese on top of the peppers about 10 minutes before they've finished baking. You can also mix and match ingredients with the stuffing, like corn, beans, and mushrooms.

1 tablespoon olive oil

1 small yellow onion, peeled and chopped

3 cloves garlic, peeled and chopped

½ teaspoon ground cumin

½ teaspoon paprika

½ teaspoon dried thyme

1 teaspoon dried basil

1 teaspoon salt

½ cup brown lentils, picked over and rinsed

1 (15-ounce) can diced tomatoes, drained

1½ cups low-sodium vegetable broth

3 cups cooked brown rice

2 medium red bell peppers, cored and seeded

2 medium green bell peppers, cored and seeded

2 medium yellow bell peppers, cored and seeded

1 cup marinara sauce

1 Heat oil in a large saucepan over medium heat. Add onion and cook for about 5 minutes until soft and translucent. Add garlic, cumin, paprika, thyme, basil, and salt. Cook until fragrant, about 30 seconds. Add lentils, tomatoes, and broth. Cover, bring to a simmer, and cook 35–40 minutes or until liquid has evaporated.

2 Add rice and stir to combine. Remove from heat.

3 Preheat oven to 375°F.

4 Add bell peppers to a 9" × 9" baking dish. Fill with rice and lentil mixture in equal amounts. Top with marinara sauce, cover with aluminum foil, and bake for 30 minutes. Serve hot.

Vegan French Toast

Don't forget the syrup! To make your toast a little sweeter, you can add 1 tablespoon maple syrup directly into the chia seed mixture. That will act as a substitute for eggs.

1 tablespoon chia seeds

1 cup unsweetened almond milk

½ teaspoon ground cinnamon

½ teaspoon vanilla extract

4 (1-ounce) slices whole-wheat bread

1 In a small bowl, combine chia seeds, milk, cinnamon, and vanilla. Refrigerate 30 minutes.

2 Grease a medium frying pan with nonstick cooking spray and heat over medium heat. Dip a bread slice into batter, making sure each side is fully coated. Transfer to frying pan and cook 5 minutes, then flip and cook an additional 5 minutes. Repeat with remaining slices.

SERVES 2

Per Serving:

Calories	195
Fat	6g
Protein	7g
Sodium	390mg
Fiber	7g
Carbohydrates	30g
Sugar	11g
Net Carbs	23g

Vegetarian Baked Ziti with Lentils

SERVES 6

Per Serving:

Calories	438
Fat	14g
Protein	26g
Sodium	270mg
Fiber	10g
Carbohydrates	52g
Sugar	2g
Net Carbs	42g

For extra flavor, cook the lentils in onions, garlic, salt, and red pepper flakes. It adds a burst of Italian flavor to give the dish a more powerful taste.

1 pound cooked ziti

3½ cups cooked green lentils

2 cups shredded mozzarella cheese, divided

3 cups marinara sauce, divided

1 cup part-skim ricotta cheese

1 Preheat oven to 350°F.

2 In a large bowl, combine ziti, lentils, and ½ cup mozzarella cheese. Pour 1 cup marinara into a 9" × 13" pan. Pour lentil mixture over sauce, spread evenly, then top with ricotta.

3 Pour remaining 2 cups marinara sauce over top in an even layer, then add remaining 1½ cups mozzarella. Cover with aluminum foil, making sure it doesn't touch the cheese. Bake 30 minutes, remove foil, and bake another 10 minutes.

CHAPTER 10

Got a Date?

Broccoli au Gratin

SERVES 2

Per Serving:

Calories	294
Fat	21g
Protein	10g
Sodium	508mg
Fiber	6g
Carbohydrates	19g
Sugar	5g
Net Carbs	13g

This dish is simple yet impressive enough for any special guest. You can use steamed cauliflower or asparagus instead of broccoli.

2 tablespoons unsalted butter

1 tablespoon all-purpose flour

6 tablespoons whole milk

⅛ teaspoon garlic powder

¼ teaspoon salt

¼ teaspoon ground black pepper

⅓ cup shredded Cheddar cheese

2 tablespoons sour cream

2 cups chopped steamed broccoli

1   Melt butter in a medium saucepan over low heat. Stir in flour and cook 2 minutes, whisking constantly. Whisk in milk, garlic powder, salt, and pepper. Raise heat to medium and bring to a boil, whisking continuously.

2   Whisk in cheese and sour cream. Bring to a boil, stir in broccoli, and serve hot.

Aloha Shrimp

SERVES 2

Per Serving:

Calories	369
Fat	4g
Protein	51g
Sodium	2,525mg
Fiber	2g
Carbohydrates	24g
Sugar	17g
Net Carbs	22g

For best results, cover the shrimp and chill for 2 hours before cooking. These also work great on the grill for a summertime seafood snack.

⅓ cup low-sodium soy sauce

1 tablespoon cooking sherry

2 teaspoons light brown sugar

1 pound large shrimp, peeled and deveined

½ medium red bell pepper, seeded and roughly chopped

1 cup pineapple chunks, drained

1   Combine soy sauce, sherry, and brown sugar in a small bowl.

2   Preheat oven broiler. Place a shrimp on a metal skewer, followed by red pepper piece, then pineapple chunk. Repeat with remaining ingredients. Brush soy sauce mixture over kebabs. Broil 5–8 minutes, turning occasionally and brushing with more sauce.

Crab Rangoon

Sweet-and-sour sauce, hot chili sauce, or soy sauce are all great dipping sauce choices for these Crab Rangoons. If you'd rather not fry these, you can always bake them. Brush them with sesame or canola oil, then bake at 425°F for 10 minutes.

4½ cups canola oil

¼ cup fresh crabmeat, drained

½ medium scallion, sliced

¼ cup cream cheese

½ teaspoon Worcestershire sauce

¼ teaspoon garlic powder

12 wonton wrappers

1 large egg, lightly beaten

1 Heat oil in a wok or large saucepan over high heat.

2 In a small bowl, add crabmeat and lightly shred with a fork. Add scallion, cream cheese, Worcestershire sauce, and garlic powder. Mix well until fully combined.

3 Lay a wonton wrapper on a work surface in a diamond shape. Gently wet edges with egg. Spoon crabmeat mixture onto wrapper, spreading outward, making sure to leave ½" of room around edges. Fold corners up to make a peak, then pinch edges closed to seal. Repeat with remaining wrappers and crabmeat mixture.

4 Carefully slide 4–5 wontons into hot oil. Deep-fry until golden brown, about 2–3 minutes. Remove with a slotted spoon, then drain on paper towels. Repeat with remaining wontons.

SERVES 2	
Per Serving:	
Calories	222
Fat	16g
Protein	10g
Sodium	268mg
Fiber	0g
Carbohydrates	7g
Sugar	2g
Net Carbs	7g

Turkey and Spinach Pasta

SERVES 2

Per Serving:

Calories	627
Fat	16g
Protein	36g
Sodium	937mg
Fiber	4g
Carbohydrates	94g
Sugar	5g
Net Carbs	90g

While steak and seafood are nice, you don't need to splurge to cook a romantic meal for two. Shredded turkey combines nicely with spinach and pasta in this simple but flavorful dish.

2 teaspoons olive oil

1 clove garlic, peeled and chopped

¼ cup chopped yellow onion

1 medium Roma tomato, sliced

½ cup condensed cream of mushroom soup

½ cup water

1 cup shredded cooked turkey

¼ teaspoon dried parsley

⅛ teaspoon salt

½ cup frozen spinach, thawed and drained

8 ounces bow tie pasta, cooked

1 Heat oil in a medium frying pan over medium heat. Add garlic, onion, and tomato and cook for about 5 minutes, until onion is soft and translucent.

2 Stir in soup, water, turkey, parsley, salt, and spinach. Cover and simmer 10 minutes. Remove from heat, then pour over pasta. Mix well and serve hot.

Zucchini Lemon Chicken

Add some chopped garlic and the zest from your lemons for a bit of extra flavor. Garnish this dish with a couple sprigs of thyme, and any date will be impressed!

4 tablespoons fresh lemon juice, divided

2 (6-ounce) boneless, skinless chicken breasts

2 teaspoons olive oil

½ small yellow onion, peeled and chopped

1 medium zucchini, sliced

½ cup low-sodium chicken broth

2 tablespoons tomato sauce

¼ teaspoon salt

¼ teaspoon ground black pepper

1 Place 2 tablespoons lemon juice in a resealable plastic bag and add chicken. Seal the bag and refrigerate 1 hour, turning occasionally so chicken is completely covered in juice. Remove chicken from refrigerator and pat dry.

2 Heat oil in a medium frying pan over medium heat. Add onion and cook for about 5 minutes until soft and translucent. Add chicken and cook 5 minutes, then add zucchini and cook 1 minute.

3 Add broth, tomato sauce, remaining 2 tablespoons lemon juice, salt, and pepper. Cover and simmer 20 minutes. Serve hot.

SERVES 2

Per Serving:

Calories	255
Fat	10g
Protein	35g
Sodium	986mg
Fiber	2g
Carbohydrates	11g
Sugar	5g
Net Carbs	9g

CITRUS YIELDS

A lemon usually contains about 3 tablespoons of juice and about 1 table-spoon of zest. Limes have 2 tablespoons juice and 1½ teaspoons of zest.

Creamy Chicken with Noodles

The sauce in this recipe can be used for other meals quite easily by leaving out the frozen spinach. Experiment with a different combination of seasonings, such as cayenne pepper or hot sauce.

SERVES 2

Per Serving:

Calories	594
Fat	27g
Protein	47g
Sodium	874mg
Fiber	3g
Carbohydrates	44g
Sugar	5g
Net Carbs	41g

3 tablespoons all-purpose flour, divided

¼ teaspoon salt

¼ teaspoon ground black pepper

½ teaspoon dried parsley

2 (6-ounce) boneless, skinless chicken breasts, cut into bite-sized pieces

2½ tablespoons butter, divided

¾ cup whole milk

¼ cup grated Parmesan cheese

¼ teaspoon paprika

2 ounces frozen spinach, thawed and drained

8 ounces egg noodles, cooked

1 In a large resealable plastic bag, combine 2 tablespoons flour, salt, pepper, and dried parsley. Add chicken, seal, and shake thoroughly until chicken is fully coated.

2 Heat 1 tablespoon butter in a medium frying pan over medium-high heat. Remove chicken from bag and place in pan. Cook about 5 minutes, then flip and cook 5 more minutes or until cooked through. Remove from heat.

3 Melt remaining 1½ tablespoons butter in a small saucepan over low heat. Stir in remaining 1 tablespoon flour. Cook 3 minutes, whisking constantly. Gradually whisk in milk, then cheese, stirring until thickened. Stir in paprika and spinach. Pour sauce over chicken and noodles. Serve hot.

Shrimp and Rice Skillet

Curried shrimp and rice make a nice combination in this simple one-dish meal. You can use either white or brown rice and add a little bit of pineapple for some sweetness.

2 tablespoons olive oil

½ medium yellow onion, peeled and chopped

2 cloves garlic, peeled and chopped

1½ pounds shrimp, peeled and deveined

½ cup tomato sauce

½ cup low-sodium chicken broth

1 teaspoon curry powder

1 teaspoon dried parsley

½ teaspoon salt

¼ teaspoon ground black pepper

1 cup cooked long-grain white rice

½ tablespoon unsalted butter

SERVES 2

Per Serving:

Calories	580
Fat	20g
Protein	65g
Sodium	869mg
Fiber	3g
Carbohydrates	36g
Sugar	7g
Net Carbs	33g

1 Heat oil in a medium frying pan over medium heat. Add onion and cook for about 5 minutes or until soft and translucent. Add garlic and cook for 30 seconds, stirring constantly. Add shrimp and cook 2–3 minutes. Flip and cook another 2–3 minutes, until shrimp turn pink.

2 Stir in tomato sauce, broth, curry powder, parsley, salt, and pepper. Cook 2–3 minutes, then stir in rice and butter. Cook 5 minutes or until heated through. Serve warm.

Spaghetti with Meatballs

Feel free to load up this basic spaghetti sauce recipe with your favorite vegetables and pasta seasonings. Green and red bell peppers, dried parsley, and even spicy chili powder will all work perfectly.

8 ounces spaghetti

2 teaspoons olive oil

¼ cup chopped yellow onion

1 clove garlic, peeled and chopped

6 medium portobello mushrooms, sliced

1 cup tomato sauce

¾ cup water

¼ teaspoon dried oregano

¼ teaspoon dried basil

½ teaspoon salt

¼ teaspoon ground black pepper

6 frozen Italian meatballs, thawed

1 Cook spaghetti according to package instructions. Drain spaghetti, rinse with cold water, and drain again. Set aside.

2 Heat oil in a large frying pan over medium heat. Add onion and cook for about 5 minutes or until soft and translucent. Add garlic and sauté 30 seconds, then add mushrooms and cook 5 minutes.

3 Add tomato sauce, water, oregano, basil, salt, and pepper. Stir well.

4 Add meatballs. Reduce heat to medium-low and simmer 15 minutes, until sauce is thickened and meatballs are cooked through. Add spaghetti and serve hot.

SERVES 2

Per Serving:

Calories	670
Fat	19g
Protein	26g
Sodium	1,792mg
Fiber	9g
Carbohydrates	101g
Sugar	13g
Net Carbs	92g

AL DENTE ALL THE WAY

Al dente means "to the tooth" in Italian, meaning the pasta is soft but still has a bite to it when you chew. Cooking pasta al dente gives you the most amount of flavor and the perfect texture for almost every pasta dish. Cooking time will vary depending on the type of pasta, but most packages will include these directions.

Chocolate-Covered Strawberries

SERVES 2

Per Serving:

Calories	616
Fat	38g
Protein	5g
Sodium	14mg
Fiber	9g
Carbohydrates	80g
Sugar	67g
Net Carbs	71g

Feel free to experiment with different flavors of chocolate chips and other types of fresh fruit, such as banana slices and pineapple chunks for dipping in the warm chocolate.

8 ounces semisweet chocolate chips

2 teaspoons shortening

½ pound (about 16) fresh strawberries

1 Lay a sheet of wax paper on a 9" × 13" baking sheet. Keep the baking sheet near where you will be cooking the chocolate.

2 Fill a heavy pot halfway with water and bring to a boil over high heat. In a medium metal bowl, combine chocolate and shortening. Reduce heat to low and place the bowl on top of the pot. Melt chocolate for roughly 10 minutes, stirring regularly with a rubber spatula, until completely melted. Remove from heat.

3 Dip each strawberry into chocolate and set on prepared baking sheet. Let cool in refrigerator 15 minutes or until chocolate has hardened. Serve chilled.

Decadent Chocolate Fondue

For best results, serve the fondue in a ceramic dessert fondue pot heated by an open flame. This fondue works with just about any fruit or sweet treat. You can use strawberries, pineapple, oranges, or even marshmallows. Whatever tastes great with chocolate will work.

1 (6-ounce) semisweet chocolate bar, broken into chunks

½ cup plus 2 tablespoons half-and-half

3 medium bananas, diagonally sliced

1 Fill a heavy pot halfway with water and bring to a boil over high heat. In a medium metal bowl, combine chocolate and half-and-half. Reduce heat to low and place the bowl on top of the pot. Melt chocolate for roughly 10 minutes, stirring regularly with a rubber spatula, until completely melted. Remove from heat.

2 Pour melted chocolate into a serving bowl. Use a fondue dipping fork to spear banana slices and dip them in warm chocolate.

SERVES 2

Per Serving:

Calories	437
Fat	18g
Protein	4g
Sodium	46mg
Fiber	5g
Carbohydrates	71g
Sugar	44g
Net Carbs	66g

Shrimp Creole

SERVES 2

Per Serving:

Calories	433
Fat	9g
Protein	27g
Sodium	490mg
Fiber	2g
Carbohydrates	60g
Sugar	4g
Net Carbs	58g

If you like your dishes a little more garlicky, add in an extra clove. It won't unbalance the flavor at all. If you want a little extra spice, you can use cayenne pepper instead of paprika.

3 teaspoons olive oil, divided

2 cups peeled and deveined shrimp

¼ cup chopped red onion

1 clove garlic, peeled and chopped

1 large tomato, sliced

1 medium celery stalk, sliced

¼ cup water

¼ teaspoon paprika

½ teaspoon dried thyme

2 cups cooked white rice

1 Heat 1 teaspoon oil in a medium frying pan over medium heat. Add shrimp and cook 2–3 minutes. Flip and cook another 2–3 minutes, until shrimp turn pink.

2 Push shrimp to the side of the frying pan and add remaining 2 teaspoons oil. Add onion and cook for about 5 minutes or until soft and translucent. Add garlic and sauté for 30 seconds.

3 Add tomato, celery, water, paprika, and thyme. Gently push down on tomato slices to break them up and squeeze out the juice. Reduce heat to low, cover, and simmer for about 15 minutes, until tomatoes are tender and juice from tomatoes is thoroughly mixed with water. Mix sauce with shrimp and serve over rice.

Eggplant Parmigiana

This cheesy eggplant delight may seem fancy, but it's a breeze to make. It's perfect served alone or alongside some vegetables, like green beans or asparagus.

1 cup tomato sauce

½ teaspoon onion powder

½ teaspoon garlic powder

½ teaspoon dried basil

½ teaspoon dried oregano

⅛ teaspoon salt

⅛ teaspoon ground black pepper

1 medium eggplant, cut into ¼" slices

6 (2-ounce) slices mozzarella cheese

¼ cup grated Parmesan cheese

SERVES 2

Per Serving:

Calories	786
Fat	48g
Protein	60g
Sodium	2,427mg
Fiber	17g
Carbohydrates	43g
Sugar	13g
Net Carbs	26g

1 Preheat oven to 350°F and spray an 8" × 8" baking pan with non-stick cooking spray.

2 In a medium bowl, add tomato sauce, onion powder, garlic powder, basil, oregano, salt, and pepper. Mix well.

3 Place eggplant flat on prepared baking pan. Spoon sauce onto eggplant. Cover eggplant with aluminum foil and bake 20 minutes or until tender. Remove from oven.

4 Remove foil and place mozzarella slices on top. Bake another 3–5 minutes, until mozzarella melts. Sprinkle with Parmesan cheese and serve hot.

Perfectly Cooked Steak

MAKE MINE MEDIUM RARE!

Ever wonder what the true difference is between "rare" and "well done"? It all comes down to cooking temperature. Rare steak is cooked to an internal temperature of 125°F, while the internal temperature of well-done steak is 160°F. Medium-rare, medium, and medium-well steaks are cooked to internal temperatures of 135°F, 145°F, and 155°F, respectively.

Steak is easier than you think, and it's a great meal for a first date. Add a nice side like rice, mashed potatoes, or some steamed vegetables to really impress your date.

½ teaspoon curry powder
¼ teaspoon salt
¼ teaspoon ground black pepper
4 tablespoons all-purpose flour
2 pounds round steak, sliced
3 tablespoons olive oil
1 small yellow onion, peeled and chopped
1 (10.75-ounce) can condensed cream of celery soup
1⅓ cups water
2 tablespoons Worcestershire sauce

1 In a small bowl, combine curry powder, salt, pepper, and flour. Coat beef in flour mixture.

2 Heat oil in a large skillet over medium heat and cook steak until browned, about 8 minutes per side. Remove steak from heat and wrap in aluminum foil.

3 Add onion and cook for about 5 minutes until soft and translucent.

4 Add soup, water, and Worcestershire sauce and stir. Cover and cook 20 minutes. Turn heat up to medium-high and cook for another 10 minutes.

5 Remove steak from aluminum foil and place on serving plate. Pour sauce over steak and serve hot.

Elegant Pot Roast

This recipe takes a while to cook, but it takes almost no time to put together. Once you get it going on the stove, you can sit back and relax for a bit before it's ready. Turn this into a complete meal by adding some small red potatoes and baby carrots to the pan with the roast.

1 (3-pound) chuck beef roast, patted dry

1 teaspoon salt

1 teaspoon ground black pepper

2 tablespoons all-purpose flour

2 tablespoons olive oil

1 (2-ounce) package instant onion soup mix

2 medium yellow onions, peeled and chopped

1 Rub roast with salt and pepper, then dust with flour.

2 Heat oil in a large frying pan over medium-high heat, then add roast. Brown roast on all sides, about 5 minutes per side.

3 Fill a medium saucepan halfway with water and bring to a boil. Add soup mix and stir to combine until fully dissolved. Simmer, uncovered, for 10 minutes and remove from heat.

4 Add 2 cups soup mixture and onions to the roast. Reduce heat to medium-low, cover, and simmer for 1½ hours or until meat is tender. Turn meat occasionally while simmering and add remaining soup mixture if needed. Serve hot.

SERVES 4

Per Serving:

Calories	647
Fat	46g
Protein	66g
Sodium	2,103mg
Fiber	3g
Carbohydrates	16g
Sugar	4g
Net Carbs	13g

Keto Bacon-Wrapped Chicken

SERVES 2

Per Serving:

Calories	275
Fat	13g
Protein	38g
Sodium	313mg
Fiber	0g
Carbohydrates	0g
Sugar	0g
Net Carbs	0g

THE CHURCH OF BACON

There's an officially sanctioned United Church of Bacon with more than twenty-five thousand members all following the eight bacon commandments. They're ordained to perform various religious services including weddings, baptisms, and funerals.

This simple chicken recipe is so easy and takes less than 5 minutes to prep. Serve with a keto-approved side like steamed broccoli for a complete meal.

4 (3-ounce) boneless, skinless chicken thighs
4 slices thin-cut bacon

1 Preheat oven to 375°F. Spray a 9" × 13" baking dish with nonstick cooking spray.

2 Wrap each chicken thigh in a slice of bacon. Place seam-side down in baking dish. Bake 20–30 minutes or until cooked through. Remove from oven and serve immediately.

Chicken Creole

GF

SERVES 4

Per Serving:

Calories	512
Fat	20g
Protein	39g
Sodium	1,337mg
Fiber	6g
Carbohydrates	47g
Sugar	9g
Net Carbs	41g

This recipe is designed to provide lots of sauce to mix in with the risotto. For extra flavor, use a flavored risotto package, like cheese or chicken.

1 tablespoon plus 1 teaspoon olive oil, divided

4 (7-ounce) bone-in, skinless chicken thighs

2 cloves garlic, peeled and chopped

1 small yellow onion, peeled and chopped

4 medium celery stalks, sliced into 1" pieces

1 medium green bell pepper, seeded and chopped

1¾ cups crushed tomatoes, with liquid

¼ teaspoon cayenne pepper

½ teaspoon dried thyme

½ teaspoon dried parsley

1 bay leaf

½ teaspoon salt

½ teaspoon ground black pepper

4 cups Herb Risotto (see recipe in chapter 6)

1 Heat 1 teaspoon oil in a large, deep-sided frying pan over medium-high heat. Add chicken and cook until browned, about 5 minutes. Flip and cook another 5 minutes until browned on both sides. Transfer to a plate.

2 Scrape off brown bits in the frying pan and discard. Heat remaining 1 tablespoon oil over medium heat. Add garlic and onion and cook for about 5 minutes, until onion is soft and translucent. Add celery, bell pepper, tomatoes, cayenne pepper, thyme, parsley, bay leaf, salt, and black pepper.

3 Return chicken to pan and reduce heat to medium-low. Cover and simmer 25 minutes. Remove bay leaf and serve over risotto.

Teriyaki Shrimp

Here's a super-quick dish for date night! Serve the shrimp with rice and steamed vegetables. If the sauce isn't sweet enough for you, just add 2 tablespoons maple syrup.

½ cup low-sodium soy sauce

2 tablespoons plus 2 teaspoons cooking sherry

2 cups small frozen raw shrimp, thawed, peeled, and deveined

2 tablespoons olive oil

1   Combine soy sauce and cooking sherry in a small bowl, then pour into a large resealable plastic bag. Place shrimp in marinade and shake until shrimp are fully coated. Refrigerate for 30 minutes.

2   Heat oil in a medium frying pan over medium heat. Sauté shrimp until they turn pink. Serve hot.

SERVES 2	
Per Serving:	
Calories	423
Fat	21g
Protein	41g
Sodium	1,978mg
Fiber	0g
Carbohydrates	10g
Sugar	3g
Net Carbs	10g

Gluten-Free Five-Cheese Pasta

This one-step recipe is perfect for a busy day. If you have the extra time, you can make your own marinara sauce by combining tomato sauce, olive oil, garlic, red pepper flakes, basil, and a pinch of salt.

1 (25-ounce) jar marinara sauce

1 teaspoon garlic powder

1 tablespoon Italian seasoning

¼ cup shredded mozzarella cheese

¼ cup part-skim ricotta cheese

¼ cup grated Parmesan cheese

¼ cup shredded fontina cheese

¼ cup shredded Asiago cheese

8 ounces gluten-free penne, cooked

SERVES 2	
Per Serving:	
Calories	758
Fat	20g
Protein	31g
Sodium	879mg
Fiber	12g
Carbohydrates	121g
Sugar	0g
Net Carbs	109g

Heat a large skillet over medium heat. Add marinara sauce, garlic powder, and Italian seasoning and cook about 5 minutes, until heated through. Add cheeses and cook until melted together, about 10 minutes. Stir in cooked penne and toss. Serve immediately.

Chicken Lo Mein

SERVES 2

Per Serving:

Calories	526
Fat	19g
Protein	43g
Sodium	2,045mg
Fiber	7g
Carbohydrates	46g
Sugar	9g
Net Carbs	39g

This recipe makes great leftovers, so feel free to double the recipe and save some for later in the week. If the sauce isn't sweet enough for you, add a teaspoon of granulated sugar to the chicken broth mixture. If you like more spice, add ⅛ teaspoon of red pepper flakes.

2 (6-ounce) boneless, skinless chicken breasts, cubed

1 tablespoon low-sodium soy sauce

2 (3-ounce) packages ramen noodles

½ cup low-sodium chicken broth

2 tablespoons oyster sauce

1 tablespoon canola oil

2 cups frozen broccoli

1 cup frozen carrots

2 medium scallions, cut into 1" pieces

1 In a small bowl, toss chicken with soy sauce. Cover and refrigerate 30 minutes.

2 Cook ramen according to package instructions. Drain pasta, rinse with cold water, and drain again. Set aside.

3 In a small bowl, combine broth and oyster sauce. Set aside.

4 Heat oil in a medium frying pan over medium-high heat. Add chicken and sauté about 10 minutes until cooked through.

5 Add broccoli and carrots. Cook 1 minute, then add chicken broth mixture. Bring to a boil, reduce heat to medium-low, and simmer for 5 minutes.

6 Stir in noodles and scallion. Cook until heated through, about 3 minutes. Serve hot.

Dairy-Free Fettuccine Alfredo

This creamy Alfredo sauce is rich and smooth, but it doesn't have any harmful dairy. Feel free to add in some chopped chicken breasts for extra protein.

½ pound fettuccine

2 teaspoons olive oil

½ medium yellow onion, peeled and finely chopped

3 cloves garlic, peeled and chopped

1 tablespoon plus 2 teaspoons all-purpose flour

½ (13.5-ounce) can full-fat coconut milk

½ cup low-sodium chicken broth

2 teaspoons lemon juice

¼ teaspoon salt

¼ teaspoon ground black pepper

1 tablespoon chopped parsley

⅛ teaspoon red pepper flakes

SERVES 2	
Per Serving:	
Calories	731
Fat	31g
Protein	16g
Sodium	348mg
Fiber	5g
Carbohydrates	103g
Sugar	9g
Net Carbs	98g

1 Cook fettuccine according to package instructions. Drain, then rinse with cold water, and drain again. Set aside.

2 Heat oil in a large skillet over medium heat. Add onion and garlic and cook for about 5 minutes, until onion is soft and translucent. Add flour and cook for about 3 minutes until golden brown, whisking constantly.

3 Add milk and broth and bring to a simmer. Reduce heat to low and cook 10 minutes, stirring constantly until thickened. Stir in lemon juice, salt, black pepper, parsley, and red pepper flakes. Pour over fettucine and toss to combine. Serve warm.

Dairy-Free Chicken Cacciatore

This classic Italian dish will ensure you get another date. The rustic flavors in the sauce meld perfectly with the vegetables and seasoning to create a wonderful comfort food.

½ teaspoon olive oil

4 (3-ounce) boneless, skinless chicken thighs

1 medium yellow onion, peeled and chopped

1 clove garlic, peeled and chopped

½ (26-ounce) can strained tomatoes

½ cup diced tomatoes

½ cup low-sodium beef broth

1 bay leaf

⅛ teaspoon red pepper flakes

1 Heat oil in a large skillet over medium-high heat. Add chicken and cook for about 5 minutes until browned. Flip and cook another 5 minutes, until browned. Remove from pan and set aside.

2 Add onion and garlic to skillet and cook 3 minutes, then add strained tomatoes, diced tomatoes, broth, bay leaf, red pepper flakes, and chicken. Reduce heat to medium, cover, and cook 20 minutes or until chicken is cooked through. Remove bay leaf. Serve immediately.

Keto Balsamic Chicken

DF K

This simple balsamic glaze pairs perfectly with the milder flavor of chicken.

¼ cup olive oil

2 tablespoons low-sodium soy sauce

½ cup balsamic vinegar

2 cloves garlic, peeled and chopped

1 small yellow onion, peeled and sliced

2 teaspoons dried oregano

¼ teaspoon ground black pepper

4 (6-ounce) boneless, skinless chicken breasts

SERVES 2	
Per Serving:	
Calories	665
Fat	36g
Protein	69g
Sodium	1,167mg
Fiber	1g
Carbohydrates	21g
Sugar	11g
Net Carbs	20g

1 Preheat oven to 375°F. Spray an 8" × 8" baking pan with nonstick cooking spray.

2 In a small bowl, combine oil, soy sauce, vinegar, garlic, onion, oregano, and pepper. Add chicken to pan, top with onion mixture, and bake 35–40 minutes or until chicken is cooked through. Serve immediately.

Chicken Cordon Bleu

This classic French dish is just as good the next day. Double the recipe so you have an easy late-night snack or quick lunch.

2 (6-ounce) boneless, skinless chicken breasts

¼ teaspoon salt

⅛ teaspoon ground black pepper

4 (2-ounce) slices Swiss cheese

4 (2-ounce) slices deli ham

¼ cup dried bread crumbs

SERVES 2	
Per Serving:	
Calories	759
Fat	42g
Protein	85g
Sodium	2,408mg
Fiber	1g
Carbohydrates	13g
Sugar	1g
Net Carbs	12g

1 Preheat oven to 350°F and grease an 8" × 8" baking dish.

2 Using a meat mallet or rolling pin, pound chicken breasts to ¼" thickness, then season with salt and pepper. Place 2 slices cheese and 2 slices ham on top of each, then roll up chicken. Place chicken seam-side down in prepared baking dish.

3 Sprinkle bread crumbs on top and bake 30–35 minutes or until chicken is cooked through. Serve immediately.

Honey Lemon Salmon

Add some extra lemon slices for garnish and a side of risotto for a perfect date night. You can double the recipe and use leftovers to make a salad for the next day.

2 tablespoons honey

1½ tablespoons fresh lemon juice

2 tablespoons low-sodium soy sauce

1 clove garlic, peeled and chopped

1 tablespoon olive oil

2 (6-ounce) salmon fillets

½ teaspoon salt

¼ teaspoon ground black pepper

1 In a small bowl, combine honey, lemon juice, soy sauce, and garlic.

2 Heat oil in a large skillet over medium-high heat. Add salmon skin-side down, then sprinkle with salt and pepper. Cook 5–7 minutes, until flaky and crispy. Add honey-lemon mixture, then flip salmon, cooking another 2 minutes. Serve immediately.

SERVES 2

Per Serving:

Calories	469
Fat	21g
Protein	46g
Sodium	1,151mg
Fiber	0g
Carbohydrates	21g
Sugar	19g
Net Carbs	21g

HEALTHY FISH

Fish like salmon, tuna, and cod are perfect sources of lean protein with plenty of omega-3 fats and vitamin D. Try to incorporate at least one serving of fish per week. If you choose a type of fish with a mild taste (tilapia, trout, haddock), you can personalize the flavor however you want!

Flatbread Pizzas

SERVES 4

Per Serving:

Calories	368
Fat	14g
Protein	19g
Sodium	565mg
Fiber	3g
Carbohydrates	44g
Sugar	3g
Net Carbs	41g

Flatbreads make an easy substitute for pizza dough, letting you whip up a healthy pizza from your own kitchen. No more delivery! Feel free to add whatever toppings you'd like.

4 (7") flatbreads
1 cup marinara sauce
1½ cups shredded mozzarella cheese

1 Preheat oven to 375°F.

2 Place flatbreads on an ungreased rimmed baking sheet. Add 4 tablespoons sauce to each flatbread and spread evenly, making sure to leave ½" of room around the edges. Top each flatbread with equal amounts of cheese. Bake 10–15 minutes or until cheese is melted and bubbly.

Honey Mustard Chicken

SERVES 4

Per Serving:

Calories	369
Fat	12g
Protein	44g
Sodium	1,141mg
Fiber	0g
Carbohydrates	17g
Sugar	17g
Net Carbs	17g

Honey and mustard is a classic combination, the sweetness of the honey mixing perfectly with the spiciness of the mustard. Add rice and steamed vegetables for a complete and healthy date night meal.

¼ cup Dijon mustard
¼ cup honey
1 tablespoon olive oil
1 teaspoon salt
2 pounds boneless, skinless chicken thighs

1 Preheat oven to 350°F.

2 In a small bowl, combine mustard, honey, oil, and salt.

3 Add chicken to a 9" × 13" baking dish then coat with honey mustard sauce. Bake 35–45 minutes or until the internal temperature reaches 165°F. Remove from oven and serve immediately.

Seared Scallops and Mashed Potatoes

Add more whole milk or butter if your mashed potatoes are too dry. You can make them a bit fancier by adding some herbs, like chives, parsley, or rosemary.

1 pound Yukon gold potatoes, peeled and cubed

1½ teaspoons salt, divided

½ teaspoon ground black pepper, divided

2 teaspoons garlic powder

⅔ cup whole milk

¼ cup unsalted butter

1 tablespoon olive oil

8 medium sea scallops

½ medium yellow onion, peeled and chopped

SERVES 2

Per Serving:

Calories	597
Fat	32g
Protein	28g
Sodium	1,497mg
Fiber	4g
Carbohydrates	48g
Sugar	7g
Net Carbs	44g

1 Place potatoes in a large pot and cover with cold water and ½ teaspoon salt. Bring to a boil over high heat, then cook for about 10 minutes or until potatoes are easily pierced with a fork. Drain and return to the pot.

2 Add another ½ teaspoon salt, ¼ teaspoon pepper, garlic powder, milk, and butter and mash well until potatoes are smooth.

3 Heat oil in a large frying pan over medium-high heat. Add scallops and season with remaining ½ teaspoon salt and remaining ¼ teaspoon pepper. Add onion and cook 4–5 minutes, until golden brown. Flip scallops and cook 4–5 minutes, until golden brown on both sides. Serve scallops over mashed potatoes.

Steak Salad

SERVES 4

Per Serving:

Calories	599
Fat	44g
Protein	33g
Sodium	1,928mg
Fiber	5g
Carbohydrates	22g
Sugar	10g
Net Carbs	17g

HOW TO CUT BEEF ACROSS THE GRAIN

If you look at a piece of steak, you will see lines running across it. These are the muscle fibers, or "grains." To cut beef across the grain, simply cut across—not parallel to—the muscle fibers. This helps tenderize the beef by shocking the muscle fibers.

This salad is light enough for lunch but hearty enough for a special dinner. To give the dressing a bit more kick, add 1 minced garlic clove, 1 tablespoon lime juice, and 1 tablespoon Dijon mustard.

1 (12-ounce) top sirloin steak

2 teaspoons salt

1 teaspoon ground black pepper

6 tablespoons olive oil, divided

¼ cup balsamic vinegar

¼ cup chopped fresh cilantro

1 cup halved cherry tomatoes

½ cup chopped red onion

1 cup crumbled feta cheese

1 medium cucumber, sliced into half moons

1 medium head butter lettuce, chopped

1 medium avocado, peeled, pitted, and sliced

1 Heat a medium frying pan over medium-high heat. Rub steak with salt, pepper, and 1 tablespoon oil on all sides. Place steak in pan and cook for 10 minutes on each side.

2 Using a meat thermometer, check steak at its thickest portion to make sure the internal temperature is at least 165°F. Transfer to a cutting board to rest for at least 5 minutes, then slice against the grain.

3 In a small bowl, combine remaining 5 tablespoons olive oil, vinegar, and cilantro. Set aside.

4 In a large bowl, add tomatoes, onion, cheese, cucumber, lettuce, and avocado. Toss to mix. Divide equally into two serving bowls and top with sliced steak and dressing.

CHAPTER 11

When the Parents Visit

Sunday French Toast

SERVES 4

Per Serving (2 slices):	
Calories	320
Fat	15g
Protein	12g
Sodium	529mg
Fiber	2g
Carbohydrates	33g
Sugar	7g
Net Carbs	31g

Feel free to experiment with different types of bread, such as French or sourdough.

4 large eggs, beaten

¼ teaspoon salt

¼ teaspoon ground black pepper

½ cup whole milk

½ cup half-and-half

1 teaspoon vanilla extract

2 tablespoons unsalted butter

8 (1-ounce) slices white bread

1 In a shallow bowl, whisk together eggs, salt, pepper, milk, half-and-half, and vanilla.

2 Heat butter in a large frying pan over medium-low heat. Dip 4 slices bread in egg mixture, then lay flat in the frying pan.

3 Cook about 5 minutes, until bread is browned, then flip and cook an additional 5 minutes. Repeat with remaining bread and egg mixture.

Chili con Carne

SERVES 4

Per Serving:	
Calories	473
Fat	23g
Protein	31g
Sodium	621mg
Fiber	9g
Carbohydrates	34g
Sugar	7g
Net Carbs	25g

Serve chili with a dollop of sour cream, and a sprinkling of shredded Cheddar cheese and sliced scallions.

2 tablespoons unsalted butter

1 pound 85% lean ground beef

½ medium red onion, peeled and chopped

½ medium green bell pepper, seeded and chopped

1 tablespoon chili powder

½ teaspoon ground cumin

½ teaspoon garlic powder

2 cups canned kidney beans, with liquid

2 cups canned crushed tomatoes, drained

1 Melt butter in a medium saucepan over medium heat. Add ground beef and sauté 4 minutes. Add onion and bell pepper and sauté 2 minutes, until beef is fully cooked and no longer pink. Drain.

2 Stir in chili powder, cumin, garlic powder, beans, and tomatoes. Reduce heat to low, cover, and simmer for 30 minutes. Serve hot.

Baked Potato

After cooking, you can load the potato with sour cream, bacon bits, chives, shredded cheese, or your own favorite toppings! You can use sweet potatoes instead of russet, but bake them at 425°F instead.

4 medium russet potatoes

2 tablespoons unsalted butter

1 Preheat oven to 400°F.

2 Pierce potatoes four times with a fork. Transfer to an ungreased baking sheet and place on middle oven rack.

3 Bake 45 minutes or until a fork inserted into potato goes through easily. Remove from oven and cut in half lengthwise. Add butter evenly between potatoes and serve hot.

SERVES 4	
Per Serving:	
Calories	160
Fat	6g
Protein	3g
Sodium	0mg
Fiber	2g
Carbohydrates	26g
Sugar	1g
Net Carbs	24g

Gourmet Vegetable Medley

Steaming vegetables in chicken broth instead of water gives them extra flavor. Before serving, you can toss them with some salt, pepper, garlic powder, and butter. Your parents will be impressed!

1 cup low-sodium chicken broth

1½ teaspoons dried parsley

2 medium carrots, peeled and cut into ¼" slices

1 medium green bell pepper, seeded and cubed

2 medium zucchini, cut into thin diagonal slices

1 Add chicken broth and parsley to a medium saucepan. Place metal steamer inside the pan, making sure the bottom doesn't touch the broth. Bring broth to a boil over medium-high heat.

2 Add carrots to steamer. Cover and cook for about 2 minutes, then add peppers. Cook for another 2 minutes, then add zucchini. Continue steaming until vegetables are tender, about 2 minutes. Drain and serve hot.

SERVES 4	
Per Serving:	
Calories	46
Fat	0g
Protein	2g
Sodium	74mg
Fiber	3g
Carbohydrates	8g
Sugar	5g
Net Carbs	5g

Baked Ham with Soy Glaze

SERVES 4	
Per Serving:	
Calories	445
Fat	18g
Protein	61g
Sodium	4,137mg
Fiber	0g
Carbohydrates	10g
Sugar	9g
Net Carbs	10g

This is a great recipe for those occasions when you want to entertain your parents instead of being stuck in the kitchen cooking. You can have the ham prepared in advance, then pop it in the oven 45 minutes before you're ready to eat.

2 tablespoons low-sodium soy sauce

1 teaspoon honey mustard

2 teaspoons light brown sugar

1 teaspoon pineapple juice

1 (3-pound) precooked ham

1 Preheat oven to 325°F. Grease a 9" × 13" baking dish with nonstick cooking spray.

2 In a small bowl, combine soy sauce, mustard, sugar, and pineapple juice. Place ham in prepared baking dish and baste with glaze.

3 Bake 45 minutes, brushing with glaze several times until the internal temperature reaches 145°F. Remove from oven, slice, and serve hot.

Nutmeg Mashed Potatoes

SERVES 4	
Per Serving:	
Calories	425
Fat	15g
Protein	8g
Sodium	612mg
Fiber	5g
Carbohydrates	67g
Sugar	3g
Net Carbs	62g

An old tradition calls for sprinkling mashed potatoes with nutmeg for good luck!

4 large russet potatoes, peeled and cut into quarters

4 tablespoons unsalted butter

2½ tablespoons heavy cream

¼ teaspoon ground nutmeg

1 teaspoon salt

½ teaspoon ground black pepper

1 Fill a medium saucepan with enough water to cover potatoes and bring to a boil over medium-high heat.

2 Add potatoes and boil until tender, about 5 minutes. Drain and transfer to a medium bowl.

3 Add butter. Mash potatoes and butter using a fork. Add cream a bit at a time as you are mashing until potatoes are fluffy. Stir in nutmeg, salt, and pepper and serve.

Beef Stew

Beef Stew is a great meal for cold winter days. Serve this to your parents after the big football game! Store the leftovers in a sealed container in the refrigerator to enjoy during the week.

2 pounds cubed stewing beef

2 tablespoons all-purpose flour

2 tablespoons olive oil

½ medium white onion, peeled and diced

1½ cups low-sodium beef broth

2 cups tomato sauce

2 tablespoons low-sodium soy sauce

2 tablespoons light brown sugar

1 teaspoon salt

1 teaspoon ground black pepper

1 cup baby carrots

4 large russet potatoes, peeled and cubed

SERVES 4

Per Serving:

Calories	752
Fat	17g
Protein	61g
Sodium	2,243mg
Fiber	8g
Carbohydrates	92g
Sugar	17g
Net Carbs	4g

1 Toss beef with flour to lightly coat. Heat oil in a large saucepan over medium heat.

2 Add onion and cook for about 5 minutes, until soft and translucent. Add beef and brown on all sides, about 5 minutes per side.

3 Pour broth over beef. Add tomato sauce, soy sauce, brown sugar, salt, and pepper. Bring to a boil. Reduce heat to low, cover, and simmer for 1 hour.

4 Add carrots and potatoes. Cook for another 30 minutes or until potatoes are tender. Serve immediately.

Bacon and Mushroom Stuffing for Turkey

MAKES 7 CUPS

Per Serving (½ cup):

Calories	119
Fat	5g
Protein	6g
Sodium	307mg
Fiber	1g
Carbohydrates	9g
Sugar	1g
Net Carbs	8g

HOW TO STUFF A TURKEY

Baking stuffing alongside a turkey is the easiest way to prepare it. But if you prefer your stuffing to cook inside the bird, here's how to do it: Hold the turkey so the neck is facing upward. Loosely fill the neck cavity with the stuffing; the stuffing should fill the turkey without being packed tightly. Tie the drumsticks together with string to seal the opening. After roasting, make sure that the interior of the stuffing reaches 165°F and the thickest part of the turkey thigh registers 180°F on a food thermometer.

Not sure how much stuffing to make? A general rule of thumb is to prepare ½ cup of stuffing per pound of turkey. This recipe makes just the right amount for a 14- or 15-pound turkey.

¾ **pound bacon, chopped**

1 cup chopped yellow onion

1 cup chopped celery

1 cup chopped portobello mushrooms

8 cups dried bread cubes

1 tablespoon dried sage

1 teaspoon dried rosemary

1 teaspoon dried thyme

½ **teaspoon salt**

1 cup low-sodium chicken broth, warmed

1 Preheat oven to 400°F. Spray a 9" × 13" baking dish with nonstick cooking spray.

2 Heat large frying pan over medium-high heat. Add bacon and cook 7–8 minutes or until crispy, stirring occasionally. Reduce heat to medium and add onion and celery. Cook 3 minutes, then add mushrooms. Cook for about 2 minutes or until onion is soft and translucent. Transfer to a large mixing bowl.

3 Add bread cubes to mixing bowl. Stir in sage, rosemary, thyme, and salt. Slowly add broth, mixing to combine.

4 Transfer stuffing to prepared baking dish. Cover tightly with foil and bake 25 minutes. Remove foil and bake 15–20 minutes longer or until the edges start to brown.

Garden Salad

For a flavorful homemade salad dressing, combine ½ cup olive oil, 2 tablespoons lemon juice, ½ teaspoon garlic powder, ½ teaspoon salt, 2 teaspoon ground mustard, and 2½ tablespoons honey. Whisk it together and pour over the salad.

8 cups chopped iceberg lettuce leaves

1 pint grape tomatoes, halved

4 medium celery stalks, chopped

2 cups sliced button mushrooms

2 cups chopped baby carrots

2 medium cucumbers, cut into half moons

6 medium radishes, halved lengthwise and sliced

½ medium red onion, peeled and sliced

1 cup large croutons

½ cup grated Parmesan cheese

SERVES 4	
Per Serving:	
Calories	165
Fat	3g
Protein	9g
Sodium	339mg
Fiber	6g
Carbohydrates	24g
Sugar	11g
Net Carbs	18g

Combine all ingredients in a large bowl. Mix well.

Roasted Chicken

Once you've mastered the basic skill of roasting chicken, try a few creative variations, such as placing lemon slices underneath the skin for extra flavor.

1 (5-pound) whole chicken

1½ tablespoons olive oil

2 teaspoons dried rosemary

2 teaspoons dried thyme

SERVES 4	
Per Serving:	
Calories	324
Fat	17g
Protein	41g
Sodium	522mg
Fiber	0g
Carbohydrates	1g
Sugar	0g
Net Carbs	1g

1 Preheat oven to 375°F. Remove the chicken giblets.

2 Rub oil, rosemary, and thyme over the chicken. Place chicken on a rack in a 15" × 9" roasting pan and bake for 1 hour. Using a meat thermometer, check chicken at its thickest portion to make sure the internal temperature is at least 175°F. Transfer to large plate and let rest for 5 minutes before serving.

Sweet-and-Sour Pork

SERVES 4

Per Serving:

Calories	504
Fat	12g
Protein	27g
Sodium	152mg
Fiber	1g
Carbohydrates	68g
Sugar	12g
Net Carbs	67g

A VERSATILE SAUCE

The secret to this popular Chinese takeout dish is the sauce. Once you know how to make it, you can create variations using chicken, shrimp, or tofu.

This sweet-and-sour recipe doesn't use cornstarch, which means your sauce won't be as thick as the traditional dish, but it will be much healthier. For a slightly different flavor, try using brown sugar instead of white granulated sugar.

⅓ cup white vinegar

2 tablespoons ketchup

3 tablespoons granulated sugar

⅓ cup water

2 tablespoons canola oil

1 (1-pound) pork tenderloin, cubed

½ large green bell pepper, seeded and cubed

¼ cup halved baby carrots

1 medium scallion, diced

4 cups cooked white rice

1 In a small bowl, combine vinegar, ketchup, sugar, and water. Set aside.

2 Heat oil in a medium frying pan over medium heat. Add pork and cook about 3 minutes per side, until browned. Drain off excess fat from pan.

3 Add ketchup sauce to the pan. Reduce heat to medium-low, cover, and simmer for 45 minutes or until tender.

4 Raise heat to medium and add green pepper and carrots. Cover and simmer for 10 minutes or until vegetables are tender. Stir in scallion and serve hot over rice.

Chicken Risotto with Vegetables

SERVES 4

Per Serving:

Calories	440
Fat	8g
Protein	43g
Sodium	860mg
Fiber	3g
Carbohydrates	47g
Sugar	6g
Net Carbs	44g

If you prefer, you can leave the skin on the chicken, but make sure to spoon out any excess fat from the saucepan before adding the carrots and other vegetables.

1 tablespoon olive oil

2 cloves garlic, peeled and chopped

½ small yellow onion, peeled and chopped

4 (6-ounce) boneless, skinless chicken breasts, cut into bite-sized pieces

2 medium tomatoes, chopped

4 medium carrots, peeled and diced

½ teaspoon salt

¼ teaspoon ground black pepper

1½ cups arborio rice

4½ cups low-sodium chicken broth, divided

2 teaspoons dried parsley

1. Heat oil in a large saucepan over medium heat. Add garlic and onion and cook for about 5 minutes until onion is soft and translucent. Add chicken breasts and cook 5 minutes, then flip and cook an additional 5 minutes.

2. Add tomatoes, carrots, salt, and pepper and stir. Cook 1 minute, then stir in rice and 1 cup broth. Bring to a boil, then reduce heat to medium-low. Stir in parsley and cook 5 minutes, stirring constantly, until broth is nearly absorbed. Add ½ cup broth and cook 3 minutes, until broth is nearly absorbed. Repeat with remaining 3 cups broth until rice is thick and creamy, about 20 minutes.

3. Using a meat thermometer, check chicken at its thickest portion to make sure the internal temperature is at least 165°F. Remove from heat and let rest for 5 minutes before serving.

Steak and Potatoes in Mushroom Sauce

This classic meal is about as simple and delicious as it gets. You can use sweet potatoes instead of baking potatoes if you prefer a sweeter taste. For extra flavor, add in some chopped onion with the mushrooms.

4 (10-ounce) boneless rib-eye steaks

4 cloves garlic, peeled and halved

½ cup barbecue sauce, divided

4 large russet potatoes

½ teaspoon salt

½ teaspoon ground black pepper

4 tablespoons olive oil

8 ounces fresh brown mushrooms, sliced

1 Preheat oven broiler.

2 Rub steaks with garlic, then place steaks in a 9" × 13" broiling pan and brush tops with 4 tablespoons barbecue sauce. Broil 8–10 minutes, then flip and brush with remaining 4 tablespoons barbecue sauce. Broil an additional 8–10 minutes. Remove from oven and set aside.

3 Pierce potatoes four times with a fork. Place potatoes on microwave-safe plate and cook on high heat 4–6 minutes. Slice potatoes open and season with salt and pepper.

4 Heat oil in a medium frying pan over medium-low heat. Add mushrooms and sauté 5 minutes until browned and tender. Place steaks and potatoes on two large plates, then spoon mushrooms on top. Serve immediately.

SERVES 4

Per Serving:

Calories	859
Fat	51g
Protein	46g
Sodium	708mg
Fiber	5g
Carbohydrates	44g
Sugar	12g
Net Carbs	39g

QUICK AND CHEESY MAC

Use this recipe as an ultra-speedy side dish! Combine 4 cups cooked penne, ¼ cup low-fat plain yogurt, 2 cups shredded Cheddar cheese, 1 teaspoon garlic powder, 1 teaspoon onion powder, 1 teaspoon salt, and 1 teaspoon ground black pepper in a large saucepan and heat over low heat until cheese is melted into a sauce.

Beef Stroganoff

SERVES 4	
Per Serving:	
Calories	904
Fat	33g
Protein	51g
Sodium	542mg
Fiber	5g
Carbohydrates	84g
Sugar	7g
Net Carbs	79g

For more sauce to coat the noodles, add an extra ½ cup of both the beef broth and the sour cream. Garnish with chopped chives and an extra dollop of sour cream.

1 pound egg noodles

2 tablespoons all-purpose flour

½ teaspoon salt

½ teaspoon ground black pepper

½ teaspoon dried basil

2 pounds cubed stewing beef

4 tablespoons olive oil, divided

1 clove garlic, peeled and chopped

1 medium yellow onion, peeled and chopped

2 cups fresh portobello mushrooms, sliced

1 cup low-sodium beef broth

½ cup sour cream

1 Cook noodles according to package instructions. Drain and keep warm.

2 In a small bowl, combine flour, salt, pepper, and basil. Toss beef in flour mixture until fully coated.

3 Heat 2 tablespoons oil in a medium frying pan over medium heat. Add beef and brown on all sides, about 5 minutes per side. Remove beef and set aside.

4 Scrape off brown bits in the frying pan and discard. Heat remaining 2 tablespoons oil over medium heat. Add garlic, onion, and mushrooms and cook for about 5 minutes, until onion is soft and translucent.

5 Return beef to the pan and add broth. Cook about 5–7 minutes, until heated through, then stir in sour cream. Heat 5 minutes, stirring occasionally, until warmed through. Serve hot over noodles.

Chicken in Walnut Sauce

Walnut crumbs are available in most grocery stores, but you can also buy walnut pieces and crush them into crumbs. Feel free to add more chili sauce if you like the heat.

3 teaspoons olive oil

8 (3-ounce) boneless, skinless chicken thighs

½ small white onion, peeled and chopped

2 cloves garlic, peeled and chopped

1 cup low-sodium chicken broth

4 tablespoons walnut crumbs

1 teaspoon chili sauce

2 ounces blanched snow peas

1 cup cooked white rice

SERVES 4

Per Serving:

Calories	388
Fat	25g
Protein	24g
Sodium	142mg
Fiber	1g
Carbohydrates	17g
Sugar	2g
Net Carbs	16g

1   Heat oil in a large, deep-sided frying pan over medium heat. Add chicken thighs and cook 7 minutes per side, until browned on both sides. Transfer to a large plate covered with a paper towel and set aside.

2   Reduce heat to low and add onion and garlic to pan. Cook for about 5 minutes or until onion is soft and translucent. Add broth, walnut crumbs, and chili sauce. Raise heat to medium-high and bring to a boil, stirring constantly.

3   Add snow peas and chicken thighs and reduce heat to medium-low. Cover and simmer for about 15 minutes, stirring occasionally. Using a meat thermometer, check chicken at its thickest portion to make sure the internal temperature is at least 165°F. Serve hot over rice.

Sausage and Tortellini Soup

SERVES 6	
Per Serving:	
Calories	365
Fat	10g
Protein	24g
Sodium	1,610mg
Fiber	6g
Carbohydrates	44g
Sugar	9g
Net Carbs	38g

This hearty soup freezes well, so you can make a large pot and have leftovers ready for a quick meal. Serve with a crusty bread, like sourdough or a French baguette.

1 pound sweet Italian sausage

3 large carrots, peeled and finely chopped

1 large yellow onion, peeled and chopped

1 medium celery stalk, chopped

2 cloves garlic, peeled and chopped

1½ teaspoons Italian seasoning

1 teaspoon salt

3 cups low-sodium beef broth

1 (28-ounce) can diced tomatoes, with liquid

1 cup tomato sauce

1 cup sliced zucchini

3 cups cheese tortellini

1 Heat a large pot over medium-high heat. Add sausage and sauté about 10 minutes, until browned. Drain excess fat, reserving 1 tablespoon in the pot.

2 Add carrots, onion, celery, and garlic and sauté for about 5 minutes or until onions are soft and translucent. Add Italian seasoning, salt, broth, tomatoes, and tomato sauce, stirring well. Bring to a boil, reduce heat to medium-low, and simmer for 25 minutes or until carrots are tender.

3 Add zucchini, stir, and cook 15 minutes, then add tortellini and cook another 10 minutes. Serve warm.

Dairy-Free Garlic Shrimp Pasta

If you can find dairy-free grated Parmesan cheese, feel free to sprinkle some on top of the pasta. For some extra vegetables, add in 2 cups fresh mixed vegetables, like carrots, broccoli, and green beans.

1 pound linguine

¼ cup olive oil

4 cloves garlic, peeled and chopped

½ teaspoon red pepper flakes

1 cup low-sodium chicken broth

½ cup plus 2 tablespoons chopped fresh parsley, divided

1 pound raw large shrimp, peeled and deveined

2 tablespoons lemon juice

1 teaspoon salt

¼ teaspoon ground black pepper

SERVES 4	
Per Serving:	
Calories	690
Fat	18g
Protein	43g
Sodium	951mg
Fiber	4g
Carbohydrates	87g
Sugar	5g
Net Carbs	83g

1. Cook linguine according to package instructions. Drain, then rinse with cold water, and drain again. Set aside.

2. Heat oil in a large skillet over medium heat. Add garlic and red pepper flakes and sauté about 1 minute until fragrant, stirring constantly. Add broth and ½ cup parsley and bring to a low simmer. Add shrimp and cook for about 5 minutes, until shrimp are pink.

3. Remove from heat, then add linguine, lemon juice, salt, and black pepper. Toss to mix, then transfer to serving bowls. Top with remaining 2 tablespoons parsley and serve.

Dairy-Free Morning Coffee Cake

This coffee cake is perfect for a weekend breakfast. You can also substitute in ⅔ cup applesauce instead of the oil for an even healthier version.

2 cups all-purpose flour

2 teaspoons baking soda

1 teaspoon baking powder

½ tablespoon plus ½ teaspoon cinnamon, divided

1 teaspoon salt

⅔ cup canola oil

1 cup full-fat coconut milk, room temperature

½ cup plus ½ tablespoon granulated sugar, divided

2 large eggs

1 teaspoon vanilla extract

1. Preheat oven to 375°F. Line an 8" × 8" baking pan with parchment paper.

2. In a small bowl, add flour, baking soda, baking powder, ½ tablespoon cinnamon, and salt. Mix well.

3. In a large bowl, combine oil, milk, ½ cup sugar, eggs, and vanilla. Whisk until fully combined, then add in flour mixture. Stir until combined. Pour batter into prepared baking pan.

4. In a small bowl, combine remaining ½ teaspoon cinnamon and remaining ½ tablespoon sugar. Sprinkle over batter. Bake 30–40 minutes or until a toothpick inserted into the middle comes out clean. Cool in pan for 5 minutes, then transfer to a wire rack. Serve warm or at room temperature.

SERVES 8

Per Serving:	
Calories	393
Fat	25g
Protein	5g
Sodium	394mg
Fiber	1g
Carbohydrates	37g
Sugar	14g
Net Carbs	36g

EXPENSIVE EXTRACT

Vanilla is the second most expensive flavor in the world after saffron. It's incredibly labor-intensive to produce, with each flower being individually hand-pollinated and hand-picked. It can often take as long as three years between planting and sale of a vanilla bean.

Mustard Salmon and Orzo

HOW TO BUY SALMON

It's best to purchase wild-caught salmon rather than farmed salmon, as the wild-caught variety offers better nutritional content and has a safer, more regulated catching process. Make sure the salmon doesn't have any brown spots and looks moist. Choose king salmon for its large size or sockeye for its stronger flavor.

To save some time, you can buy prepackaged flavored risotto instead of the orzo. This meal goes great with some steamed vegetables, like asparagus, green beans, or broccoli.

2 tablespoons unsalted butter

1 medium yellow onion, peeled and chopped

1½ cups orzo

1½ teaspoons salt, divided

2½ cups water

¼ cup chopped parsley

2 tablespoons Dijon mustard

2 tablespoons olive oil

4 (6-ounce) salmon fillets

1 Preheat oven to 425°F. Line a baking sheet with aluminum foil.

2 Melt butter in a medium saucepan over medium heat. Add onion and sauté for 5 minutes until soft and translucent. Add orzo, 1 teaspoon salt, and water. Stir and bring to a boil. Cover, then reduce heat to low and simmer for 8–10 minutes. Stir in parsley and keep warm.

3 Combine mustard and olive oil in a small bowl. Place salmon skin-side down on prepared baking sheet. Season with mustard mixture and remaining ½ teaspoon salt. Bake 8–10 minutes or until flaky and crispy. Serve on top of orzo.

Gluten-Free Chicken Divan

This casserole dish comes together in no time at all! If you'd like, you can add 1 cup cooked rice to the mix for some extra texture.

¾ cup sour cream

¾ cup mayonnaise

1 tablespoon onion powder

2 teaspoons garlic powder

1 teaspoon salt

½ teaspoon ground black pepper

3 cups cooked cubed chicken breasts

1¼ pounds steamed broccoli

1¼ cups shredded Cheddar cheese, divided

SERVES 6	
Per Serving:	
Calories	493
Fat	38g
Protein	28g
Sodium	848mg
Fiber	3g
Carbohydrates	10g
Sugar	3g
Net Carbs	7g

1 Preheat oven to 350°F and grease a 9" × 13" baking dish with nonstick cooking spray.

2 In a large bowl, combine sour cream, mayonnaise, onion powder, garlic powder, salt, pepper, chicken, broccoli, and 1 cup cheese. Mix well and transfer to prepared baking dish. Top with remaining ¼ cup cheese. Bake for 30 minutes or until fully cooked through.

Cilantro Lime Chicken

Cilantro isn't for everyone, but it adds a nice fresh flavor that goes well with the lime juice. If you really dislike cilantro, you can substitute parsley.

4 tablespoons olive oil

6 cloves garlic, peeled and chopped

1 teaspoon ground cumin

1 teaspoon salt

½ cup fresh lime juice

⅓ cup chopped fresh cilantro

4 (3-ounce) bone-in, skin-on chicken thighs

SERVES 4	
Per Serving:	
Calories	299
Fat	23g
Protein	19g
Sodium	863mg
Fiber	0g
Carbohydrates	4g
Sugar	1g
Net Carbs	4g

1 Combine oil, garlic, cumin, salt, lime juice, and cilantro in a medium bowl. Add chicken and toss to coat in marinade. Cover and refrigerate for at least 30 minutes.

2 Heat large skillet over medium heat. Add chicken and cook 5–7 minutes on each side, until crispy and cooked through. Serve hot.

Spinach and Ravioli

SERVES 4

Per Serving:	
Calories	359
Fat	17g
Protein	12g
Sodium	436mg
Fiber	3g
Carbohydrates	38g
Sugar	4g
Net Carbs	35g

This simple meal is rich in vitamins and nutrients and comes together in a flash.

18 ounces cheese ravioli

4 tablespoons unsalted butter

½ cup chopped yellow onion

2 cloves garlic, peeled and chopped

½ teaspoon red pepper flakes

¼ teaspoon salt

¼ teaspoon ground black pepper

4 cups baby spinach leaves

1 Cook ravioli according to package instructions. Drain, then rinse with cold water, and drain again. Set aside.

2 Melt butter in a large skillet over medium heat. Add onion and cook for about 5 minutes, until soft and translucent. Add garlic, red pepper flakes, salt, and black pepper and cook another minute.

3 Add ravioli and spinach and cook 5 minutes. Serve hot.

Baked Pork Chops

SERVES 4

Per Serving:	
Calories	257
Fat	18g
Protein	23g
Sodium	1,392mg
Fiber	1g
Carbohydrates	3g
Sugar	1g
Net Carbs	2g

These Baked Pork Chops are perfectly seasoned and easy to put together.

2 teaspoons salt

1 teaspoon ground black pepper

1 teaspoon smoked paprika

1 teaspoon onion powder

1 teaspoon garlic powder

4 (4-ounce) pork chops

4 tablespoons olive oil

1 Preheat oven to 400°F. Grease a baking sheet with nonstick cooking spray.

2 In a small bowl, mix together salt, pepper, paprika, onion powder, and garlic powder. Rub each pork chop with oil, then generously coat with seasoning mixture. Place on prepared baking sheet and bake for 15–20 minutes until the internal temperature reaches 145°F. Let rest for 5 minutes before serving.

Gluten-Free Baked Ziti with Turkey

This extra-cheesy, gluten-free casserole is perfect for a crowd, even if you're not gluten-free yourself. Top it with ½ cup gluten-free bread crumbs for some more crunch.

12 ounces gluten-free ziti

1 pound lean ground turkey

1 clove garlic, peeled and chopped

½ cup chopped green bell pepper

3 cups chopped baby spinach leaves

1½ cups ricotta cheese

¼ cup shredded Parmesan cheese

1 large egg

¼ teaspoon salt

¼ teaspoon ground black pepper

¼ teaspoon garlic powder

¼ teaspoon onion powder

⅛ teaspoon red pepper flakes

2½ cups gluten-free marinara sauce

1½ cups shredded mozzarella cheese

SERVES 6

Per Serving:	
Calories	542
Fat	23g
Protein	35g
Sodium	459mg
Fiber	4g
Carbohydrates	53g
Sugar	1g
Net Carbs	49g

WHAT IS GLUTEN?

Gluten is a group of proteins found in wheat, rye, oats, and barley. It's what gives bread its elasticity and allows it to rise. Those with celiac disease are allergic to the proteins, and those with gluten sensitivities often find it difficult to digest, as it can cause inflammation in the digestive tract.

1 Preheat oven to 350°F. Grease a 9" × 13" baking dish with non-stick cooking spray.

2 Cook ziti according to package instructions. Drain, then rinse with cold water, and drain again. Set aside.

3 Heat large frying pan over medium heat. Add turkey and sauté, using a large spoon to break up turkey into small chunks. Cook for 5 minutes, then add garlic, bell pepper, and spinach. Cook for another 5 minutes or until turkey is browned. Remove from heat and set aside.

4 In a large bowl, add ricotta cheese, Parmesan cheese, egg, salt, black pepper, garlic powder, onion powder, and red pepper flakes. Mix well.

5 Add half the penne to the bottom of prepared baking dish. Pour half the sauce on top, then add ricotta mixture and spread evenly. Add half the turkey mixture, then top with half the mozzarella. Repeat layers.

6 Cover with aluminum foil and bake for 20 minutes, then remove foil and bake another 5 minutes, until cheese is melted.

Healthy Philly Cheesesteaks

These Healthy Philly Cheesesteaks are delicious whether you're from Boston, New York, Los Angeles, or Philadelphia. For a lighter version, use lettuce wraps instead of sub rolls.

2 tablespoons olive oil, divided

12 ounces flank steak, thinly sliced across the grain

¼ teaspoon salt

¼ teaspoon ground black pepper

1 medium yellow onion, peeled and sliced

1 medium green bell pepper, seeded and sliced

2 cloves garlic, peeled and chopped

½ teaspoon Worcestershire sauce

½ teaspoon low-sodium soy sauce

4 (1-ounce) slices provolone cheese

4 (8") toasted sub rolls

1 Heat 1 tablespoon oil in a large frying pan over medium-high heat. Season steak with salt and black pepper, then cook for about 3 minutes on each side or until no longer pink. Remove from pan and keep warm.

2 Heat remaining 1 tablespoon oil and add onion and bell pepper. Cook for about 5 minutes or until onion is soft and translucent. Add cooked steak, garlic, Worcestershire sauce, and soy sauce. Mix well.

3 Evenly divide steak and vegetable mixture into quarters. Top each with a slice of cheese. Cook 5 minutes, until cheese softens. Transfer steak and cheese to sub rolls. Serve warm.

Gluten-Free Chili Zucchini Boats

GF

Choose your favorite type of chili for this recipe. It calls for Chili con Carne, but you can also use Texas Chili (see recipe in Chapter 8) or Vegetarian Chili (see recipe in Chapter 9). Top the boats with some crushed Fritos for extra crunch.

4 medium zucchinis, sliced lengthwise

4 cups leftover Chili con Carne (see recipe in this chapter)

1 cup shredded Cheddar cheese

1 Preheat oven to 350°F. Line a baking sheet with parchment paper.

2 Scoop out center of each zucchini half, removing all seeds. Place on prepared baking sheet, then spoon in chili. Top with cheese. Bake 20 minutes or until cheese is melted. Remove from oven and serve hot.

SERVES 8	
Per Serving:	
Calories	309
Fat	17g
Protein	20g
Sodium	411mg
Fiber	6g
Carbohydrates	20g
Sugar	6g
Net Carbs	14g

French Onion Soup

To make a more classic version of this recipe, ladle your soup into oven-safe serving bowls and top each bowl with 2 slices of baguette and 2 slices of provolone cheese. Broil for about 5 minutes.

2 tablespoons unsalted butter

4 large yellow onions, peeled and thinly sliced

1 clove garlic, peeled and chopped

¼ teaspoon salt

1 teaspoon ground black pepper

4 cups low-sodium beef broth

2 tablespoons Worcestershire sauce

SERVES 4	
Per Serving:	
Calories	134
Fat	6g
Protein	5g
Sodium	358mg
Fiber	3g
Carbohydrates	17g
Sugar	8g
Net Carbs	14g

Melt butter in a large saucepan over medium heat. Add onions and cook for about 5 minutes or until soft and translucent. Add garlic, salt, and pepper and cook another 1 minute or until fragrant. Add broth and Worcestershire sauce and bring to a simmer. Cover and simmer for 10 minutes. Transfer to serving bowls and serve hot.

Chicken and Waffles

SERVES 4

Per Serving:

Calories	700
Fat	12g
Protein	53g
Sodium	2,234mg
Fiber	9g
Carbohydrates	96g
Sugar	15g
Net Carbs	87g

EXTRA-FLUFFY WAFFLES AND PANCAKES

In order to make your waffles or pancakes fluffier, you have to make sure they're full of air. And since you can't just add air as an ingredient, you have two options: beat your egg whites until stiff before you add them in or add extra baking soda. Either option will create air pockets, making light and fluffy waffles or pancakes.

This healthy version of the classic Southern dish uses baked chicken instead of fried and applesauce instead of oil in the waffles. Serve the two together with some maple syrup.

2½ cups white whole-wheat flour, divided

1¼ teaspoons salt, divided

1 teaspoon ground black pepper

¼ teaspoon red pepper flakes

4 large eggs, divided

2 cups crushed cornflakes

4 (6-ounce) boneless, skinless chicken breasts

1 teaspoon ground cinnamon

2 teaspoons baking powder

1½ teaspoons baking soda

2 cups unsweetened almond milk

1 teaspoon vanilla extract

2 tablespoons honey

⅓ cup applesauce

1 Preheat oven to 425°F. Line a baking sheet with aluminum foil and grease with nonstick cooking spray.

2 Add ½ cup flour, 1 teaspoon salt, black pepper, and red pepper flakes to a small bowl. Add 1 egg to a separate small bowl and beat. Add cornflakes to a third small bowl. Coat each chicken breast in flour mixture, then egg, and then cornflakes, and place on prepared baking sheet. Bake for 20–30 minutes, until fully cooked, and remove from oven. Using a meat thermometer, check chicken at its thickest portion to make sure the internal temperature is at least 165°F. Transfer to large plate and keep warm.

3 Preheat waffle maker and spray with nonstick cooking spray. In a large bowl, combine remaining 2 cups flour, cinnamon, baking powder, baking soda, and remaining ¼ teaspoon salt. In a small bowl, combine milk, vanilla, honey, applesauce, and remaining 3 eggs. Pour milk mixture into flour mixture and mix well. Cook batter according to waffle maker instructions.

CHAPTER 12

Desserts

Rice Cereal Squares

MAKES 24 SQUARES

Per Serving (1 square):

Calories	80
Fat	2g
Protein	1g
Sodium	55mg
Fiber	0g
Carbohydrates	14g
Sugar	6g
Net Carbs	14g

We all know Rice Cereal Squares make for a wonderful midnight snack. You can easily alter this recipe by adding M&M's, peanut butter, or chocolate chips.

⅓ cup unsalted butter

4½ cups mini marshmallows

6 cups puffed rice cereal, such as Kellogg's Rice Krispies

1 Line a 9" × 13" baking pan with parchment paper.

2 Melt butter and marshmallows in a large, heavy skillet over low heat. Sauté for about 5 minutes, until marshmallows have completely melted. Remove from heat.

3 Stir in cereal and mix thoroughly. Spread mixture evenly in prepared baking pan. Chill in refrigerator for 1 hour. Cut into squares and serve.

Blueberry Banana Parfait

SERVES 4

Per Serving:

Calories	122
Fat	4g
Protein	3g
Sodium	37mg
Fiber	2g
Carbohydrates	21g
Sugar	14g
Net Carbs	19g

This simple dessert is so easy to personalize. Add in your favorite fruits, like peaches, pineapple, strawberries, raspberries, or kiwi. For a more ice cream–like texture, chuck the yogurt in the freezer for about 30 minutes before serving.

1 cup sliced bananas

1 cup fresh blueberries

1 cup vanilla full-fat Greek yogurt

1 tablespoon fresh lime juice

1 tablespoon lime zest

¼ cup sweetened coconut flakes

Divide sliced banana between four wine or parfait glasses. Add blueberries, then top with yogurt. Drizzle with lime juice. Sprinkle lime zest and coconut on top. Chill in refrigerator for at least 15 minutes, and serve.

Apple Crisp

Can't you just taste the fall? Serve this easy Apple Crisp warm, topped with a dollop of vanilla ice cream and maybe a drizzle of caramel sauce.

¾ cup all-purpose flour

¾ cup quick-cooking oats

¾ cup light brown sugar

¼ cup granulated sugar

¾ teaspoon ground cinnamon

½ teaspoon ground nutmeg

½ teaspoon ground allspice

½ cup unsalted butter, chilled

2 (20-ounce) cans apple pie filling

1 Preheat oven to 375°F. Grease a 9" × 9" baking pan.

2 Combine flour, oats, brown sugar, granulated sugar, cinnamon, nutmeg, and allspice in a medium bowl. Add butter. Using two knives, cut butter repeatedly until it's in pea-sized chunks, mixing with flour mixture until crumblike and slightly moist.

3 Evenly spread 1 can apple pie filling on prepared baking pan. Sprinkle half the crumb mixture on top until pie filling is completely covered. Evenly spread remaining can apple pie filling on top of crumb mixture. Top with remaining crumb mixture to cover filling.

4 Bake for 30 minutes or until browned, then remove from oven. Let cool on a wire rack for at least 15 minutes.

SERVES 8

Per Serving:

Calories	422
Fat	12g
Protein	2g
Sodium	76mg
Fiber	3g
Carbohydrates	79g
Sugar	47g
Net Carbs	76g

CRISP OR COBBLER?

It can be hard to tell the difference between a crisp and a cobbler. Both have a fruit filling topped with flour and spices, and both are served bubbling hot with whipped cream or ice cream. The main difference lies in the topping. Crisp toppings consist mainly of flour and sugar, while cobblers are topped with biscuit dough.

Perfect Peanut Butter Cookies

MAKES 40 COOKIES

Per Serving (1 cookie):

Calories	114
Fat	7g
Protein	2g
Sodium	73mg
Fiber	1g
Carbohydrates	10g
Sugar	6g
Net Carbs	9g

These taste delicious served warm from the oven or after they've cooled off a bit. To make the classic peanut butter kiss cookie, press a Hershey's Kiss into each cookie as they're cooling.

1 cup chunky peanut butter

¾ cup unsalted butter, room temperature

⅔ cup packed light brown sugar

⅓ cup granulated sugar

1 large egg

½ teaspoon vanilla extract

½ cup chopped pecans

1½ cups all-purpose flour

½ teaspoon baking soda

½ teaspoon salt

1   Preheat oven to 350°F. Grease a 9" × 13" baking sheet with non-stick cooking spray.

2   In a large bowl, combine peanut butter, butter, brown sugar, and granulated sugar until smooth. Add egg and vanilla, mixing until fully combined. Stir in pecans.

3   In a medium bowl, sift together flour, baking soda, and salt. Gradually add flour mixture to peanut butter mixture, stirring thoroughly.

4   Roll dough into balls about 1"–1½" in diameter. Place on prepared baking sheet, approximately 2" apart, and press down in the middle with a fork. Bake for 12 minutes or until a toothpick inserted into the middle of a cookie comes out clean. Cool on baking sheet for 5 minutes, then transfer cookies to a wire rack. Serve warm or at room temperature.

Double Chocolate Chip Peppermint Drop Cookies

These Double Chocolate Chip Peppermint Drop Cookies are perfect for the cold holiday season or really any random peppermint craving you might have during the year.

½ cup plus 2 tablespoons unsalted butter, room temperature

⅔ cup light brown sugar

⅓ cup granulated sugar

2 tablespoons unsweetened cocoa powder

1 large egg

1 teaspoon vanilla extract

1 teaspoon peppermint extract

1½ cups all-purpose flour

½ teaspoon baking soda

½ teaspoon salt

1 cup semisweet chocolate chips

1 Preheat oven to 350°F. Grease a 9" × 13" baking sheet with non-stick cooking spray.

2 In a large bowl, combine butter with brown sugar, granulated sugar, and cocoa powder until smooth. Add egg, vanilla extract, and peppermint extract, mixing until fully combined.

3 In a medium bowl, sift together flour, baking soda, and salt. Gradually add flour mixture to butter mixture, stirring thoroughly until blended into a soft dough. Stir in chocolate chips.

4 Roll dough into balls about 1"–1½" in diameter. Place on prepared baking sheet, approximately 2" apart, and press down in the middle with a fork. Bake for 10–12 minutes or until a toothpick inserted into the middle of a cookie comes out clean. Cool on baking sheet for 5 minutes, then transfer cookies to a wire rack. Serve warm or at room temperature.

MAKES 48 COOKIES

Per Serving (1 cookie):

Calories	77
Fat	4g
Protein	1g
Sodium	40mg
Fiber	1g
Carbohydrates	10g
Sugar	7g
Net Carbs	9g

VERSATILE VANILLA EXTRACT

The modern-day substitute for the vanilla bean, vanilla extract is used to heighten the taste of everything from ice cream to chocolate. Although pure vanilla extract is best, it's also more expensive. Synthetic vanilla extract—sold as vanilla flavoring or imitation vanilla—can be used instead.

Lemon Crisp Cookies

MAKES 48 COOKIES

Per Serving (1 cookie):

Calories	72
Fat	4g
Protein	1g
Sodium	33mg
Fiber	0g
Carbohydrates	9g
Sugar	5g
Net Carbs	9g

HOW TO SOFTEN BUTTER

The easiest way to soften butter is just to leave it out until it reaches room temperature. But if you're a bit pressed for time, you can soften it quickly by microwaving 2 cups of water for 2–3 minutes until boiling. Remove the water and place the butter in the microwave, closing the door quickly to trap the hot air. Let the butter sit for 10 minutes and it will be perfectly softened.

The yellow food coloring is optional, so no worries if you don't have any. All it does is add color to the cookies to represent the lemon flavor.

1 cup granulated sugar

16 tablespoons unsalted butter, softened

3 teaspoons lemon juice

5 drops yellow food coloring

1 large egg

2 cups all-purpose flour

¾ teaspoon baking soda

¼ teaspoon salt

⅓ cup powdered sugar

1 Preheat oven to 350°F. Grease a 9" × 13" baking sheet.

2 In a large bowl, combine sugar and butter until smooth. Blend in lemon juice, food coloring, and egg. In a medium bowl, combine flour, baking soda, and salt.

3 Gradually add flour mixture to butter mixture, stirring thoroughly until blended into a soft dough.

4 Roll dough into balls about 1"–1½" in diameter. Place on prepared baking sheet, approximately 1½" apart, and press down in the middle with a fork. Bake for 9–10 minutes or until a toothpick inserted into the middle of a cookie comes out clean. Cool on baking sheet for 2 minutes, then transfer cookies to a wire rack. Dust cookies with powdered sugar. Serve warm or at room temperature.

Cinnamon Chocolate Brownies

These chocolaty brownies combine a bunch of wonderful flavors that all work in harmony with one another. The spicy cinnamon pairs perfectly with the creamy pecans.

MAKES 16 BROWNIES

Per Serving (1 brownie):

Calories	173
Fat	12g
Protein	2g
Sodium	61mg
Fiber	1g
Carbohydrates	15g
Sugar	11g
Net Carbs	14g

THE GREAT POWER OF GREASING

Greasing is an essential step of almost every recipe to prevent your food from sticking to your pans and baking dishes. If you don't have non-stick cooking spray, you can coat your pan with butter and sprinkle flour on top.

½ cup all-purpose flour

¼ teaspoon salt

½ teaspoon baking powder

½ teaspoon ground cinnamon

4 (4-ounce) squares semisweet chocolate, chopped

8 tablespoons unsalted butter

2 large eggs

1 teaspoon vanilla extract

¾ cup granulated sugar

1 cup chopped pecans

1 Preheat oven to 325°F. Grease a 9" × 9" baking pan.

2 In a small bowl, combine flour, salt, baking powder, and cinnamon until well blended.

3 Fill a large heavy pot halfway with water and bring to a boil over high heat. In a medium metal bowl, combine chocolate and butter. Reduce heat to low and place the bowl on top of the pot. Melt chocolate for roughly 10 minutes, stirring regularly with a rubber spatula until completely melted. Remove from heat.

4 Beat in eggs, vanilla, and sugar. Blend in flour mixture, then gently stir in pecans.

5 Spread batter evenly in prepared baking pan. Bake on middle rack of oven for 30 minutes or until a toothpick inserted in the middle of a brownie comes out clean. Cool in pan for 5 minutes, then cut into sixteen bars. Serve warm or at room temperature.

Chocolate Mousse

For best results, thicken further by chilling in the freezer for 10–15 minutes before eating. You can use a blender in place of an electric mixer, if you don't have a mixer. Top it off with some mint leaves and sliced strawberries for a decadent dessert.

½ cup heavy whipping cream

2 tablespoons powdered sugar

2 tablespoons unsweetened cocoa powder

½ teaspoon vanilla extract

Combine all ingredients in a small bowl. Blend with an electric mixer on low until mixture thickens. Chill for 30 minutes in the refrigerator before serving.

SERVES 1	
Per Serving:	
Calories	490
Fat	46g
Protein	5g
Sodium	48mg
Fiber	4g
Carbohydrates	22g
Sugar	16g
Net Carbs	18g

Mocha Shake

For best results, use high-quality ice cream and your favorite coffee for this Mocha Shake. You can even try adding a little caramel drizzle and a couple of drops of mint extract to the mix for extra flavor.

2 cups vanilla ice cream

½ cup chilled coffee

2 teaspoons unsweetened cocoa powder

2 crushed ice cubes

Blend ice cream, coffee, and cocoa powder in a blender until combined. Add ice and pulse three to four times until smooth. Chill for at least 30 minutes or until ready to serve.

SERVES 2	
Per Serving:	
Calories	294
Fat	16g
Protein	5g
Sodium	117mg
Fiber	2g
Carbohydrates	35g
Sugar	31g
Net Carbs	33g

S'mores

SERVES 2

Per Serving:

Calories	389
Fat	20g
Protein	1g
Sodium	91mg
Fiber	5g
Carbohydrates	60g
Sugar	39g
Net Carbs	55g

Looking for a quick and easy snack for late-night study binges? Microwaved S'mores take mere minutes to make. Feel free to experiment with different flavors of chocolate chips, such as peppermint.

8 mini marshmallows
½ cup semisweet chocolate chips
2 graham crackers, halved

1 Combine marshmallows and chocolate chips in a small microwave-safe bowl. Microwave on high heat for 1½ minutes. Stir, and microwave for an additional 1½ minutes in 30-second intervals, stirring each time, until chocolate and marshmallows are melted.

2 Let chocolate and marshmallows cool for 2 minutes, stir until combined, and spread evenly on graham cracker halves.

Chocolate Banana Ice Cream

SERVES 2

Per Serving:

Calories	350
Fat	10g
Protein	8g
Sodium	82mg
Fiber	11g
Carbohydrates	69g
Sugar	33g
Net Carbs	58g

Make sure you're using a high-power blender or food processor in order to get the right texture. You can replace the peanut butter with almond butter if you'd like.

4 medium frozen bananas, peeled
¼ cup unsweetened cocoa powder
2 tablespoons smooth peanut butter
½ teaspoon vanilla extract
3 tablespoons sweetened almond milk

Combine bananas, cocoa powder, peanut butter, and vanilla in a blender and pulse for 30 seconds. Add 1 tablespoon almond milk and pulse for 30 seconds. Repeat with remaining milk until you get a creamy texture. Serve cold.

Dairy-Free Chocolate Mousse

If your mousse texture doesn't set in the beginning, just pop it in the refrigerator until it's ready. Top with mint leaves if you're feeling extra fancy!

1 (13.5-ounce) can full-fat coconut milk, chilled

2 tablespoons confectioners' sugar

3 tablespoons unsweetened cocoa powder

¼ teaspoon salt

¼ teaspoon vanilla extract

2 ounces 70% dark chocolate squares, finely chopped

SERVES 4	
Per Serving:	
Calories	336
Fat	30g
Protein	2g
Sodium	163mg
Fiber	3g
Carbohydrates	22g
Sugar	11g
Net Carbs	19g

Open coconut milk, making sure not to shake it. Scoop out cream sitting on top and transfer to a small bowl. Add sugar and mix with a hand mixer until a whipped cream is formed, about 1 minute. Add cocoa powder, salt, and vanilla, mixing well, then fold in chocolate. Serve chilled.

Baked Peaches 'n' Cream

Sprinkle a little extra cinnamon and nutmeg on top of your vanilla ice cream when serving for a little extra spice.

4 medium peaches, halved and pitted

2 tablespoons light brown sugar

¼ teaspoon ground cinnamon

2 tablespoons salted butter, cut into eight pieces

4 cups vanilla ice cream

SERVES 4	
Per Serving:	
Calories	425
Fat	22g
Protein	6g
Sodium	167mg
Fiber	3g
Carbohydrates	55g
Sugar	50g
Net Carbs	52g

1 Preheat oven to 325°F. Place peaches skin-side down in a 9" ×13" baking dish.

2 In a small bowl, combine sugar and cinnamon. Place 1 piece butter in the middle of each peach, then sprinkle sugar mixture evenly over peaches. Bake for about 35–40 minutes or until peaches are tender. Serve with vanilla ice cream.

Dairy-Free Coconut Green Tea Ice Cream

Who knew green tea could turn into such a delicious ice cream? Because matcha powders will vary in bitterness, start with a little bit of sugar, then work your way up depending on how sweet you like it. You can also use 4 tablespoons maple syrup instead of granulated sugar.

1 (13.5-ounce) can full-fat coconut milk

2 teaspoons matcha green tea powder

¼ cup granulated sugar

½ teaspoon vanilla extract

1 teaspoon lemon juice

⅛ teaspoon salt

Add all ingredients into a blender and blend until smooth, about 1 minute. Transfer to a shallow dish, cover, and freeze for 3 hours, stirring every hour. Let sit at room temperature for at least 5 minutes to soften. Serve cold.

SERVES 4

Per Serving:

Calories	206
Fat	15g
Protein	1g
Sodium	93mg
Fiber	1g
Carbohydrates	15g
Sugar	14g
Net Carbs	14g

MATCHA POWDER POWER

Matcha powder comes from high-quality green tea leaves that have been pulverized into small dust. It's absolutely packed with antioxidants, which help prevent cancer, heart disease, and other chronic diseases. It's also been shown to protect your liver, boost brain functions, and help you lose weight.

Vegan Cookie Dough Bites

MAKES 10 BITES

Per Serving (1 bite):

Calories	165
Fat	7g
Protein	2g
Sodium	1mg
Fiber	1g
Carbohydrates	24g
Sugar	8g
Net Carbs	23g

To make this recipe gluten-free, you can substitute oat flour or super-fine almond flour. To melt the coconut oil, just heat 3 tablespoons in the microwave for about 20 seconds, then measure to make sure you have enough.

1⅔ cups all-purpose flour

3 tablespoons maple syrup

3 tablespoons melted coconut oil

1½ teaspoons vanilla extract

⅓ cup semisweet vegan chocolate chips

1 Line a baking sheet with parchment paper.

2 In a medium bowl, combine flour, maple syrup, oil, and vanilla. Using a rubber spatula, mix ingredients well until they form a dough-like consistency. Gently stir in chocolate chips.

3 Roll dough into balls about 1" in diameter, then place on prepared baking sheet. Refrigerate for 15 minutes. Serve chilled.

Raspberry Lemon Sorbet

SERVES 2

Per Serving:

Calories	176
Fat	4g
Protein	15g
Sodium	40mg
Fiber	12g
Carbohydrates	27g
Sugar	10g
Net Carbs	15g

The sourness in the raspberry and lemon blend together to create a nice, smooth palate cleanser. To make this dairy-free, simply use a dairy-free yogurt, like almond yogurt.

2½ cups frozen raspberries

1 cup plain low-fat Greek yogurt

1½ tablespoons fresh lemon juice

2 tablespoons fresh lemon zest

Add raspberries, yogurt, and lemon juice to a blender. Blend on high until smooth and creamy, about 2 minutes. Garnish with lemon zest and serve chilled.

Gluten-Free Chocolate Chip Cookies

These chocolate chip cookies can help satisfy your sweet tooth, even if you're avoiding gluten and dairy. For a Paleo version, replace the canola oil, brown sugar, and peanut butter with coconut oil, coconut sugar, and almond butter, respectively.

1 cup blanched almond flour

¼ cup coconut flour

1 teaspoon baking soda

¼ teaspoon salt

6 tablespoons canola oil

¾ cup packed light brown sugar

6 tablespoons peanut butter

1½ teaspoons vanilla extract

1 large egg

1 cup semisweet dairy-free chocolate chips

MAKES 16 COOKIES

Per Serving (1 cookie):

Calories	244
Fat	17g
Protein	3g
Sodium	153mg
Fiber	3g
Carbohydrates	23g
Sugar	18g
Net Carbs	20g

1 Preheat oven to 350°F. Line a baking sheet with parchment paper.

2 In a medium bowl, combine almond flour, coconut flour, baking soda, and salt. Set aside.

3 In a large bowl, blend together oil and sugar with a hand mixer or stand mixer on medium speed until fully combined, about 1 minute. Add almond butter and vanilla and mix again, then add egg and mix on low for another minute. Fold in chocolate chips.

4 Roll dough into balls about 1"–1½" in diameter. Place on prepared baking sheet, approximately 4" apart, and press down gently on each ball with your fingertips. Bake for 14–17 minutes or until a toothpick inserted into the middle of a cookie comes out clean. Cool on baking sheet for 5 minutes, then transfer cookies to a wire rack. Serve warm or at room temperature.

Paleo Sweet Potato Brownies

MAKES 16 BROWNIES

Per Serving (1 brownie):

Calories	95
Fat	6g
Protein	2g
Sodium	73mg
Fiber	1g
Carbohydrates	10g
Sugar	7g
Net Carbs	9g

Sweet potato? In brownies? You betcha. Sweet potato is the perfect flour substitute for all those grain-free people out there and there's no change in flavor.

1 large sweet potato
3 large eggs, beaten
⅓ cup melted coconut oil
⅓ cup honey
2 teaspoons vanilla extract
3 tablespoons coconut flour
4 tablespoons unsweetened cocoa powder
½ teaspoon baking powder
¼ teaspoon ground cinnamon
¼ teaspoon salt

1 Preheat oven to 425°F. Line an 8" × 8" baking pan with parchment paper.

2 Pierce potato four times with a fork. Transfer to a baking sheet and place on middle oven rack. Bake for 25–30 minutes or until cooked through, and remove from oven. Let cool 5 minutes.

3 Remove skin and place pulp in a large bowl. Mash with a fork. Turn oven heat down to 350°F.

4 Add eggs, oil, honey, and vanilla to mashed sweet potato and mix thoroughly.

5 In a small bowl, combine flour, cocoa powder, baking powder, cinnamon, and salt and mix well. Add to potato mixture and mix well, then pour into prepared baking pan. Bake for 30 minutes or until a toothpick inserted into the middle of the brownies comes out clean. Serve warm or at room temperature.

Chocolate Cake in a Mug

If you don't have maple syrup, you can use honey or Swerve sweetener, a sugar substitute for keto dieters. Feel free to swap out the almond flour for 1 tablespoon coconut flour and add some sugar-free chocolate chips.

1 tablespoon unsalted butter

3 tablespoons almond flour

1 large egg, beaten

2 tablespoons maple syrup

½ teaspoon baking powder

⅛ teaspoon salt

1 tablespoon unsweetened cocoa powder

Add butter to a 16-ounce mug and melt in the microwave for 10 seconds. Add remaining ingredients and mix well, then microwave again for 1 minute. Serve immediately.

SERVES 1	
Per Serving:	
Calories	414
Fat	27g
Protein	12g
Sodium	616mg
Fiber	4g
Carbohydrates	37g
Sugar	26g
Net Carbs	33g

Keto Fudge

Want some extra flavor in this super-chocolaty, keto-friendly dessert? Add ½ cup peanut butter or sprinkle some chopped nuts on top.

½ cup plus 1 tablespoon unsalted butter

4 ounces cream cheese

2 cups sugar-free chocolate chips

1 teaspoon vanilla extract

1 Line an 8" × 8" baking pan with parchment paper.

2 Heat a small saucepan over low heat. Add all ingredients to saucepan and mix thoroughly, making sure to not burn mixture. Cook until ingredients are melted. Pour into prepared baking pan and refrigerate 1 hour. Slice and serve cold.

SERVES 16	
Per Serving:	
Calories	222
Fat	18g
Protein	3g
Sodium	23mg
Fiber	2g
Carbohydrates	19g
Sugar	1g
Net Carbs	17g

Vegan Coconut Avocado Lime Ice Cream

SERVES 2

Per Serving:

Calories	451
Fat	32g
Protein	4g
Sodium	20mg
Fiber	5g
Carbohydrates	37g
Sugar	26g
Net Carbs	32g

If you don't have coconut milk, you can just use water. Keep in mind this is the no-churn version of ice cream, so the consistency will be a little different than you're used to.

1 (5.4-ounce) can coconut cream

½ large avocado, peeled and pitted

3 tablespoons lime juice

2 tablespoons lime zest

2 tablespoons full-fat coconut milk

¼ cup granulated sugar

¼ cup shredded unsweetened coconut

Place coconut cream, avocado, lime juice, lime zest, coconut milk, and sugar in a blender and blend until smooth, about 3 minutes, stopping every 30 seconds to scrape the sides. Transfer to a shallow dish, cover, and freeze for 2 hours. Let sit at room temperature for at least 5 minutes to soften. Garnish with coconut and serve.

Gluten-Free Pie Crust

Check the ingredient list on your all-purpose flour. If it doesn't include xanthan gum, add ½ teaspoon to the flour mixture. It'll help hold your crust together. You can also add 2 teaspoons lemon juice or vinegar, so your crust doesn't turn tough.

2 cups all-purpose gluten-free flour

½ teaspoon salt

2 teaspoons granulated sugar

½ cup unsalted butter, chilled

1 large egg, beaten

⅔ cup cold water

1   In a large bowl, combine flour, salt, and sugar. Using two knives, cut butter repeatedly until it's in pea-sized chunks, then add to flour mixture and mix until crumblike and slightly moist. Add in egg and mix again.

2   Add water 1 tablespoon at a time, until mixture turns into a dough, making sure it's not too dry. Cut dough in half and roll into two balls. Place dough balls in two large bowls, cover, and refrigerate for least 1 hour.

3   Remove dough balls from refrigerator and let sit at room temperature for 10 minutes. Coat a flat surface with flour and place 1 dough ball on surface. Begin rolling out dough until it's ¼" thick. Repeat with second dough ball.

MAKES 2 PIE CRUSTS

Per Serving (⅛ of one crust):	
Calories	112
Fat	6g
Protein	1g
Sodium	81mg
Fiber	1g
Carbohydrates	12g
Sugar	1g
Net Carbs	11g

UNSALTED BUTTER BENEFITS

The name says it all—unsalted butter has no added salt. It's usually better for baking, as salt can overpower butter's naturally sweet flavor. The only drawback is that unsalted butter is more perishable—the salt in salted butter acts as a preservative. For long-term storage, keep unsalted butter in the freezer.

Dairy-Free Strawberry Shortcakes

SERVES 6

Per Serving:

Calories	458
Fat	21g
Protein	5g
Sodium	660mg
Fiber	3g
Carbohydrates	61g
Sugar	28g
Net Carbs	58g

POPULAR BERRIES

Strawberries are grown in every state in the US, and Americans love to eat them! According to the US Department of Agriculture they eat an average of 3.4 pounds of strawberries every year.

Love strawberries? You'll love this Dairy-Free Strawberry Shortcake recipe. The sugar crystalizes with the strawberry juices, creating a perfectly sweet sauce that coats the biscuits.

4 cups sliced strawberries

½ cup plus 2⅔ tablespoons granulated sugar, divided

2 tablespoons lemon juice

2 tablespoons lemon zest

2 cups all-purpose flour

3 teaspoons baking powder

1 teaspoon salt

⅓ cup shortening

⅓ cup unsweetened almond milk

1 (14-ounce) can full-fat coconut milk, refrigerated

1 teaspoon vanilla extract

1 In a medium bowl, combine strawberries, ½ cup sugar, lemon juice, and lemon zest. Let sit 1 hour.

2 Preheat oven to 450°F. Line a baking sheet with parchment paper.

3 In a large bowl, combine flour, 2 tablespoons sugar, baking powder, salt, and shortening. Using two knives, cut shortening repeatedly until it's in pea-sized chunks, and the mixture is crumblike and slightly moist. Stir in almond milk.

4 Place dough on a floured flat surface and roll into a ball. Knead with your hands for about 1 minute, then roll out until ½" thick. Using the rim of a glass, cut out six circles about 2½"–3" in diameter. Place 1" apart on prepared baking sheet. Bake 10–12 minutes or until golden brown. Cool on baking sheet for 5 minutes, then transfer biscuits to a wire rack.

5 Open coconut milk, making sure not to shake it. Scoop out cream sitting on top and transfer to a small bowl. Add vanilla and remaining ⅔ tablespoon. Beat with a hand or stand mixer until mixture is thick and creamy, about 3 minutes.

6 Cut each shortcake in half lengthwise and place bottom half in shallow bowls or plates. Fill shortcakes with strawberry mixture and half the coconut cream, then top with other shortcake half and drizzle remaining coconut cream on top.

Peanut Butter Chocolate Cake

SERVES 6

Per Serving:

Calories	425
Fat	16g
Protein	9g
Sodium	573mg
Fiber	9g
Carbohydrates	72g
Sugar	35g
Net Carbs	63g

CHOCOLATE IS HEALTHY?!

Well, not all chocolate. Dark chocolate specifically has some health benefits when eaten in moderation. You can find lots of iron and magnesium in dark chocolate, making it a perfect snack or dessert! Just make sure you don't get milk chocolate, which is loaded with unhealthy sugar.

With chocolate chips on top, you don't even need icing! Make sure your bananas are nice and ripe—the riper the bananas, the sweeter your cake will be.

3 medium ripe bananas, peeled
½ cup full-fat vanilla Greek yogurt
⅓ cup packed light brown sugar
1 teaspoon vanilla extract
3 tablespoons smooth peanut butter
1 large egg
1½ cups whole-wheat all-purpose flour
⅓ cup cocoa powder
1½ teaspoons baking soda
½ teaspoon salt
¾ cup semisweet chocolate chips, divided

1 Preheat oven to 350°F. Grease an 8" round cake pan with nonstick cooking spray.

2 Add bananas, yogurt, sugar, vanilla, peanut butter, and egg to a large bowl and blend with a hand or stand mixer until smooth, about 2 minutes.

3 In a small bowl, combine flour, cocoa powder, baking soda, and salt. Mix well. Add flour mixture to yogurt mixture and mix until fully combined. Fold in ½ cup chocolate chips.

4 Pour batter into cake pan and sprinkle remaining ¼ cup chocolate chips on top. Bake for 25–30 minutes or until a toothpick inserted into the middle comes out clean. Cool in pan for 5 minutes, then transfer cake to a wire rack. Serve warm or at room temperature.

Gluten-Free Cheesecake

For best results, gradually add in the whipping cream while slowly increasing the speed of the mixer. This will give you a thicker and creamier cheesecake.

1½ cups almond flour

¼ cup granulated sugar

4 tablespoons unsalted butter, melted

¼ teaspoon salt, divided

2 (8-ounce) packages cream cheese, room temperature

⅔ cup confectioners' sugar

2 teaspoons lemon juice

2 teaspoons vanilla extract

2 cups heavy whipping cream

2 tablespoons lemon zest

1 Preheat oven to 350°F. Grease an 8" springform pan with non-stick cooking spray.

2 In a small bowl, combine flour, granulated sugar, butter, and ⅛ teaspoon salt. Press mixture into bottom of prepared pan. Bake 15 minutes. Set aside to cool.

3 In a large bowl, beat cream cheese until smooth using a hand or stand mixer. Add confectioners' sugar, lemon juice, vanilla, and remaining ⅛ teaspoon salt and beat until smooth. Gradually pour in cream and continue to mix until thick and creamy.

4 Pour batter over crust. Sprinkle lemon zest on top. Refrigerate at least 5 hours before serving.

SERVES 12

Per Serving:

Calories	425
Fat	38g
Protein	6g
Sodium	183mg
Fiber	2g
Carbohydrates	16g
Sugar	13g
Net Carbs	14g

Greek Yogurt Fruit Tart

SERVES 8

Per Serving:

Calories	308
Fat	18g
Protein	3g
Sodium	175mg
Fiber	2g
Carbohydrates	34g
Sugar	21g
Net Carbs	32g

PANDORA'S BOX OF YOGURTS

Yogurt is an amazing source of protein, but not all yogurts are created equal. Some are chock-full of added sugars and chemicals from processing. Greek yogurt is the best choice, as it has the fewest artificial additives with the most protein. If you're feeling extra healthy, opt for a plain nonfat Greek yogurt.

Any fruit will work in this tart. Try it with peaches or raspberries.

10 graham crackers, crushed

2 tablespoons granulated sugar

6 tablespoons unsalted butter, melted

⅛ teaspoon salt

1 (14-ounce) can full-fat coconut milk, refrigerated

1½ cups full-fat vanilla Greek yogurt

3 tablespoons honey, divided

1 cup blueberries

6 medium strawberries, leaves removed and sliced

2 medium kiwis, peeled and sliced

1 Preheat oven to 350°F.

2 In a large bowl, combine crackers, sugar, butter, and salt. Transfer to a 9" pie pan. Press crust into the bottom and up the sides of the pan. Bake 8–10 minutes until golden and crispy. Remove from oven and let cool completely.

3 Open coconut milk, making sure not to shake it. Scoop out cream sitting on top and transfer to a large bowl. Add yogurt and 2 tablespoons honey. Mix well, then pour over crust. Top with blueberries, strawberries, and kiwis, and drizzle remaining 1 tablespoon honey on top. Refrigerate at least 1 hour before serving.

Churro Banana Bites

Melt ¼ cup semisweet chocolate chips to serve on the side as a dipping sauce. If you don't have coconut oil, you can use nonstick cooking spray.

2 tablespoons granulated sugar

2 teaspoons ground cinnamon

1 tablespoon coconut oil

2 medium ripe bananas, peeled and cut into ½" slices

1 In a small bowl, mix together sugar and cinnamon, then set aside.

2 Heat coconut oil in a large frying pan over medium heat. Add bananas and fry 1 minute. Sprinkle half the cinnamon-sugar mixture on top, flip, and sprinkle with remaining cinnamon-sugar mixture. Cook an additional 1 minute, then remove from heat and serve.

SERVES 2

Per Serving:

Calories	225
Fat	7g
Protein	1g
Sodium	0mg
Fiber	4g
Carbohydrates	43g
Sugar	28g
Net Carbs	39g

Carrot Cake Cookies

MAKES 36 COOKIES

Per Serving (1 cookie):

Calories	108
Fat	4g
Protein	1g
Sodium	76mg
Fiber	1g
Carbohydrates	16g
Sugar	9g
Net Carbs	15g

BAKING WITH GLASS VERSUS METAL

There actually is a difference when baking with glass or metal pans. When using glass, it's best to reduce the cooking temperature by 25°F and be prepared to take out your food up to 10 minutes earlier than its original baking time. Glass doesn't heat up as quickly, but it retains heat better, so it reaches a higher temperature in the oven compared to metal pans.

For a quick glaze to add on top of the cookies, combine 1 cup powdered sugar, 1 ounce softened cream cheese, and 3 teaspoons whole milk until smooth. Drizzle on top after baking but before the cookies cool.

¾ cup unsalted butter, softened

1 cup packed light brown sugar

½ cup granulated sugar

2 large eggs

1 teaspoon vanilla extract

1½ cups all-purpose flour

1 teaspoon baking soda

1 teaspoon ground cinnamon

¼ teaspoon ground nutmeg

¼ teaspoon ground cloves

½ teaspoon ground ginger

½ teaspoon salt

1 cup shredded carrots

2 cups quick-cooking oats

1 Preheat oven to 350°F. Line a baking sheet with parchment paper.

2 In a large bowl, combine butter, brown sugar, and granulated sugar using a hand or stand mixer until smooth and creamy. Add 1 egg and mix well, until fully combined. Add remaining 1 egg and mix well until fully combined. Mix in vanilla.

3 In a small bowl, combine flour, baking soda, cinnamon, nutmeg, cloves, ginger, and salt. Add flour mixture to egg mixture and stir until fully combined.

4 Stir in carrots and oats. Roll dough into balls about 1"–1½" in diameter. Place on prepared baking sheet, approximately 2" apart, and press down in the middle with a fork. Bake for 15 minutes or until golden brown. Cool on baking sheet for 5 minutes, then transfer cookies to a wire rack. Serve warm or at room temperature.

STANDARD US/METRIC
MEASUREMENT CONVERSIONS

VOLUME CONVERSIONS

US Volume Measure	Metric Equivalent
⅛ teaspoon	0.5 milliliter
¼ teaspoon	1 milliliter
½ teaspoon	2 milliliters
1 teaspoon	5 milliliters
½ tablespoon	7 milliliters
1 tablespoon (3 teaspoons)	15 milliliters
2 tablespoons (1 fluid ounce)	30 milliliters
¼ cup (4 tablespoons)	60 milliliters
⅓ cup	90 milliliters
½ cup (4 fluid ounces)	125 milliliters
⅔ cup	160 milliliters
¾ cup (6 fluid ounces)	180 milliliters
1 cup (16 tablespoons)	250 milliliters
1 pint (2 cups)	500 milliliters
1 quart (4 cups)	1 liter (about)

WEIGHT CONVERSIONS

US Weight Measure	Metric Equivalent
½ ounce	15 grams
1 ounce	30 grams
2 ounces	60 grams
3 ounces	85 grams
¼ pound (4 ounces)	115 grams
½ pound (8 ounces)	225 grams
¾ pound (12 ounces)	340 grams
1 pound (16 ounces)	454 grams

OVEN TEMPERATURE CONVERSIONS

Degrees Fahrenheit	Degrees Celsius
200 degrees F	95 degrees C
250 degrees F	120 degrees C
275 degrees F	135 degrees C
300 degrees F	150 degrees C
325 degrees F	160 degrees C
350 degrees F	180 degrees C
375 degrees F	190 degrees C
400 degrees F	205 degrees C
425 degrees F	220 degrees C
450 degrees F	230 degrees C

BAKING PAN SIZES

American	Metric
8 × 1½ inch round baking pan	20 × 4 cm cake tin
9 × 1½ inch round baking pan	23 × 3.5 cm cake tin
11 × 7 × 1½ inch baking pan	28 × 18 × 4 cm baking tin
13 × 9 × 2 inch baking pan	30 × 20 × 5 cm baking tin
2 quart rectangular baking dish	30 × 20 × 3 cm baking tin
15 × 10 × 2 inch baking pan	30 × 25 × 2 cm baking tin (Swiss roll tin)
9 inch pie plate	22 × 4 or 23 × 4 cm pie plate
7 or 8 inch springform pan	18 or 20 cm springform or loose bottom cake tin
9 × 5 × 3 inch loaf pan	23 × 13 × 7 cm or 2 lb narrow loaf or pate tin
1½ quart casserole	1.5 liter casserole
2 quart casserole	2 liter casserole

APPENDIX A
Good Sources of Nutrients

GOOD SOURCES OF VITAMIN A
- Apricot
- Broccoli
- Cantaloupe
- Carrot
- Collards
- Kale
- Mango
- Pumpkin
- Spinach
- Squash, winter
- Sweet potato
- Tomato
- Turnip greens
- Watermelon

GOOD SOURCES OF VITAMIN C
- Apple with skin
- Apricot, dried
- Banana
- Beans, lima
- Broccoli
- Cantaloupe
- Collards
- Grapefruit
- Grapefruit juice
- Honeydew melon
- Kale
- Kiwi
- Orange
- Orange juice
- Pear with skin
- Peas, green
- Peppers
- Potato, with skin
- Spinach
- Squash, winter
- Strawberries
- Sweet potato
- Tomato
- Turnip greens
- Watermelon

GOOD SOURCES OF FOLATE
- Beans, dry
- Black-eyed peas
- Broccoli
- Lentils
- Mustard greens
- Orange
- Orange juice
- Peas, green
- Peas, split
- Spinach
- Turnip greens

GOOD SOURCES OF POTASSIUM
- Apricot, dried
- Banana
- Beans, dry
- Black-eyed peas
- Cantaloupe
- Grapefruit juice
- Honeydew melon
- Lentils
- Orange juice
- Peas, green
- Peas, split
- Plantain
- Potato
- Potato with skin
- Prune juice
- Spinach, cooked
- Squash, winter
- Sweet potato
- Tomato

GOOD SOURCES OF DIETARY FIBER
- Apple with skin
- Apricot, dried
- Banana
- Beans, dry
- Beans, lima
- Black-eyed peas
- Broccoli
- Carrot
- Lentils
- Orange
- Pear with skin
- Peas, green
- Peas, split
- Potato with skin
- Prune
- Spinach
- Squash, winter
- Strawberries
- Sweet potato
- Tomato

Note: A good source of a vitamin or mineral contributes at least 10 percent of its Percent Daily Value per serving. A good source of dietary fiber contributes at least 2 grams of dietary fiber per serving.

APPENDIX B
Glossary of Basic Cooking Terms

baste:
To spoon or brush a liquid over food—usually meat—during cooking. Basting prevents food from drying out while being cooked. The basting liquid can be anything from a prepared sauce to the pan juices from meat that is cooking.

blanch:
To plunge vegetables and other food briefly into boiling water. Blanching seals in the color and textures of tender-crisp vegetables, such as asparagus. It's also a quick and easy way to loosen the skins on nuts, tomatoes, and other fruits, and to remove the salty flavor from foods such as ham. Blanched food that isn't going to be cooked immediately should be plunged into ice cold water. This "shocks" the food and stops the cooking process.

boil:
To heat a liquid until bubbles form on the surface, or to cook food by placing it in liquid that is boiling. In a "rolling boil" the entire liquid is boiling, not just the surface. Stirring with a spoon won't cause the liquid to stop boiling.

broil:
To cook food right above or under a heat source. Food can be broiled in an oven or on a grill. When broiling meat, use a rack or broiling pan so the fat from the meat can drain.

brown:
To briefly fry meat in oil until it has a brown crust on both sides but is not cooked through. Browning meat removes excess fat and helps keep it tender by sealing in its natural juices.

chop:
To cut food into small pieces, not necessarily of a uniform size. Garlic is frequently chopped before frying.

cream:
To mix together butter and sugar until a fluffy light-yellow mixture forms.

cut:
To combine a solid shortening and dry mixture together using two knives, cutting the shortening repeatedly until the mixture resembles pea-sized crumbs.

dice:
To cut food into small cubes no larger than ¼".

drain:
To remove the water from blanched, washed, rinsed, or boiled food. For hassle-free draining, purchase a colander. Depending on your budget, several varieties are available, from stainless steel to inexpensive plastic.

marinate:
To soak food in a liquid before cooking, both to tenderize it and add flavor. Most marinades contain an acidic ingredient such as lemon juice, wine, or vinegar.

mince:
To cut food into very small pieces. Minced food is cut more finely than chopped food.

sauté:
To quickly cook food in a pan in a small amount of oil, butter, or other fat.

sear:
To cook a piece of meat over high heat until the outside forms a brown crust.

simmer:
To cook food in liquid that is almost, but not quite, boiling.

steam:
To cook food in the steam given off by boiling water. Unlike boiling, in steaming, the food never comes into direct contact with the hot water.

Index